Moreau Lislet:
The Man Behind The Digest of 1808

Revised edition of *Moreau Lislet, Foster Father of Louisiana Civil Law, 1996*

Alain Levasseur
with the assistance of
Vicenç Feliú

Baton Rouge
CLAITOR'S PUBLISHING DIVISION
2008

Revised/Reprinted, 2008
by
Claitor's Publishing Division

ISBN : 1-59804-446-X

Copyright 1996, Allain A. Levasseur
All rights reserved.

Published and for sale by:
CLAITOR'S PUBLISHING DIVISION
P.O. Box 261333, Baton Rouge, LA 70826-1333
800-274-1403 (In LA 225-344-0476)
Fax: 225-344-0480
Internet address:
e mail: claitors@claitors.com
World Wide Web: http://www.claitors.com

(original title page)

Louis Casimir Elisabeth

MOREAU - LISLET

FOSTER FATHER

OF

LOUISIANA CIVIL LAW

ALAIN A. LEVASSEUR
Hermann Moyse, Sr. Professor of Law
Associate Director, Center of Civil Law
Studies

The Louisiana State University
Law Center Publications Institute

1996

copyright 1996, Alain A. Levasseur
All rights reserved.

L. Moreau Lislet (1818)

Source: Masonic Temple, New Orleans

PREFACE

The Louisiana legal system is unique in the United States and legal scholars and others throughout the country have been interested in learning how this situation came to pass. Most assume that Louisiana lawyers know the answer, and with surprising frequency we, of the legal profession, are asked when we travel around the country, "What is the origin of your jural system?" (or, sometimes, pejoratively, "Where did you get your crazy laws"?). Our answers are usually vague and incomplete (e.g. "We adopted the Code Napoléon") or desperately wrong (e.g. "The Acadians brought their laws with them when they migrated to Louisiana in 1755"). Even legal scholars who are steeped in Louisiana law have a hard time answering questions about the roots of our legal system. Indeed, as this excellent little book demonstrates, there has been disagreement among this elite group as to how these questions should be answered.

It is, therefore, fair to say that, until now, the origins of the Louisiana legal system have been shrouded in mystery. This book does not have a title that is overreaching: it resolves the riddle in a most persuasive way. It accomplishes this goal in the old-fashioned way of painstaking research that carefully and diligently delves into minute matters that sometimes, in and of themselves, have been enigmatic and important, at least in a secondary way. For example, was Moreau Lislet, the single most important individual in the development of our law, a person of African antecedence, as contended by the great legal scholar Mitchell Franklin, or a caucasian, as commonly assumed? What kind of a scholar was he? Was he respected by his peers? Was he capable of deceit?

This book, of course, will be of intense interest to members of the legal profession, at least those who are not preoccupied with money making. (Even these lawyers may find the book rewarding by uncovering here or there a nugget of wisdom that will be of tangible benefit to their entrepreneurial skills of selling their legal product). Outside the legal profession, the book will be attractive to anyone who is interested in the history of an important period- namely of the early 19th century- of our state and nation. At bottom this work is as much a book of history as it is of law and will be of great value to those who are interested in either or both of these disciplines.

William D. Hawkland
Chancellor Emeritus and Boyd Professor Emeritus
Louisiana State University
Law Center

Acknowledgments

My "academic and scholarly debts" are to my colleagues Chancellor W.D. Hawkland, Chancellor W.R. Day, Professors Robert A. Pascal and Thomas A. Harrell, for their unyielding support and their insightful observations. I owe a special debt of gratitude to Tanya Shively for her dedicated and passionate involvement in the cause of the Louisiana Civil Law system which she exhibited through this work she helped me nurture. My indebtedness also goes to Barbara C. Prout, a diligent, meticulous and multilingual assistant, who contributed her skills to bring this work to its present form.

Preface to the reprint edition
Acknowledgements

This new edition is dedicated, to a large extent, to the De La Vergne family and mostly to Louis de la Vergne whose erudition and perseverance have greatly motivated us in undertaking a new version of our original book on "Louis Casimir Elizabeth Moreau Lislet: Foster Father of Louisiana Civil Law" (1996).

Sincere thanks to Bob Claitor and Claitor's Publishing for their contribution to Louisiana legal history through the publication of this book.

Alain Levasseur
Vicenç Feliú

INTRODUCTION

"Calumny never dared to aim its shafts at him".
C.

The history of the legal system of the State of Louisiana is still very young: not even three centuries old. And, yet, despite the rather close temporal proximity of its original sources, this "History" has remained shrouded in the cloud of a tenacious but serene and soothing mystery. A "mystery", indeed, it has been, fueling speculations of all sorts by a few prominent legal scholars and drawing intellectual cleavages of substantial magnitude between a handful of legal historians. The serenity of that mystery instills a feeling of comfort, righteousness and strength; why should one be willing to attempt to explain that mystery that "time", apparently, does not wish to unravel?

Although the Louisiana civil law system is inherently different from the common law system prevailing in the other states of the United States, we are nevertheless very much alike a multitude of other legal systems such as those prevailing on the Latin American continent, in the province of Quebec and through most of Europe. Furthermore, we can trace our legal history several centuries back, to the Emperor Justinian and his Corpus Juris Civilis of the VIth century A.D.. Our history ties us also more specifically to two of the oldest and, at one time, most powerful European nations, France and Spain. That feeling of "belonging" is comforting as it provides a feeling of lasting identity while it is, at the same time, a source of pride. Indeed, Louisianians have legitimate grounds to be proud of the past legal history of their state as they should be looking forward to experiencing the benefits of a mixed legal culture. Standing at the crossroads of two major legal traditions, Louisiana may even be setting the modern trend that will become the destiny of all existing legal systems.

Yet, the tenacity of the mystery still surrounding the history of Louisiana law must be challenged and piece by piece carved out of its shroud. Louisianians will then find even greater pride in their mixed legal system and, hopefully, stand strong in its defense, as it was, at one time, in the hands of a few great men who fashioned the Louisiana legal system out of "the Roman law which formed the basis of the civil and political laws of all the civilized nations of Europe".

Ever since the adoption of the Louisiana Digest in 1808, the mystery of the Louisiana legal system has been built on theories or propositions which have had, and still continue to have, their advocates. The publication, in 1971, of Professor Batiza's meticulous textual analysis of the " Louisiana Civil Code of 1808: its actual sources and present relevance" triggered another round of debates among legal historians and scholars. The issue was simple to state but difficult to solve: were the sources of the Louisiana Civil Code of 1808, French or Spanish? In this respect, Professor Batiza advanced two conclusions, one direct and "mathematical" whereas the second was somewhat veiled and fundamentally "subjective".

The first direct and mathematical conclusion was that the "French Projet of the year VIII is the source of 807 provisions; the French Civil Code of 1804 is the source of 709 provisions. Thus, the French Projet and Code, combined, account for 1,516 provisions, or about 70 percent of the Louisiana Code of 1808" out of the 2,081 provisions, or 97 percent, that Professor Batiza was able to "identify".

The second conclusion, veiled and subjective, was, in our opinion, much more serious since it impugned the integrity and moral character of the two drafters of the Louisiana Civil Code, but one, Moreau Lislet, more specifically than the other, James Brown. This second conclusion, bordering on an accusation, was that, actually, Moreau Lislet had betrayed the trust placed in him by the Louisiana legislature which appointed him in 1806 with the mission to draft a Code based on the laws then in force in the "Territory of Orleans", meaning Spanish law and Roman law. So, Professor Batiza implied, in writing 70 percent of the Civil Code articles on the basis of French sources, Moreau Lislet had violated the trust placed in him by his peers and the citizenry of the Territory. Moreau Lislet was, in fact, charged with deceit, misrepresentation, not to mention "fraud".

This veiled but inevitable conclusion appeared to us, in 1971, to be excessive and even outrageous. It was based exclusively on "words", on matching "texts", on the outward look of the texts of law without enough attention being paid either to the "substance" of the law or to the actual drafting and matching process that might have been used by Moreau Lislet and James Brown. Our immediate reaction was to side with the "accused" who was denied his right to due process of law and to be represented before the court of twentieth century scholars.

We decided to attempt to find out, exclusively at the outset, who was this "Moreau Lislet", who was "the man", where did he come from, what had he done and, hopefully, develop a rational and accurate feel for that unknown but remarquable man and his work. Following a great amount of research and many months of disillusionment, this is what we believe we have accomplished in the second part of this work.

The next step in our research was inevitably dictated to us by the conclusions we had reached on the personality of Moreau Lislet. Having concluded that he was a man of the utmost integrity, a scholar most admired and a gentle loving man, we attempted to walk in the steps taken by Moreau Lislet in his actual drafting of the Digest of 1808. What did his peers think of his work on the Digest? What were the political, professional and social circumstances surrounding Moreau Lislet while he was drafting the Digest and thereafter? How was the Digest implemented by the courts?. In the third part of this work we could only conclude that "grandeur", "integrity and honesty" were on Moreau Lislet's side and that there had been no "mockery" on his part. In our opinion, the judgment of "History" exonerates Moreau Lislet of any wrongdoing!

The first part of this book was undertaken last, out of necessity. Indeed, the relationship between the first and the third parts of this research can be found in the conclusion reached in the first part that the law of Louisiana in between the years 1803 and 1808 was <u>definitely</u> Spanish. There was, therefore, continuity in the law of Louisiana through the good offices of Moreau Lislet. We hope to have proven "beyond a reasonable doubt" that, in this crucial year of 1803, the French government did not repeal Spanish law so that the laws of Spain were the law of the Territory during the formative years, 1803 to 1808, of the Louisiana legal system. Thereby, another controversy that had arisen as to whether or not French law had been substituted to Spanish law in 1803, should also be put to rest.

TABLE OF CONTENTS

TITLE PAGE
PREFACE (original and revised)

INTRODUCTION i

PART I - THE MAJOR PERIODS OF LOUISIANA LEGAL HISTORY 1

Chapter I - The French Period 1

Chapter II - The Spanish Period 8

Chapter III - The Transitional Period:
   The Fate of Louisiana 13

Chapter IV - Louisiana Under American Domination:
   The First Years: 1803-1808 39

PART II - A "CIVIL LAW" LAWYER: LOUIS CASIMIR MOREAU LISLET 69

Chapter I - Louis Casimir Moreau Lislet:
   A Family Tree 71

Chapter II - Louis Casimir Moreau Lislet:
   Uncertainties of the Early Years 79

Chapter III - From Dondon to New Orleans 95

Chapter IV - The First Years of Integration 114

Chapter V - The Rewarding Years 134

Chapter VI - Poverty and Greatness 154

PART III - GRANDEUR OR MOCKERY? 167

Chapter I - "The Tournament of Scholars" 170

Section I - Professor Batiza's Theory of the French Origin of the Digest of 1808 171

Section II - Professor Pascal's Theory of the Spanish Origin of the Digest of 1808 176

Section III - Form Versus Substance 184

Chapter II - 19th and 20th Centuries Variation on the Same Theme 207

Section I - Moreau Lislet and the Spanish Sources of the Digest of 1808: 19th Century Spanish Variations 208

Section II - Moreau Lislet and the French Sources of the Digest of 1808: 19th Century French Variations 221

Section III - 20th Century Variations on the Same Theme 229

Chapter III - The Digest of 1808 and the Courts 236

Section 1 - The Digest of 1808 and the Superior Court of the Territory of Orleans: 1808-1812 . 237

Section 2 - The Sources of the Digest of 1808 and the Supreme Court of the State of Louisiana: 1812-1823 243

CONCLUSION 257

APPENDICES 281
    New Appendix – Spanish Sources of Law ... 304
    of the Digest of 1808 (Feliú)

PART I

THE MAJOR PERIODS OF LOUISIANA LEGAL HISTORY

CHAPTER I.

THE FRENCH PERIOD

Although 1682 marked the year in which René Cavelier Sieur de La Salle claimed, officially in the name of King Louis XIV of France, the vast stretch of land extending from the Gulf of Mexico to the Great Lakes in the northern half of the United States, it was not actually until 1699, following the truce of Riswick, that this land truly underwent colonization and development.[1]

The first French settlement along the Gulf Coast was founded at this time by Pierre Le Moyne, Seigneur d'Iberville, and established in Biloxi, now in Mississippi. That settlement, which consisted of a military outpost, and other posts along the Mississippi River that were later added so as to establish a link with the northern part of the country, were the symbols of France's control of this territory. On September 14, 1712, a royal edict granted to Antoine Crozat, a wealthy French merchant, commercial and economic control over the colony, and at the same time provided that the legal system of

---

[1] *See generally* Charles Gayarré, *Histoire de la Louisiane*, 2 Volumes, 1846-1847; Gayarré, *History of Louisiana*, 4 Volumes, 1879; François Xavier Martin, *The History of Louisiana*, 1882; Marcel Giraud, *Histoire de la Louisiane Française*, 4 Volumes, 1953-1974; Henry Plauché Dart, *The Legal Institutions of Louisiana*, 1918; *Louisiana Historical Quarterly* Vol. 2, p. 72 *et seq.*

Louisiana would be the Custom of Paris.² The Superior Council, whose structure and powers were defined in patent letters dated December 18, 1717, was entrusted with the administration of this Custom, which thus represented the first legal system to be enforced in the territory of Louisiana. A royal edict issued September 10, 1716, had declared the Superior Council to be a permanent body, after the model set up in the other French colonies.³ In August, 1717, the colony was turned over to the Company of the Western Indies and the financier John Law. Then in August and September of 1719 a new royal edict and letters patent were issued,⁴ confirming the existence of the Superior Council, extending its powers, and raising it to the status of a legal institution. The Council was to remain in existence until 1763, a year that marked the end of the first period of the French presence in Louisiana.

The Superior Council, which functioned as the court of last resort, was composed primarily of non-lawyers who were representatives of the Company. The Council had jurisdiction over both civil and criminal cases applying the royal civil ordinance and the royal criminal ordinance of 1670 and judging according to the rules of procedure in use at the Châtelet, in Paris.

Within the smaller districts of Louisiana, the military commanders acted as Justices of the Peace, referring the more important cases to the Superior Council. By virtue of a royal edict issued in 1725, a special court was established in New Orleans. The function of this court was to relieve the

---

[2] Dart, op. cit. p. 74 *et seq*; Giraud, op. cit. vol. 1, p. 279.

[3] Giraud, op. cit. vol. 2, p. 85.

[4] Id. vol. 3, p. 292; Dart, op. cit. p. 86.

Louisiana after being driven out of their land by British troops. This influx of new French blood, together with the fact that the entire year of 1765 passed without a Spanish governor assuming control of the territory, gave the local French-speaking population hope that the treaty of cession to Spain would not be carried out.

On March 5, 1766, however, Don Antonio de Ulloa arrived in Louisiana to assume power in the name of the King of Spain. Although Ulloa was received with due respect, there was an undercurrent of disdain and hostility. Ulloa, realizing that he could not assume immediate and effective control of the reins of government, thought it wiser to leave intact, at least temporarily, the institutions in force and seek the good graces of the French commander Aubry, successor of D'Abbadie, who had died a few months earlier. Thus, Ulloa was the governor in title but Aubry was the actual authority. Ulloa refused to recognize the Superior Council as a representative part of the former colonial government, except in its capacity as a court. Nevertheless, by its very rejection and the humiliation felt by its members, the Superior Council gained an important political power.

Quite naturally the local population, hostile to the new Spanish government, put its trust in the Superior Council rather than in Aubry, who was suspected of being an agent of the Spanish crown. These suspicions, which ultimately became justified by a series of events, were based upon Aubry's clear disregard for the instructions that the King of France had given to Aubry's predecessor, D'Abbadie, on April 21, 1764.[9] This clear and open hostility expressed by most of the Creole population was deeply rooted in its fear of the Spanish system of administration of colonies, which many associated with a total denial of their rights as persons or as owners. The overt conflict between the two parties to this

---

[9] Id. p. 167 *et seq.*

Superior Council of some of its responsibilities and to expedite the administration of justice in certain matters.[5]

The Company of the Western Indies experienced economic and financial difficulties and, in 1731, surrendered the administration of the colony back to the French crown. For the next thirty years (from 1731 to 1762), few changes occurred within the government of Louisiana, aside from the fact that the officers of the French crown took over the former functions of the representatives of the Company of the Western Indies.

On November 3, 1762, by virtue of the treaty of Fontainebleau, the King of France ceded to his cousin, the King of Spain, the Louisiana territory. This "gift" was to remain a secret between the two kings until the signing of the treaty of Paris on February 10, 1763.[6] On April 21, 1764, King Louis XV of France wrote a letter to the French military commander, D'Abbadie,[7] instructing him to transfer his powers over the colony of Louisiana to the representatives of the Spanish monarch upon their arrival. When the news of the cession became known to the French inhabitants of the territory, they were stunned and deeply disturbed.[8] The feeling that they were being treated as mere objects of bargaining between France, England and Spain made them wonder with anxiety what would become of their form of government, their laws, and their customs. It was precisely at this time, moreover, that several hundred exiles from the Canadian province of Nova Scotia, or Acadia, fled to

---

[5] Dart, p. 95.

[6] Gayarré, op. cit. vol. II, p. 91 *et seq.*

[7] Id. p. 109; Martin, op. cit. p. 196 *et seq.*

[8] Id. p. 112.

"forced coexistence" reached its peak in October of 1768 when the Superior Council decided to expel Ulloa from Louisiana.[10] Some six hundred plantation owners and merchants had sent a petition to the Superior Council, asking that certain rights and liberties be restored to them and that Ulloa, along with the other Spanish officers, be expelled from Louisiana. Lafrénière, who was the assistant public prosecutor at the Superior Council, as well as a gifted speaker, charged the Spanish authorities, and Ulloa in particular, with having violated both the spirit and letter of the treaty of transfer of Louisiana from France to Spain, and of having encroached upon the rights, customs and privileges of its inhabitants. In a word, Lafrénière accused Ulloa of having usurped his power and of having behaved like a despot. Despite the strong protests raised by Aubry, the Superior Council ordered the expulsion of Ulloa on October 29, 1768. Ulloa was to leave Louisiana shortly thereafter.

This revolution was actually no more than the rebellion of a few who would soon pay dearly — some with their lives — for their insubordination. Backed by the approval of France and the determination of the Duke of Choiseul (the French Minister in charge of the colonies) to abide by the provisions of the treaty of transfer, the Spanish government decided to resort to force and to subdue the colony. This mission was entrusted to General Alexander O'Reilly.

On August 18, 1769, the new Spanish governor landed in New Orleans heading a cohort of officials and an impressive army. On August 21, General O'Reilly had the leaders of the October, 1768 rebellion arrested and brought before a court.[11]

---

[10] Martin, op. cit. p. 201; Gayarré, op. cit. vol. II, p. 189 *et seq*.

[11] Martin, op. cit. p. 205 *et seq*; Preface to the English translation of *Las Siete Partidas*, p. XIX.

Once order had been restored and his power secured, O'Reilly undertook a thorough reform of the military, administrative, financial and judicial structures of the colony, in accordance with the instructions given to him and the powers vested in him.[12]

This period in Louisiana political and legal history has been summarized in the following words by Baron Pierre de Coubertin:

Quoique, d'ailleurs, on affectât de nier à Madrid que l'attachement pour la nation française et pour le Souverain eut été la cause du crime et que même on y considérât comme pleinement prouvé que la patrie et le souverain étaient des objets très indifférents pour tous les chefs du soulèvement, le gouvernement espagnol n'essaya pas de s'en autoriser pour entreprendre l'hispanisation de la Louisiane. O'Reilly parait avoir mesuré d'un coup d'oeil l'impossibilité d'en venir à bout, car il posa les bases d'un régime qui ne devait avoir d'espagnol que le titre et qui, pour le reste, demeurerait entièrement français. . .[13]

---

[12] The text of this commission, which is dated April 16, 1769, has been translated into English and appears in the *Inter-American Law Review*, vol. IV, p. 143 *et seq.* in an article entitled "The Unity of Private Law in Louisiana Under the Spanish Rule" by Rodolfo Batiza.

[13] *Revue des Deux Mondes*, 1904-2, p. 814. "L'Amérique Française et le Centenaire de la Louisiane," by Pierre de Courbertin, p. 805. The following is the author's translation:

Although an attempt was made in Madrid to deny that the affection for the French nation and sovereign had been the cause of the criminal act and even though it was considered to be proven that the motherland and sovereign were unimportant

Those words express an opinion that is shared by some and criticized by others, with respect to the scope and depth of the reforms, especially legal, that were introduced by O'Reilly in the early part of the Spanish colonization of Louisiana.

---

to the leaders of the uprising, the Spanish government did not attempt to take advantage of it to undertake the hispanisation of Louisiana. O'Reilly seems to have immediately realized that it was impossible to do it, since he laid down the basis of a system which would be Spanish in title only, and which would otherwise remain entirely French...

CHAPTER II.

THE SPANISH PERIOD

Opinions concerning the extent of the legal reforms introduced by O'Reilly, such as the replacement of the Custom of Paris with the law of "La Recopilacion de las Indias," are often one-sided.[14] Our purpose here is not to undertake an analysis of these opinions but rather to give as impartial an overview as possible of the essential aspects of the legal administration of the colony under Spanish rule.

One of the first reforms that O'Reilly implemented in order to better establish his authority was to abolish the Superior Council. This institution had been the source of many difficulties for the former governor, Ulloa, and had been the instigator of the October 1768 uprising against the Spanish crown. It was no surprise, then, that on November 25, 1769, O'Reilly issued a proclamation defining the colony's new form of government:

[i]t is indispensable to abolish the said Council, and to establish in its stead that form of political Government and administration of justice prescribed by our wise laws. . . We establish . . . a city council or cabildo, for the administration of justice and preservation of order in this city. . . Because of the lack of lawyers in this country, and the little knowledge which his new subjects possess of the Spanish laws might render a strict observance of them difficult, and as every abuse is contrary to the intentions of his Majesty, we have thought it useful, and even necessary to issue a summary or proclamation drawn from the said laws . . . until a better knowledge of the Spanish language may enable every one, by the perusal of the

---

[14] These opinions, of which there are essentially three, will be presented in a subsequent chapter.

aforesaid laws, to gain a better understanding of the details.[15]

On that same day, Don Alexander O'Reilly published a series of instructions bearing on the procedure to be followed in civil and criminal trials "in accordance with the laws of the Nueva Recopilacion de Castilla and la Recopilacion de Las Indias. . .".[16] With respect to the law applicable to the merits of a case or the substantial issues raised, O'Reilly, who had been fully authorized to act according to the circumstances,[17]

---

[15] *The Louisiana Law Journal*, Vol. 1, No. 2, 1841, "Ancient Jurisprudence of Louisiana," pages 1 through 27.

[16] Id. pages 27 through 60. Aside from presenting the rules of procedure, these instructions included a sixth section on wills, which dealt not only with the form of wills but, also with provisions of substance relating to the transmission of successions.

[17] Royal patent issued at Aranjuez, on April 16, 1769. "The Unity of Private Law in Louisiana under the Spanish Rule," *Inter-American Law Review*, Vol. IV, p. 145.
The powers vested in O'Reilly by Charles III were neither specific nor restricted. On the contrary, O'Reilly received "full powers" in all areas, especially legal. The extent of these powers contrasts with the more restrictive nature of the powers vested in Ulloa on March 22, 1769. With respect to the introduction of Spanish law in Louisiana, Ulloa was entrusted with ensuring...
   6. That civil and criminal lawsuits and proceedings instituted between natives of the country, or when a Spaniard or foreigner is involved, be commenced, continued and decided according to the laws and customs having a constant and uninterrupted force in the colony, and in situations which are either doubtful or have not been specifically contemplated,

informed the Council of the Indies that "In all respects I deem it necessary that this Province be governed by the same laws as those in force in the other dominions of His Majesty in America, and that everything be written in the Spanish language; in this manner it will be easier to appeal to the superior courts . . ., otherwise the king would have to establish new courts with judges familiar with different laws and foreign languages . . ."[18] O'Reilly's suggestions received the formal approval of the King of Spain on January 27, 1770.[19]

according to the Laws of the New Compilation of the Indies; but when the lawsuit be instituted between Spaniards, it shall be decided according to the said Laws of the Indies...

Therefore, the powers which were vested in O'Reilly included and exceeded those which had been vested in Ulloa. It is not surprising, then, that, although no official document has yet been discovered to confirm this allegation, O'Reilly introduced the Spanish law into Louisiana, as he had the general power to do, and as it was later confirmed by Louis Moreau Lislet that he had done:

From the time of the promulgation of O'Reilly's proclamation of November 25, 1769 until now, the French laws ceased to have any authority in this country, and all controversies were tried and decided conformably to the Spanish laws, by a tribunal, of which the governor was the only judge, though he was bound to take the advice of a lawyer appointed and commissioned to that effect, by the King of Spain... (Preface to the English translation of Las Siete Partidas, 1820, p. XX and XXI).

[18] Batiza, op. cit. p. 146.

[19] Id. p. 147.

The documents summarized above, whose authenticity is beyond doubt, prove in a clear and definite manner that O'Reilly received the authority to initiate any reform which he deemed necessary to ensure the proper administration of Louisiana. Of course, the fact that O'Reilly had been given the power to replace the Custom of Paris with "la Recopilacion de las Indias" and other sources of Spanish law, does not necessarily mean that he actually made use of this power. But, then, why would a "general" ask to be granted certain powers from his superiors if he did not intend to use them in order to serve the best interests of a cause which he, himself, was defending? Why would O'Reilly have gone to such length to explain the reasons for his petition to the King of Spain if he had not considered all the advantages that his administration would gain by the change that he contemplated?

The wording of the last few sentences of the preamble of the proclamation of November 25, 1769, quoted above, is very instructive: on the one hand, it illustrates the skill with which O'Reilly introduced a change into Louisiana's legal system, taking his time and beginning with an "abstract" of the Spanish laws that everyone could understand;[20] and, on the other hand, it reflects the determination with which he began this reform, addressing the settlers in French, thereby preventing them from claiming ignorance of the Spanish language as an excuse for disregarding the new law.[21] In the end, "time brought familiarity [with the Spanish law] and before the close of the first decade the French inhabitants and

---

[20] This "abstract" is accompanied by numerous references to the various Spanish laws.

[21] The proclamation of November 25, 1769 was published in both French and Spanish. Henry Plauché Dart, "Courts and Law in Colonial Louisiana", *Report of the Louisiana Bar Association*, 1921, p. 54.

the Spanish system became friends, the people began to understand and to take advantage of the laws of the Indies and the laws of Spain, finding after all that there was no fundamental difference, or at least no such difference as to justify their original disgust at the change of rulers and systems."[22]

It appears that the various governors who succeeded O'Reilly after 1772[23] did not bring about any major reform to the legal system introduced by O'Reilly in 1769. This suggests that the local population had finally accepted the Spanish laws. However, the history of Louisiana law was not to end there. During the last few months that marked the turn of the century, the settlers had reason to believe that their hopes, which had for so long been disappointed, their wishes so long disregarded, were about to be fulfilled: Napoléon Bonaparte apparently wished to integrate Louisiana into the Empire that he was beginning to build.

---

[22] Dart, "Colonial Legal System of Arkansas, Louisiana and Texas," *Report of the Louisiana Bar Association*, 1926, p. 56.

[23] The governors were: Unzaga 1772-1776; Galvez 1777-1783; Miro 1784-1791; Carondelet 1792-1797; Gayoso 1797-1799; Casa Calvo 1799-1801 and Salcedo 1801-1803.

CHAPTER III.

THE TRANSITIONAL PERIOD: THE FATE OF LOUISIANA

Based on all of the information he had received, particularly that contained in a thorough and convincing report drawn up by De Pontalba, a resident of Louisiana for quite some time,[24] Bonaparte concluded that France's repossession of this territory, which held a strategic position on the vast American continent, could greatly contribute to the expansion of French industry and trade. Therefore, by virtue of a treaty concluded on the 1st of October, 1800, at San Ildefonso, Spain agreed to return Louisiana to France on the basis of the territorial boundaries set by the treaty of Fontainebleau of November 3, 1762. In return, Bonaparte granted the duchy of Tuscany to the Duke of Parma, the son-in-law of the King of Spain. France and Spain agreed, however, that the treaty of San Ildefonso would remain a secret as long as England and France were at war for fear that England, mistress of the seas, would seize control of Louisiana. As a result, the Spanish government sent a new governor, Don Juan Manuel de Salcedo, to Louisiana in June of 1801.

The treaty of San Ildefonso, which was important from both a political and strategic point of view, would not remain a secret for long. The American ambassador to England[25] was quickly apprised of this news and informed his government of it in March of 1801. The American government, fully conscious of the unique position that the port of New Orleans held with respect to the great waterway, the Mississippi River, was somewhat alarmed by the news. It immediately

---

[24] Gayarré, *History of Louisiana*, Vol. III, p. 410.

[25] Rufus King-Gayarré, op. cit. Vol. III, p. 448.

dispatched Robert Livingston as its emissary to the French authorities to dissuade France and Spain from carrying out their plan and to make a bid towards a purchase of the territory on behalf of the United States.

The negotiations between France and the United States were to last over two years. In the meantime, to fill the vacuum, Louisiana was returned by Spain to France.

One of the many concerns of the French *préfet*, Clément Laussat, was the nature of the powers that he and the commissioner of justice, Aymé, had received to carry out possible reforms of the Louisiana legal system. The importance of this issue cannot be underestimated because it is at the very heart of the controversy that has divided Louisiana's scholars over the importance and the extent of Laussat's powers to modify the legal system introduced by O'Reilly as well as the extent of Laussat's use of those powers. Some official documents that were drawn up prior to Laussat's departure for Louisiana help to illustrate the problems with which the new French administrators were confronted.

In a report dated August of 1802, while still in France, Laussat wrote the following to the French Minister of the Navy, Decrès:[26]

---

[26] *Archives Nationales Colonies*, C 13, A 51. The following is the author's translation of the report:

In order to determine the judicial structure which is best suited to Louisiana, one must have lived or have spent some time there.

Nevertheless, it is clear that there are few judicial proceedings within a country in which the inhabitants live far from one another and in which the owners have no neighbors so to speak.

New Orleans represents one of the few exceptions, although

Avant d'établir l'organisation judiciaire qui convient à la Louisiane je pense qu'il faut avoir été sur les lieux.

Néanmoins, on voit aisément qu'il y a peu de procès dans un pays où les habitants vivent à de grandes distances les uns des autres et dont les propriétés n'ont pas pour ainsi dire de voisins.

La Nouvelle Orléans presque seule est dans une position différente: mais c'est surtout par son commerce qu'elle a de la population et qu'elle est le théatre de beaucoup de transactions; aussi sera-ce un bienfait très salutaire que d'y établir très promptement un tribunal de commerce sur le pied de ceux qui existent dans nos places de commerce.

---

it is mainly because it is a center of trade that it is densely populated and that so many transactions are carried out there; therefore, it would be most beneficial to establish in New Orleans, as soon as possible, a commercial court on the same scale as those which exist in our market-places.

Under the Spanish government, civil and criminal actions are heard in New Orleans by the governor and two assistants. Appeals from these decisions may be taken, first, to the Superior Council of Havana and, second, to the Council of Madrid.

The Municipal Council (Cabildo) judges in summary proceedings and cases which amount to less than 1,650 francs; in these decisions, the municipal council is presided over by the governor and assisted by a graduate who acts as an auditor.

It would appear, then, that the best thing to do would be to postpone any plan of judicial reorganization in this territory and to send
the Commissioner of Justice to Louisiana with instructions adapted to the local way of thinking.

Laussat

Sous le gouvernement espagnol, la partie civile et criminelle est exercée à la Nouvelle Orléans par le gouverneur assisté de deux assesseurs. Il y a appel de ses jugemens d'abord au Conseil Supérieur de la Havanne, et enfin au Conseil de Madrid.

Le Conseil Municipal (Cabildo) juge les causes sommaires et au dessous de 1650 francs; il est, dans ces sortes de jugemens, présidé par le gouverneur et assisté par un gradué qui a titre d'auditeur.

On voit que, tel étant l'état des choses, ce qu'on peut faire de mieux est de suspendre tout plan d'ordre judiciaire pour ce païs là, et de se contenter d'y envoyer le Commissaire de Justice avec des instructions adaptées à ces notions locales.

Laussat

The commissioner of justice submitted suggestions of instructions to the Minister of the Navy in a report of November 1802, excerpts of which are given here:

RAPPORT

Le Commissaire de Justice Aymé, par sa lettre du 17 Brumaire, demande au Ministre des Instructions sur l'organisation judiciaire et sur la législation de la Louisiane.

Il observe, au sujet de l'organisation actuelle et pour en montrer l'incompatibilité avec nos lois, "que c'est tantôt le gouverneur général officier essentiellement militaire qui juge soit au civil soit au criminel et tantôt un Alcade; que la décision n'émane presque jamais que d'un seul juge; qu'enfin les jugements sont portés par appel à la Havane et que ceux rendus par ce second tribunal vont en dernier ressort au Conseil de Castille."

Dans l'intention de présenter aux justiciables plus de motifs de confiance sans les exposer aux mêmes lenteurs, il propose, comme meilleur mode d'organisation judiciaire pour la Louisiane:

1. Un Tribunal d'Appel séant à la Nouvelle Orléans qui jugeat en dernier ressort tant au civil qu'au criminel et ne put juger qu'au nombre de Sept juges. Ce Tribunal serait composé d'un Président, de six juges, d'un commissaire du gouvernement, d'un greffier et de deux suppléants.

2. Deux Tribunaux de première instance, l'un à la Nouvelle-Orléans, l'autre au siège de la Sous-Préfecture, lesquels seront en même temps Tribunaux Civils, de Commerce et de l'Amirauté. Ils jugeraient en dernier ressort jusqu'à concurrence de 2000. Ils seraient composés chacun d'un Président, de deux juges, d'un commissaire du gouvernement, d'un greffier et de deux suppléants. Ils ne pourraient juger qu'au nombre de trois juges.

Le Commissaire de Justice s'abstient de prononcer sur ces deux questions, savoir:

1) Si le recours sera admis au Criminel

2) S'il convient de renvoyer pour le recours en cassation, en matière civile, devant le Tribunal de Cassation, ou devant le Tribunal d'Appel de la Colonie française la plus voisine qui en ferait fonction.

En considérant que la population de la Louisiane est d'origine française, qu'on y parle notre langue et que son régime a été longtemps le même que celui de nos colonies, il pense que le gouvernement trouvera convenable d'ordonner que la justice y soit rendue tant au civil qu'au criminel, suivant les formes de procéder, les Loix, Règlements et Tarifs qui étaient observés en 1789 dans les possessions rendues à la France par le traité d'Amiens...[27]

---

[27] *Archives Nationales Colonies*, C 13, A 51. The following is the author's translation of the report:

The Commissioner of Justice Aymé requests, in his letter of 17 Brumaire, that the Minister of the Navy issue some instructions on the judicial structure and legislation of

Louisiana.

He observes that the present structure is incompatible with our laws and that civil and criminal cases are decided, sometimes, by the governor-general and, sometimes, by an alcade; that the decision is almost never rendered except by only one judge; and, finally, that the judgments are appealable to Havana and may be subsequently taken in last resort to the Council of Castille.

In order to instill more confidence in the ordinary man without subjecting him to the usual delays, he proposes that the new legal structure in Louisiana consist of:

1. *A court of appeal, established in New Orleans, which would judge in last resort in both civil and criminal cases and which would require seven judges for any ruling. This court would be composed of a President, six judges, a commissioner for the government, a clerk of court, and two deputies.*

2. *Two district courts — one in New Orleans, and one at the seat of the sub-prefecture — both of which would also serve as civil courts, commercial courts and courts of admiralty. They would judge in last resort up to 2000. Each court would be composed of a President, two judges, a commissioner for the government, a clerk of court and two deputies. The court would require three judges for any ruling.*

The Commissioner of Justice will refrain from taking any position on two questions:

1. *Whether a recourse will be granted in criminal cases;*

2. *Whether appeals from judgments in civil cases should be taken to the Tribunal of Cassation or to the Court of Appeal of the nearest French colony which would act in this capacity.*

Since the inhabitants of Louisiana are of French extraction and speak French, and since the system of law in this province had long been the same as that of our colonies, he believes that the government should order that justice be dispensed, in both civil and criminal cases, in accordance with the forms of

On Brumaire 29, year 11, (November 2nd, 1802) the Minister of the Navy, Decrès, sent the following instructions to the commissioner of justice in Louisiana:[28]

---

action, the regulations and the tariffs observed in 1789 in those colonies handed over to France by virtue of the treaty of Amiens...

[28] Id. The following is the author's translation:

I reply, citizen, to your two letters of 16 V^e and 17 of this month in which you request instructions on the judicial structure and legislation of Louisiana and present some bases relating to the administering of justice in this colony.

The intention of the government is not to decide, at this time, what concerns the courts and the forms of action in Louisiana. Rather, the government before acting will wait to have those proposals submitted by you in this regard which will serve the best interests of the ordinary man, the localities, and the legislation of both the mother country and its colonies; after having discussed this at great length with the Captain-General and Colonial Prefect in meetings which observe the form prescribed by the rules governing the organization of the respective powers. You should first seek all available information from the leading citizens and public officials of this territory.

Since appeals from judgments can no longer be taken to Havana or the Council of Castille, they shall henceforth be taken to the court or courts which you in conjunction with the other two superior authorities will consider necessary and financially feasible to establish.

Appeals to the highest instance shall be taken, as in all of our colonies, to a special court in France and scheduled in accordance with the distance and estimated travel time. I do not know whether the government will eventually change this

Je réponds citoyen, à vos deux lettres des 16 V^{re} et 17 de ce mois par lesquelles vous demandez des instructions sur l'organisation judiciaire, sur la législation de la Louisiane et présentez des bases relatives à l'administration de la justice dans cette colonie.

L'intention du gouvernement n'est point de régler, en ce moment, ce qui concerne les tribunaux et les formes de procéder à la Louisiane. Il attendra, pour s'en occuper, les propositions que vous lui soumettrez, à cet égard, sous les rapports combinés du plus grant interêt des justiciables, des localités, de la législation de la métropole et de celle de ses colonies; après en avoir mûrement conféré avec le capitaine Général et le préfet Colonial, dans des assemblées communes à la forme prescrite par le règlement de l'organisation des pouvoirs respectifs. Vous devrez même, auparavant, vous entourer consultativement de toutes les lumières que vous pourrez recueillir de principaux habitants et officiers publics du pays.

---

state of things and grant the power of review or cassation from Island to Island, or from the continent to the nearest Island; at this time, however, it intends to leave fully intact the universality of powers vested in the Tribunal of Paris.

Therefore, until the Consuls of the Republic have determined the judicial structure of Louisiana, the existing structure shall be preserved and subject only to temporary modifications of an indispensable and urgent nature. Nonetheless, in your personal capacity and by virtue of your powers, you shall judge alone or together with other judges, and as their President, in all cases in which the governor-general would have judged alone or with other judges.

Those explanations should dispel any objection which you may have to the temporary preservation of the Spanish system of law.

Decrès

Le recours par voie d'appel, ne pouvant plus avoir lieu à la Havane, ni au Conseil de Castille, vous attribuerez ces recours, de concert avec les deux autres premières autorités, à celui ou à ceux des Tribunaux existans, que vous jugerez devoir déterminer, en évitant néanmoins une composition trop nombreuse et par conséquent trop onéreuse aux finances de l'état.

Quant au pourvoi en cassation, il aura lieu, comme dans toutes nos autres colonies, au Tribunal créé à cet effet en France, dans les délais que la distance des lieux vous paraitra devoir comporter. J'ignore si le gouvernement ne changera pas cet ordre de choses par la suite, en attribuant compétance de Cassation ou de révision soit d'Isle à Isle, soit de continent à l'Isle la plus voisine; mais quant à présent, son intention est de ne rien ôter à l'universalité des pouvoirs du Tribunal de Paris.

Ainsi, jusqu'à ce que les Consuls de la République ayant fixé l'organisation judiciaire de la Louisiane, celle qui subsiste aujourd'hui sera maintenue, sauf les modifications provisoires que l'administration locale aurait jugées être indispensables et ne pouvoir souffrir de retard. Néanmoins, en votre qualité personnelle et en vertu de vos attributions, vos jugerez seul ou en concurrence avec d'autres juges, et comme leur Président, dans tous les cas où le Gouverneur Général jugeait seul ou en concurrence.

Ces explications me paraissent résoudre vos objections contre la conservation temporaire du régime espagnol, sur le fait de la justice.

Decrès

Decrès' letter is important for two reasons: first, it emphasizes the fact that the French government had no intention of introducing any hasty and ill-conceived reforms. Quite to the contrary, if there were to be reforms they would not be introduced until after the commissioner of justice had completed an in-depth study and had compiled a report for the benefit of the consuls of the Republic on the alterations which ought to be made in the administration of justice in Louisiana. The second important feature of this letter is that it clearly states that Louisiana would, for the time being, remain under the Spanish legal system. It follows from this letter that O'Reilly and his successors had indeed implemented a Spanish legal system of law in Louisiana. This is confirmed by a document that was written by Decrès in November of 1802, which contains the following:[29]

---

[29] Id. The following is the author's translation:
INSTRUCTION for the Captain-General of Louisiana:
Louisiana, which is retroceded to France by virtue of article 3 of the treaty concluded at San Ildefonso between the Court of Madrid and the French Republic...
Louisiana must be considered mainly in the light of Justice, finances...
JUSTICE.

Until now, justice has been dispensed very simply, although arbitrarily, under the Spanish government.
The Commissioner of Justice, appointed by the First Consul, is entrusted with establishing a more reputable system of justice as a result of his own involvement and supervision.
His first order of business shall be to consider what must be maintained in the present organization of Louisiana's tribunals, with respect to their procedure and composition.
There is no doubt that the administration of justice in this colony should be brought closer to that of those countries subjected to the laws of the Republic, although any precipitant change has its disadvantages. However, one cannot claim that inhabitants who are scattered over a vast stretch of land, separated from one another by great distances, and suffering only minor complications of interests, should need the multiplicity of courts and legal procedures required by a large

INSTRUCTION pour le Capitaine Général de la Louisiane.
   La Louisiane qui est rétrocédée à la France par l'article 3 du Traité conclu à St. Ildelphonse entre la Cour de Madrid et la République française...
   La Louisiane doit être ici considérée surtout sous le rapport de la Justice, des finances...

JUSTICE
   L'ordre judiciaire parait avoir été réglé jusqu'à ce jour fort simplement, mais arbitrairement, sous le gouvernement espagnol.
   Cet ordre de choses va prendre un caractère respectable par les travaux et la surveillance du Commissaire de Justice nommé par le Premier Consul.
   Son premier soin devra être de considérer ce qui doit être maintenu dans l'organisation actuelle des Tribunaux de la Louisiane, dans la forme des procédures et la composition des juges.

---

population massed together in a small and confined space.
   The duties of the Commissioner of Justice, therefore, shall be limited, upon his arrival, to fulfilling those of the leading legal authority in the colony whoever were the persons who previously fulfilled these legal duties. The Commissioner of Justice shall exercise all of the powers of Title Three of the Decree of 24 fructidor.
   He shall prepare a plan for the administration of justice adapted to the colony and shall promptly send it to the Minister, who shall, in turn, submit it to the Consuls.
   He shall also send his proposals on the appointment of the judges; and until he has received the government's decision, those courts which are in existence in Louisiana shall remain in existence.
   The Minister of the Navy and the Colonies
Decrès

Nul doute que l'ordre judiciaire de cette colonie ne doive être rapproché de ce qui a lieu dans tous les pays soumis aux loix de la République, mais tout mouvement subit a ses inconvénients. On ne peut d'ailleurs se dissimuler que des habitans épars sur une grande étendue de territoire, séparés les uns des autres par de grandes distances, n'ayant que de faibles complications d'intérêts, n'ont pas besoin de la multiplicité des Tribunaux et des formes judiciaires qu'exige une population nombreuse et réunie dans un petit espace.

Les Fonctions du Commissaire de Justice, se borneront donc, à son arrivée, à remplir les fonctions de la première autorité judiciaire dans la colonie par quelques personnes qu'elles ayent été exercées précédemment, et il entrera dans la plénitude des attributions du Titre Trois de l'arrêté du 24 fructidor.

Il rédigera un plan d'ordre judiciaire adapté à la colonie et il le fera parvenir sans délai, au Ministre, pour être soumis aux Consuls.

Il enverra en même temps ses propositions pour la nomination des juges et jusqu'à ce qu'il ait reçu la décision du gouvernement, les tribunaux actuels de la Louisiane continueront à avoir leur cours. . .

Le Ministre de la Marine et des Colonies
Decrès

These instructions from Decrès define very narrowly the extent of the powers of reform vested in the future French administrators of the colony. They were instructed to proceed only with limited reforms with respect to the organization of the courts and the rules of procedure. They were not given any power to implement any change in the substance of the law and, moreover, even with respect to the rules of procedure, the Captain-General was warned to proceed with moderation because "any precipitate change has its disadvantages."

On March 26, 1803, Laussat arrived in New Orleans to assume his duties. On May 24 of that same year, Laussat addressed the following letter to "Citizen Decrès, Minister of the Navy and the Colonies":[30]

---

[30] *Archives Nationales Colonies*, C 13, A 52. The following is the author's translation:
To Citizen Decrès, Minister of the Navy and the Colonies:
Citizen Minister
According to your instructions, you wish that the system of justice in effect at this time remain temporarily the same or, to use your own words, that "those tribunals which are in existence in Louisiana shall remain in existence." I have been here for two months — I have listened and observed. It is my duty to inform your Excellency that, contrary to your instructions, the sooner the present course of things is changed, the sooner we shall bring an improvement, an improvement highly desired by the whole colony. Shall I tell you Citizen Minister? There are no tribunals in Louisiana; there is not even a shade of one.
Let me tell you how justice is administered here: it is worse than in Turkey. All judgments within the colony are rendered in the name of the governor, except in matters relating to taxes, in which case the Intentdant acts as the supreme arbitrator. The governor signs his name as a mere formality; his signature is a matter of course, for which he is paid a fee, which constitutes one of the sources of income of his office.
Beside the governor stands the auditor of war (or lieutenant-governor); he is a ranking officer; the governor cannot decide on any matter except military without first consulting with the auditor.
Moreover, the auditor is the sole judge both in civil and criminal cases. Assessors do not even act as assistants to him. What is not allowed to a justice of the peace in France for the amount of 100 is allowed to the auditor in New Orleans for

Par vos instructions, vous avez voulu qu'en ce qui est de

---

any amount.

Therefore, his judgments inspire neither respect nor confidence and, whether sound or not, they are almost always regarded with the most shameful suspicions...

The right of appeal to Cuba and Madrid is a slow and most expensive remedy...

A change in this area is considered to be one of the first benefits of a change of sovereignty.

It may be another two months before the Commissioner of Justice arrives, and then another month or two before he is able to propose another plan; and, finally, at least six or eight months before one can expect to receive your reply from France regarding these proposals.

I beg of you in the name of the entire colony, Citizen Minister, not to allow this state of things to persist — a state in which, in this regard, the colony wails. The honor of the French government requires that the colony immediately free itself from this situation.

Now that you actually know our situation here, would you be assuming any risk, Citizen Minister, if you were to order, as soon as you receive this dispatch, by an instruction issued to the Captain-General, the Commissioner of Justice, and myself, that there be immediately established here:

1. a civil tribunal composed of five judges.
2. a commercial tribunal composed of five judges selected by the merchants.
3. a justice of the peace for each district.

This proposal is so simple that it could only raise objections on account of local circumstances, practices, or oppositions.

I assure your Excellency that far from having to fear these kinds of obstacles, you would be doing a useful and urgent thing, highly desired by and most pleasant to the colony.

Greetings,
Laussat

l'ordre Judiciaire, les choses restassent provisoirement ici dans l'état où elles sont, en un mot, selon vos propres expressions, que les Tribunaux actuels de la Louisiane continuassent à avoir leur cours.

Je suis ici depuis deux mois: j'ai écouté et observé; il est de mon devoir d'avertir votre Excellence que, plutôt au contraire ce cours cessera, plutôt nous opérerons un grand bien, un bien essentiel après lequel toute la colonie soupire; car, vous le dirai-je Citoyen Ministre? il n'y a pas de Tribunaux à la Louisiane, il n'y en a même pas l'ombre.

Voici comment l'ordre judiciaire s'y exerce; c'est pis qu'en Turquie. Les jugemens de toute espèce, dans le sein de la Colonie, se rendent au nom du gouverneur, excepté en matière fiscale où l'intendant est arbitre souverain. Le gouverneur ne donne son nom que pour la forme; sa signature est un act passif auquel est attaché un salaire, qui forme l'une des branches du revenu de sa place.

Mais à côté du gouverneur est ce qu'ils appellent un auditeur de Guerre, un Lieutenant du Gouverneur; il est gradué; rien de ce qui est de la compétence du gouverneur, hors du militaire, ne peut recevoir de décision qu'après qu'il a donné son avis.

Il est d'ailleurs seul juge en fait de justice tant au civil qu'au criminel. Des assesseurs ne lui sont même pas adjoints; ce qu'un juge de paix en France ne peut se permettre pour une valeur de 100 est permis à l'auditeur de la Nouvelle Orléans pour quelle valeur que ce soit.

Aussi ses sentences n'inspirent-elles ni respect ni confiance; fondés ou non, les soupçons les plus honteux manquent rarement de les accueillir. . . .

La voie d'appel à Cuba et successivement à Madrid est un remède tardif et ruineux. . . .

On envisage un changement en cette partie comme un des premiers bienfaits du changement de domination. . . .

Il se passera peut-être deux mois avant que le Commissaire de Justice soit ici; ensuite un mois ou deux avant même qu'il puisse se reconnaitre et proposer aucun plan; enfin au moins six ou huit mois avant que nous recevions votre réponse de France sur ses propositions.

Je vous conjure au nom de la colonie entière, Citoyen Ministre, de ne pas laisser subsister si longtemps l'état dans lequel, à cet égard, elle gémit; l'honneur du gouvernement Français exige qu'elle en sorte sans délai. . . .

Maintenant que vous savez authentiquement ce qui existe ici, quel inconvénient trouveriez-vous, Citoyen Ministre, à ordonner aussitôt après la réception de cette dépêche, par une instruction commune au Capitaine Général, au Commissaire de Justice et à moi, qu'il fut établi immédiatement ici:
1. *un Tribunal Civil ordinaire composé de cinq juges.*
2. *un Tribunal de Commerce également composé de cinq juges indiqués par les négociants.*
3. *un juge de paix par arrondissement.*

Cette proposition est si simple, qu'elle n'est même susceptible d'autres objections que de celles qui seraient puisées dans les circonstances, les habitudes, les oppositions locales.

Or je garantis à votre Excellence que loin qu'elle ait à redouter des obstacles de ce genre, elle fera au contraire une chose utile, urgente, extrêmement désirée et fort agréable à la colonie.

    Salut et Respect,
    Laussat

What Laussat obviously did not know, however, was that four days before he wrote this letter Napoleon Bonaparte had ceded Louisiana to the United States by virtue of the Treaty of Paris. This cession might explain why Laussat was not to receive a reply to his letter of May 24 and why, moreover, he had not been empowered to take extreme measures, at any time, to reinstate French law in Louisiana.

Article 4 of the Treaty of Paris stipulated that the government of France was to send a commissioner to

Louisiana in order to receive possession of the province from Spain and to deliver it to the commissioners appointed on behalf of the United States. On June 6, 1803, the First Consul appointed Laussat commissioner on the part of France. Laussat was instructed by article 4 of the treaty to take only those measures that would ensure the successful cession of Louisiana to the United States. As commissioner, therefore, Laussat could not undertake any large-scale reform in a province that was soon to belong to the United States. Moreover, it was not until November 30, 1803, that Laussat officially received possession of Louisiana in the name of the French government and, therefore, only after that date that he was able to introduce some changes, the merits of which he praised in his letters to Decrès. Laussat was a loyal and faithful subject, however, and on November 30, 1803, he issued a proclamation announcing to the inhabitants of Louisiana that he was on the eve of delivering possession of the colony to the commissioners of the United States:

Louisianais

La mission qui m'avait transporté à travers 2500 lieues de mer, au milieu de vous, cette mission dans laquelle j'ai longtemps placé tant d'honorables espérances et tant de voeux pour votre bonheur, elle est aujourd'hui changée. Celle dont je suis maintenant le ministre et l'exécuteur, moins douce quoiqu'également flatteuse pour moi, m'offre une consolation: c'est qu'en général elle vous est encore plus avantageuse. . .

L'époque arrivera promptement où vous vous donnerez une forme de gouvernement particulier qui, en même temps qu'elle respectera les maximes sacrées consignées dans le pacte social de l'union fédérale, sera adaptée à vos moeurs, à vos usages, à votre climat, à votre sol, à vos localités.

Mais vous ne tarderez pas surtout à ressentir les avantages d'une justice intègre, impartiale, incorruptible, où les formes invariables de la procédure et sa publicité, où les bornes soigneusement posées à l'arbitraire de l'application des lois, concourront avec le caractère moral et national des juges et des jurés, à répondre efficacement aux citoyens de leur sûreté et de leurs propriétés. Car c'est ici un des attributs singulièrement propres à la domination sous laquelle vous passez. . ."[31]

Despite the temporary nature of his office, Laussat took his role seriously. As there was no way of knowing exactly

---

[31] Gayarré, "Essai Historique sur La Louisiane," Volumes 1-2, 1830-1831, p. 61 *et seq.* The following is the author's translation of the proclamation:

Louisianians:
The mission which has brought me to you across 2500 leagues of water, this mission upon which I have based so many high hopes and ardent wishes for your happiness, has now completely changed. The mission with which I am now charged, as minister and executor, is less gratifying but equally flattering to me, and offers me one source of consolation: it will be more advantageous to you...
The time will come when you will establish for yourselves a form of government which, while respecting the sacred maxims of the social pact of the Federal Union, will be adapted to your mores, customs, climate, soil and particular localities.
But you shall soon feel the advantages of an upright, impartial, and incorruptible administration of justice, in which the strict and invariable forms of procedure and their publicity, and in which the carefully set limits to the arbitrary application of the laws, shall concur with the moral and national character of the judges and juries, to effectively meet the citizens' needs for security and safeguard of their property. For this is one of the inherent characteristics of the rule under which you are falling. . .

when the United States Congress would ratify the treaty, Laussat reorganized the administrative structure of New Orleans, replacing the Spanish Cabildo with a mayor, two deputy mayors and a municipal council composed of ten members.[32] He also issued an important decree whose essential provisions are reproduced below:

Considérant que par la remise de possession de la Louisiane à la République Française, les officiers de Justice qui tenaient leur caractère de la Couronne Royale d'Espagne, ont dû cesser leurs fonctions, et que le pays se trouve en ce moment sans Tribunaux; que cependant le Traité de cession aux Etats-Unis touchant à son exécution, il ne peut manquer d'en résulter bientôt des changements très considérables dans l'organisation judiciaire; qu'il y aurait les plus graves inconvénients à y multiplier coup sur coup, sans une extrême nécessité, les innovations et les changements; qu'au contraire les délais sont en général dans la nature et la sagesse de sa marche, et que par conséquent on peut se permettre de lui en imposer un de quelques jours dans cette circonstance forcée et extraordinaire;

Considérant néanmoins qu'il se présente journellement quelques cas pressans auxquels il importe de pourvoir d'avance;

ARRETE:

Le Corps Municipal prononcera, en matière judiciaire, jusqu' après l'installation des Tribunaux ou jusqu'à ce qu'il en soit autrement ordonné, par un ou plusieurs commissaires choisis dans son sein, sur les causes sommaires, urgentes, et pour lesquelles il y aura péril en la demeure, et procédera à

---

[32] Decree of November 30, 1803, for the establishment of the municipal authority in New Orleans. *Louisiana Historical Quarterly*, Vol. 20, p. 170.

tous les actes de droit, sans préjudice de la juridiction qui lui appartient en fait de police. Quant au surplus des affaires pendantes et en instruction, elles demeureront en suspens, jusqu'à qu'il ait été incessament établi des Tribunaux ou des juges pour en connaître. "³³

---

³³ New Orleans Public Library, R. V. A511, 1803-1804 (*Early Printings in New Orleans*, McMurtrie, p. 114). The following is the author's translation:

Whereas by the retrocession of Louisiana to the French Republic, the judges who served the Spanish crown have been divested of their powers and whereas this province is presently without any tribunals; whereas, nonetheless, the treaty of cession to the United States shall soon be carried into effect, certain significant changes in the judicial structure of this territory are bound to occur and serious problems could arise if innovations and changes were made at the same rate as those made in the past and without dire need; on the contrary, time is generally of the nature and wisdom of the course of the territory and, consequently, one may venture to impose one more delay of several days under these strained and extraordinary circumstances;

Whereas, nonetheless, emergencies occur every day and must be provided for in advance;

It is decreed:

The Municipal body shall adjudicate, in legal matters, until the Tribunals have been established or until it has been decided otherwise, by one or several commissioners selected from amongst its members, on summary and urgent proceedings for which there is danger in delaying, and shall undertake all legal acts without prejudice to the jurisdictional powers which belong to it in police matters.

All cases that are pending or under investigation shall remain undecided until the establishment of tribunals or judges

This decree does not state that Laussat repealed the Spanish laws in force at that time in Louisiana and that he established the laws of France in their stead.[34] The proclamation issued by Laussat on November 30, 1803, along with the above decree issued on the same date in fact attest to Laussat's deep understanding of the problems to which a radical and abrupt change in the existing legal instructions would give rise, and his firm belief that it was necessary to avoid chaos at all costs.[35]

It appears, then, that more credibility can be given to the statements made in the private and official documents written at the time of the cession than to the biased, and often unfounded, opinions expressed today. It appears certain,

---

capable of deciding them.

[34] This was the opinion of John H. Tucker, Junior, although he could not support it with any other official document. *Society of Bartolus juridical studies*, "Effect on the Civil Law of Louisiana brought about by the changes in its Sovereignty," p. 48.

[35] George Dargo brings an accusation against Laussat which is unwarranted and which Dargo would certainly have expressed in more reserved terms if he had been familiar with the above decree and had weighed its provisions as well as those of the Proclamation of November 30, 1803. (*Jefferson's Louisiana*, Harvard University Press, 1974, p. 105: "Pierre Clement de Laussat, had abolished all of the existing Spanish courts and had deliberatly neglected to put French substitutes in their place. . ."). This accusation reflects one raised by Governor Claiborne (*U.S. Territorial Papers*, Vol. IX — Orleans Territory, p. 338 *et seq.*). Contra: *Wayne Law Review*, Vol. 2, p. 169-189 "Law and Government in the Louisiana Purchase, 1803-1804" by Elizabeth Gasper Brown.

moreover, that O'Reilly had in fact abrogated all French law in Louisiana in 1769.[36] The following document, which is taken from the memoirs and correspondence of Laussat, leaves very little doubt on this point:

Inventaire, Registres, documents . . . émanant des archives du gouvernement de la Louisiane que le citoyen, Pierre Clément Laussat, Préfet Colonial, Commissaire du gouvernement français reçus des mains de MM De Salcedo et le Marquis de Casa Calvo . . . ainsi qu'il suit:
. . . .

un décret abolissant le conseil français et proclamant la mise en vigueur du droit espagnol et d'un nouveau conseil à la Nouvelle Orléans en date du 21 décember 1769. . ."[37]

---

[36] This is not the opinion of Barbé Marbois, the French Minister of Finance in 1803 and one of the original signatories of the treaty of cession of Louisiana to the United States: *Histoire de la Louisiane*, p. 350: "Les Lois et les ordonances royales furent provisoirement maintenues à la Louisiane, mais pour un temps fort court. Le président et les deux chambres du Congrès ordonnèrent que les lois de l'union americaine y seraient proclamées et exécutées." The History and Development of the Louisiana Civil Code by John T. Hood Jr., 33 *Tulane Law Review*, p. 7; *Louisiana and Her Laws*, by Henry J. Levy; *The Louisiana Book, Selections from the literature of the State*, Thomas M. Caleb, 1894.

[37] Memoirs and Correspondence of Laussat, 1803-1804, to Spanish officials relative to the cession of Louisiana. Papeles de Cuba., *Legajo, 220* (5) Louisiana. Retaking of possession by France from the hands of Spain (Howard Tilton Memorial Library, Special Collections). The following is the author's translation:

It follows that, despite Laussat's admonishments, the French government, not wishing to hurry things, adopted a wait-and-see policy at the time prior to the cession, as dictated by the political bargaining engaged in at that time for the control of Louisiana.[38] Moreover, there is not the slightest reference in Laussat's memoirs to a decision of any kind to revive the influence of French law in Louisiana.[39] Such a decision would have been clearly inconsistent with the instructions given to Laussat by his government and at odds with the wisdom and moderation which he displayed in his actions. An example is the decree of December 17, 1803, which relates to the application of the Black Code in Louisiana and which Laussat issued after being pressured by the

---

Inventory, registers, documents . . . emanating from the archives of the government of Louisiana which the Citizen, Pierre Clément Laussat, Colonial Prefect, emanating Commissioner of the French government, received from the hands of Messieurs De Salcedo and the Marquis de Casa Calvo as follows, to-wit:

. . . .

Decree doing away with the French Council and proclaiming the placing in force of the Spanish law and of a new council at New Orleans, dated December 21, 1769. . .

[38] The records of the *Archives Nationales*, Série Colonies, C 13 do not appear to contain any official documents attesting to the reintroduction of the French law in Louisiana.

[39] "Mémoires sur ma vie. A mon Fils, Pendant les années 1803 et suivantes que j'ai rempli des fonctions publiques: à savoir A La Louisiane, A La Martinique, A La Guyane Française (Howard Tilton Memorial Library, Special Collection).

municipal council of New Orleans. It demonstrates the degree to which Laussat was aware of the nature of his mission, of the limitation of his powers, and of the minimal role that he was expected to play until Louisiana was to be officially ceded to the United States.[40]

---

[40] This decree reads as follows:

Au Nom de la République Française

Le Préfet Colonial, Commissaire du Gouvernement français,
Vu l'arrêté du Corps Municipal de cette ville, en date d'hier, 23 Frimaire, relatif à la Police des Esclaves.
Considérant que le Projet de Règlement, extrait de l'Edit de 1724 dont le corps municipal nous demande d'ordonner provisoirement l'exécution, contient des modifications et des additions à plusieurs Articles de cet Edit; Que, bien qu'en général elles tendent à son amélioration, le moindre changement serait un acte de Législation Suprême, qui d'un côté l'étendue d'autorité dont nous croyons pouvoir user dans les circonstances actuelles, ou supposerait de la part de la France, une sanction supérieure qu'elles ne comportent plus, et d'un autre côté réclamerait de nous une maturité d'examen à laquelle il nous est impossible maintenant de nous livrer; que, cependant...que les instructions du gouvernement français, d'accords avec une loi de la République, du 30 floréal an X, nous prescrivaient de le (Code Noir) remettre en vigueur; que le faire, en ce moment, autant qu'il est en nous, c'est donner à la Louisiane, en nous séparant d'elle, un dernier témoignage des intentions paternelles et bienveillantes de leur ancienne Mère Patrie...
Arrête
Art. ler. L'Edit donné à Versailles au mois de mars 1724, pour le gouvernement et l'administration de la Justice, Police, Discipline et Commerce des esclaves nègres, dans la province

In conclusion, it appears that Laussat did, indeed, abolish the Spanish courts which had been established by O'Reilly, and that he replaced them with a form of French court: "Le Corps Municipal prononcera, en matière judiciaire, jusqu'après l'installation des Tribunaux ou jusqu'à ce qu'il en soit autrement ordonné, par un ou plusieurs commissaires choisis, dans son sein, sur les causes sommaires et urgentes, et pour lequelles il y aura péril en la demeure..."[41] However,

---

et colonie de la Louisiane, y sera exécuté, dorénavant selon la forme et la teneur.

Art. 2. Sont néanmoins exceptées, de cette disposition générale, les dispositions du dit Edit qui supposent un culte national ou la Traite Directe des Nègres et, en un mot, toutes celles qui seraient en contradiction avec aucun des Articles de la Constitution des Etats-Unis, sous l'empire de laquelle La Louisiane est à la veille de passer.

Donné à Nouvelle Orléans, le 24 Frimaire an XII et 17 décembre 1803.
Laussat

[41] See footnote 10, Part I, Chap. III. "L'installation des Tribunaux" to which Laussat refers never occurred: See footnote 12, Part I, Chap. III. Barbé Marbois wrote that the appointed judges merely administered justice in summary and urgent matters.

The following is the author's translation of the relevant language of the decree cited above at footnote 10:
The Municipal body shall adjudicate, in legal matters, until the tribunals have been established or until it has been decided otherwise, by one of several commissioners selected from amongst its members, on summary and urgent proceedings for which there is danger in delaying.

Laussat did not restore the preeminence of French substantive law in Louisiana; it had been repealed by O'Reilly in 1769 and was never formally reinstated.

The twenty days during which France temporarily held official control of Louisiana would prove more significant in the history of the law of the State than the hundred or so years of prior French and Spanish government. When Governor William C. C. Claiborne took possession of Louisiana in the name of the United States on December 20, 1803, he certainly had no idea that his government would be the source and the cause of serious political turmoil, as well as the instrument by which a Civil Code and the civil law system would be introduced into Louisiana, adding further to the elements of originality and singularity which characterize this North American state.

CHAPTER IV.

LOUISIANA UNDER AMERICAN DOMINATION: THE FIRST YEARS: 1803-1808

During the short period that preceded the official cession of Louisiana to the United States, President Thomas Jefferson set out to learn how this newly acquired territory was being governed, what legal system was in force and how justice was being dispensed. The American governor, W.C.C. Claiborne, to whom these questions were being directed, sent the President a report in which he wrote the following about the Louisiana legal system:

Louisiana, like most other Countries which have undergone a change of Masters, derives many of its Municipal Customs and regulations from different sources; By what kind of Laws, the French formerly governed the Province is unknown to me. After its session [sic] by them to Spain, General O'Reilly the Governor of the Province, published a Collection of Laws (as I am informed) of a general nature, but few in number. But whether that small Code was a selection from the previous Laws of the Country, to which he intended to give new force, or were certain Ordinances, then for the first time promulgated by the authority of the new Government, I have not ascertained.

....

There are in Louisiana, both Civil and Ecclesiastical Courts, the respective Jurisdictions of which, are I presume, separated by the usual Lines of distinction. Many of the officers of Government civil and Military, are vested, according to Circumstances, with inferior judicial Authority. In the several divisions of the Province, the Commandants, and other Persons commissioned only as Alcaldes or Majistrates [sic], hold petty courts of limited Jurisdiction. From these petty Courts an Appeal lies to the Governor General, who is invariably assisted with the Advice of a Counsellor called the Auditore. — From the decision of the Governor General, an appeal formerly lay to the Governor of the Havana; but now lies to the King and Council only ....

Fame accuses these Courts with Corruption, and I fear, many notorious facts support the Suspicion . . . "[42]

In a report in which he addressed himself to these same questions, Daniel Clark wrote the following:

The Code of laws is derived from the Recopilacion de Indias, & Leyes de Castilla & les uses & Coutumes de Paris for what respects usages & Customs,
The Courts in existence are:
The Governor's which has a Civil & military Jurisdiction throughout the province,
The Lewt. Governor's whose Jurisdiction extends throughout the Province in Civil affairs only,
The Tribunal of each of the two Alcades . . .
The Tribunal of the Intentioned in Admiralty & Revenue Causes . . .
   The Tribunal of the Alcade Provincial . . .
   The Ecclesiastical Tribunal . . . "[43]

Based on this firsthand but somewhat biased information, President Jefferson approved, on October 31, 1803, a resolution of Congress which provided for the temporary administration of the newly acquired territory until more permanent measures could be adopted. This resolution

---

[42] *U.S. Territorial Papers*, Vol. IX - Orleans Territory, p. 19 *et seq.*

[43] Id. p. 35 *et seq.*

stipulated, among other things, that ". . . all the military, civil, and judicial powers, exercised by the officers of the existing government of the same, shall be vested in such person and persons, and shall be exercised in such a manner, as the President of the United States shall direct for maintaining and protecting the inhabitants of Louisiana in the free enjoyment of their liberty, property and religion. . ."[44]

That same day, the President appointed William C. C. Claiborne temporary governor "to exercise within the said ceded territories all the powers and authorities heretofore exercised by the Governor and Intendant thereof . . ."[45] A few weeks later, Claiborne arrived in New Orleans and, in three days, took possession of Louisiana in the name of the United States.[46]

Claiborne was divested of his "despotic"[47] powers on March 26, 1804, when the United States Congress passed an act "for the organization of Orleans Territory and the

---

[44] Id. p. 90.

[45] Id. p. 143.

[46] On December 30, 1803, Claiborne established "a court of pleas, composed of seven justices. Its civil jurisdiction was limited to cases, which did not exceed in value three thousand dollars, with an appeal to the governor, in cases where it exceeded five hundred. Its criminal jurisdiction extended to all cases, in which the punishment did not exceed a fine of two hundred dollars and imprisonment during sixty days." (Francois Xavier Martin, *The History of Louisiana*, 1882, p.319).

[47] Gayarré, *History of Louisiana*, Vol. IV, p. 4.

Louisiana District."[48] The newly acquired territory was thus divided into two parts (the Territory of Orleans in the south, and the District of Louisiana in the north), and the executive, judicial and legislative branches of government were organized in each. The judicial power in the Territory of Orleans[49] - the only one with which we shall be concerned - was vested in a Superior Court and in such inferior courts and justices of the peace as might be deemed necessary by the Legislative Council of the territory.[50] The Superior Court was granted jurisdiction over both civil and criminal cases and consisted of three judges, any one of whom was sufficient by himself to constitute a court. These judges were appointed by the President for a period of four years. A district court consisting of one judge was established, and it held a minimum of four annual sessions in the city of New Orleans.[51]

Some of the provisions of the act of March 26, 1804, and in particular one that prohibited the importation of slaves into

---

[48] *U.S. Territorial Papers*, Vol. IX, p. 202 *et seq*.

[49] See section 5 of the Act of March 26, 1804.

[50] The Legislative Council of the Territory was composed of thirteen persons appointed annually by the President of the United States (Section 4 of the Act of March 26, 1804).

[51] Section 8 of the Act of March 26, 1804. The provisions of the section declare that the district judge shall have and exercise the same jurisdiction and powers as those exercised by the judge of the district of Kentucky, as defined in Sections 10 and 12 of the Act of September 24, 1789. (1 Stat. 77, 78, 79, 80). This judge earned an annual salary of $2,000.

the territory,[52] distressed the old French settlers, who were denied any active participation in the organization of the three branches of government.[53] Laussat, who was still in Louisiana

---

[52] Section 10 of the act prohibited any person from importing or bringing into the territory any slave or slaves.

[53] The anxiety and concern of the French colonists, who were awaiting the adoption by Congress of laws which would provide for the organization of the territory, were expressed in the following terms by the Mayor of New Orleans, Etienne Boré, in a letter addressed to the President of the United States and dated February 10, 1804:

To the President of the United States
...I Am at the head of the municipal Body of the capital of this province, that is to say of the Only body which exists there, of the Only one which Is composed of landowners and of citizens: I am qualified to speak to you of their interests...
We Are in extreme impatience for the Bills which must fix our internal Organization. The need thereof makes Itself felt more and more every day. We have extreme confidence in the Wisdom of Congress, in yours, Mr. President, who after having caused to be negotiated our union with the federation, will have it at heart that it should turn out to our good fortune. You will be anxious to cement Sentiments of fraternity between louisiana, and the other states which you govern, between their inhabitants and the louisianians...
I shall venture to represent it to you, Mr. President: it is indispensable that the heads of louisiana should know the french language, as well as the english language: if they had had this advantage, we should not have experienced the occurrences which have produced so bad a Feeling and the course of business would not languish and would not be exposed to numberless embarrassments.

in April 1804, described the dissatisfaction among the Louisianians in the following letter to Decrès:[54]

We have seen the moment when the municipal body was forced to take to you in this regard strong complaints: Mr. Claiborne began from the start by suggesting to us that we should draw up our public acts in english. A change of policy, after the discontent which this proposal excited, caused us to renounce addressing to you, Mr. President, the memoir of complaints which we had already drawn up on this Subject and preserved our liberties from this attack. A government which was despotic by its nature respected them for a long time what ought we not to expect from a Republican Government, in which the principles of natural rights have so many Safeguards and with which we are now associated Under the guarantees of a treaty which contains sacred Stipulations in our favor: we flatter ourselves generally that we Shall be erected into a Separate state, as soon as it Shall be proved that we have a Sufficient population; we have no doubt that in the meantime we shall be given what you call your Second degree of Government: it is the continual object of our hopes and of our conversations among all louisianians. Our fathers discovered, settled, cleared this region: it is watered with our Blood and our Sweat; we have caused it to flourish in spite of obstacles: worthy up to now of a better fate, we are expecting from the united states that they will appreciate the acquisition which they have made, and they will Endeavor to make it dear to us: they have a good means, for doing so by giving us a constitution in agreement with our needs our wishes our rights ... (U.S. Territorial Papers, Vol. IX, p. 184 et seq).

[54] *Archives Nationales Colonies Louisiane*, C 13, A 53.

The following is the Author's translation:

The Colonial Prefect, Commissioner of the French Republic, to the Citizen Decrès, Minister of the Navy and the Colonies:

Citizen Minister

The Louisianians, as I have already informed your Excellency, have, to their regret, been rejected once again from their mother-country. At first, they viewed and referred to this cession with much bitterness. The Spaniards secretly encouraged them to do so out of spite for the preference which Louisiana has always shown for France, as well as by a national hatred incited by the plots and acts of one of their leaders.

The tendencies and views of the Spaniards were, moreover, wonderfully assisted by the natural antipathy which the Louisianians entertained for the Americans.

Nevertheless, at the approach of a new sovereign, partly from the love of novelty, partly from the hope for those advantages which had been depicted to them, and perhaps partly from a forced resignation to a fate which they could not escape, they were about ready to acquiesce to the United States government.

But no sooner had the agents of this government assumed power that they committed one blunder after another.

I shall spare your Excellency the unnecessary details and mention only the sudden introduction of the English language, which hardly anyone understands, in the daily exercise of authority and in the most important acts of public life; brawls and commotions at public balls to decide which of the English dances or French dances would start first...the marked substitution of American for Creole majorities in the administrative and judicial bodies, the arbitrary mixture of old customs [with new ones], under the pretext that nothing has changed in the forms of the governor, — the United States

Le Prefet Colonial, Com^{re} de la République Française Au citoyen Decrès, Ministre de la Marine et des Colonies. Citoyen Ministre,

Le Louisianais, comme j'en ai déjà informé votre Excellence, se vit à regret jeté une seconde fois du sein de son ancienne mère-patrie; il interpréta et commenta en général, au premier moment, la cession avec beaucoup d'amertume. Les Espagnols l'y incitaient sourdement par dépit de la prédilection que ce pays avait toujours conservé pour la France, non moins que par une haine nationale dans laquelle les menées et les exemples très signalés d'un de leurs chefs étaient tout à fait propres à les nourrir et à les enflammer.

Le penchant et les vues des Espagnols étaient d'ailleurs merveilleusement servis par l'antipathie naturelle du Louisianais pour les américains.

Néanmoins, aux approches du changement de domination, partie amour de la nouveauté, partie espoir des avantages dont on leur dépeignait la brillante perspective, peut-être aussi résignation forcée au sort qu'il ne dépendait pas d'eux d'éviter, ils étaient assez disposés à se laisser aller sous le gouvernement des Etats-Unis.

Mais à peine ses agents eurent-ils pris les rênes qu'ils firent école sur école et faute sur faute.

J'en épargnerai à V.E. les détails inutiles.

En deux mots, introduction brusque de la langue Anglaise, que presque personne n'entend, dans l'exercice journalier de l'autorité et dans les actes les plus importants de la vie; rixes et tumultes pour savoir lesquelles l'emporteraient aux bals publics, des contredanses Anglaises ou des contredanses Françaises...substitution affectée de majorités américaines aux

---

government could hardly have had a worse beginning or have sent two men (Governor Claiborne and General Wilkinson) less suitable to conciliate their hearts...

majorités créoles dans les corps administratifs et judiciaires, mélange arbitraire d'anciens usages sous prétexte qu'il n'y a encore rien d'innové dans les formes du gouverneur, —Il n'était guère possible que le gouvernement des Etats-Unis débutat plus mal et qu'il envoyat deux hommes (Mr. Claiborne, Gouverneur et Wilkinson, Général) moins propres à lui concilier les coeurs,—".

Laussat

With the Act of March 26, 1804 of the United States Congress, the new governmental structure of the Territory of Orleans came into being as of October 1, 1804.[55] The territory was immediately divided by the Legislative Council into twelve counties; in each county an inferior court was established, presided over by one judge. The Council passed a series of acts regulating the procedure to be followed in the different courts of the territory, from the Superior Court to the justice of the peace courts.[56]

---

[55] On August 30, 1804, Thomas Jefferson appointed: Claiborne, Governor; James Brown, Secretary of the Territory; Dominic Hall, Judge of the District of Orleans; Col. Kirby and M. Prevost, judges of the Superior Court. Furthermore, he decided that, out of the thirteen members of the Legislative Council, seven would be American (constituting, thus, the majority) and six would be French. (*U.S. Territorial Papers*, Vol. IX, p. 281 *et seq*). Kirby died before taking office and Duponceau, who would have been the third judge of the Superior Court, refused his nomination.

[56] F. X. Martin, *History of Louisiana*, p. 326; Orleans Territory, Acts passed at the First Session of the Legislative Council (New Orleans 1805), pp. 144-209; 388-399.

In Section 11 of the Act of March 26, 1804, it was stipulated that "The laws in force in the said territory, at the commencement of this act, and not inconsistent with the provisions thereof, shall continue in force, until altered, modified or repealed by the legislature."[57] For the longer term, the legislative Council had the difficult mission of introducing into the Territory of Orleans a system of law which would be accepted by the old French settlers and the newcomers alike, as well as by both the Creoles and the "Americans". Furthermore, the system that was to be created had to be compatible with the United States Constitution and made easy for the recently established legal institutions to administer. The Council's efforts to carry out this mission would ultimately fan a fire of wrath and indignation which had been kindled by the political events leading up to this moment.

Whether of French or Spanish origin, the civil law was considered at that time to be the law of the Territory of Orleans. The provision of the Act of March 26, 1804 that continued that law in force was certainly not welcomed by the "Americans" who had emigrated to Louisiana and who felt totally estranged from its system of law. As a result, a confrontation arose between the partisans of the civil law system, who at that time constituted the majority, and the defenders of the common law system, who, although fewer in number, were nonetheless influential and powerful. By the nature of his duties, Governor Claiborne was caught in the middle of this dispute - to which, through his awkwardness, he added more fuel. He described the intensity of this dispute in the following passage:

In the course of my efforts to introduce the American System of Jurisprudence into the ceded Territory, I experienced many difficulties, and excited some dissatisfaction among the

---

[57] *U.S. Territorial Papers*, Vol. IX, p. 210.

people. — I sincerely wish, that the Judges may find their duties agreeable; and that the happiest result may attend their exertions for the Public Good..."[58]

The local newspapers offered advocates of the two legal systems a vehicle through which they could match their talents and express their opinions. On November 9, 1804, the following letter appeared in the *Louisiana Gazette*:[59]

By the treaty of cession Louisiana became entitled to be incorporated into the union. She was thenceforth to be considered as the germ of one, or of several states, to be assimilated, in all respects, and as soon as possible to her sister commonwealths. In all the other states the laws are founded on the common law of England...

The laws of Spain are generally excellent in themselves; for they are founded on the Roman Code, one of the most perfect and elegant systems of jurisprudence ever promulgated to the world. Its precepts are for the most part the genuine maxims of the law of nature, applied to the state of man in civil society; but the manner of carrying them into effect, adopted by the Spanish Tribunals, is perhaps the most objectionable that could have been derived. If ingenuity had been exerted to give opportunity for the corrupt administration of justice no rules of practice more efficacious for that purpose could have been framed, than those which permit the Judge to hear, to examine and decide in private ... It appears, therefore, ... that Mr. Claiborne acted right in establishing a Court, similar in many respects to those of America, in place of restoring the Tribunals which the French Prefect had abolished...

---

[58] Letter from Claiborne to James Madison, October 29, 1804, *U.S. Territorial Papers*, Vol. IX, p. 317.

[59] *The Louisiana Gazette*, Friday, November 9, 1804, No. 13. "To the Editor of the Louisiana Gazette...".

> *I admit that the introduction of the English language will occasion some inconvenience. But would not inconvenience be felt if the French language were exclusively established? Those whose native tongue is English, though they now compose but a small part, will probably form in a few years, a majority of our population. Is it not then advisable to commence with the gradual introduction of that language, which the interests of all require to become one day the general language of the Country?*
>
> Laelius

A few weeks later, the *Gazette* published a second letter expressing a counter argument:

> *On reading in your paper a piece signed LAELIUS, which has for its object a defence of the administration of Governor Claiborne, I was induced to make enquiry who Laelius was, what were his means of information, and what could induce him to volunteer in a cause, in which notwithstanding his talents he could render so little service to the person he calls his friend. I learned with surprise that Laelius was a stranger to ninety-nine hundredths of the community, a man of yesterday among us, it is said a foreigner, who has not been a resident two months in Louisiana, who had no opportunity of judging by his own experience, of any part of the administration of Governor Claiborne. . .*"[60]

The year 1805 was to be a particularly crucial year in the Claiborne administration. The proponents and opponents of the two legal systems became extremely vocal and adamant, and the long-term strategy behind which the local administration seemed to withdraw only served to aggravate

---

[60] *The Louisiana Gazette*, Friday, January 11, 1805, No. 22, "To the Editor of the Louisiana Gazette...".

the situation. Perhaps in a spirit of compromise, James Brown proposed a solution that lacked neither originality nor a certain impracticability:

Should the present system be continued until October, I have conceived that much good might be done by availing ourselves of the assistance of the Council to adopt a good code of Laws for the Government of the Territory. We possess all the materials for the able execution of such a work. The Civil law — the Spanish Ordinances — the British Statute and Common laws, and the codes of all the States are spread before us, and the people are prepared for the reception of a code ably compiled from these several systems. . ."[61]

On February 4, 1805, a joint resolution of the governor and the Legislative Council was approved, appointing a committee to compile and prepare a civil and a criminal code and "to employ two counselors-at-law to assist them in drafting the said codes."[62] The committee's plans were thwarted by Claiborne's opposition, on the one hand, and by the passing of an act of Congress, on the other hand. This act of March 2, 1805,[63] among other things, reorganized the

---

[61] James Brown, letter to Senator John Breckinridge, January 22, 1805, Vol. IX, *U.S. Territorial Papers*, p. 379.

[62] Acts passed at the first session of the Legislative Council of the Territory of Orleans. Joint resolution of February 4, 1805, p. 458. The two counselors-at-law "employed" by the committee were Edward Livingston and James Brown, *U.S. Territorial Papers*, Vol. IX, p. 379.

[63] *U.S. Territorial Papers*, Vol. IX, p. 405. This act which would become effective as of July 4, 1805, granted to the Territory of Orleans only a semblance of government

legislative branch of the Orleans Territory, creating a new assembly, to which was given the name of the "House of Representatives", and which was composed of twenty-five members who were to be elected by the people. This assembly existed side by side with the Legislative Council, which was composed of five members who were to be appointed by the President of the United States out of ten individuals selected by the House of Representatives of the territory. The act further stipulated that "The laws in force in the said territory, at the commencement of this act, and not inconsistent with the provisions thereof, shall continue in force, until altered, modified, or repealed by the legislature."[64]

The expression "laws in force" referred to the Spanish law, to the acts of the United States Congress applicable to the territory and, naturally, to those acts that had been passed by the Legislative Council of the territory from the time it first came into being. These last acts related, for the most part, to questions of criminal law and introduced elements of the common law. However, in the area of private law, no act had as yet been passed to permanently and indisputably establish the nature of this law. Thus, the French grew increasingly fearful that, through the common law rules of procedure which had now spread to the Territory of Orleans, the common law would work its way into the substantive law as well.[65] The

---

which fooled no one.

[64] Sec. 4, Act of March 2, 1805, see note 22 supra.

[65] This fear arose from what was stipulated in Section I of the Act of March 2, 1805: "...and that from and after the establishment of the said government, the inhabitants of the territory of Orleans shall be entitled to and enjoy all the rights, privileges, and advantages secured by the said ordinance, and now enjoyed by the people of the Mississippi territory."

suspicion with which many regarded Claiborne was quickly justified when, at the opening of the second session of the Legislative Council on June 22, 1805, the governor addressed the council with awkwardness and provocative determination. In his speech, the governor took pleasure in emphasizing that the act of March 2, 1805, by which the ordinances of 1787 were applied in the Territory of Orleans,[66] implied that the court to be created would have a "Common Law Jurisdiction,"[67] and that therefore, it was advisable to consider making innovations upon the present system and to take measures to allow for a gradual transition from one system of law to another.[68]

The substance of Claiborne's speech, a speech that had not been delivered by the governor with the intention of appeasing his opponents, isolated him even further and alienated him from certain important figures, such as James Brown,[69] who until then had been an ally of the governor in his effort to introduce the common law into the territory. The House of Representatives, which had been elected in the autumn of

---

Digeste General des Actes des Législatures du Territoire d'Orléans, by François Xavier Martin, 1816, p. 169 *et seq.* Elizabeth Gasper Brown, *Legal Systems in Conflict*; Orleans Territory 1804-1812, in the *American Journal of Legal History*, vol. 1, p. 45, 46 (1957).

[66] *Official Letter Books of W.C.C. Claiborne*, 1801-1816, Vol. III, p. 104.

[67] Id. at p. 104.

[68] Id. at p. 104.

[69] Letter from James Brown to John Breckinridge of September 17, 1805, *U.S. Territorial Papers*, p. 506 *et seq.*

1805, also expressed its opposition to the governor by considering a proposal "de charger le comité occupé dans ce moment à préparer un mémoire pour être présenté au Congrès des Etats-Unis, de solliciter dans ce mémoire la révocation de toute clause de l'ordonnance du 13 juillet 1787 qui tendrait à établir dans le territoire d'Orléans le système judiciaire connu sous le nom de loi commune, vu le ..., la confusion qui résulteraient d'une subversion aussi complète des lois qui ont régi ce Territoire jusqu'au quatre du présent mois..."[70]

This volcanic situation finally erupted in 1806 when the two houses of the newly-formed legislature of the territory convened together for the first time. These houses were predominantly made up of Frenchmen. On May 22, 1806, the two houses adopted a resolution "déclarant les lois qui continuent d'être en vigueur dans le Territoire d'Orléans, et les auteurs auxquels on peut se référer comme autorités en matière de droit dans le même Territoire."[71] The object of

---

[70] *Le Moniteur*, Saturday, November 16, 1805, No. 563. House of Representatives. We have been unable to determine whether the report in question had been adopted. The following is the author's translation:

...to charge the committee engaged at this time in preparing a report for the United States Congress, to request in this report the revocation of those clauses in the ordinance of July 13, 1787 which would aid in establishing in the Territory of Orleans that legal system known as the common law..., considering the confusion which would result from a radical change in the laws which had governed this Territory up until the fourth day of this month..."

[71] *National Archives*, Orleans Territorial Papers, Vol. VIII.

An Act

declaring the laws which continue to be inforce in the Territory of Orleans, and authors which may be recurred to as authorities within the same

. . .

Whereas by the effect of the reiterated changes which the government of this Territory has undergone, the divers matters which now compose its judiciary system, are in some measure, wrapped in obscurity, so that it has become necessary to present to the citizens the whole of those different parts, collected together by which they may be guided, whenever they will have to recur to the laws, untill the Legislature may form a civil code for the Territory; and whereas by the 11th section of the act of Congress, intitled "an act dividing Louisiana into two Territories and providing for the government thereof" passed the 22d march 1804, and by the 4th section of the act of the said Congress, intitled "an act further providing for the government of the Territory of Orleans" it is said, that the laws which shall be inforce in the said Territory, at the commencement of the said acts, and which shall not be contrary to the dispositions thereof, shall continue to be in force untill altered, modified or repealed by the Legislature of the Territory.

Sect. 1st. Be it therefore declared by the legislative Council and the House of Representatives of the Territory of Orleans in general assembly convened, that by virtue of the said dispositions, the laws which remain in force, and those which can be recurred to as authorities in the tribunals of this Territory, save the changes and modifications which may have already been made by the Legislatures of the said Territory, save also whatever might be contrary to the constitution of the United States, to the laws of the federal government which have been extended to the said Territory by Congress, and to the acts of the said Congress which direct the present government of the said Territory, and save therefore the modifications, which necessarily result from the introduction which the act of the 22d march 1804, has made into the said Territory of the two most important principles of the judiciary system of the common law, to wit, the writ of habeas corpus, and the trial by jury, are the laws and authorities following, to wit: 1. The roman Civil code, as being the foundation of the spanish law, by which this country was governed before its cession to France and to the United States, which is composed of the institutes, digest and code of the emperor Justinian, aided by the authority of the commentators of the civil law, and particularly of Domat in his treaty of the Civile laws; the whole so far as it has not been derogated from by the spanish law; 2. The Spanish law, consisting of the books of the recopilation de Castille and autos acordados being nine books in the whole; the seven parts or partidas of the king Don Alphonse the learned, and the eight books of the royal statute (fueroreal) of Castille; the recopilation de indias, save what is therein relative to the enfranchisement of Slaves, the laws de Toro, and finally the ordinances and royal orders and decrees, which have been formally applied to the colony of Louisiana, but not otherwise; the whole aided by the authority of the reputable commentator admitted in the courts of Justice.

Sect. 2. And be it further declared, that in matters of commerce the ordinance of Bilbao is that which has full authority in this Territory, to decide all contestations relative thereto; and that wherever it is not sufficiently explicit, recourse may be had to the roman laws; to Beawes lex mercatoria, to Park on insurance, to the treatise of the insurances by Emorigon, and finally to the commentaries of Valin, and to the respectable authors consulted in the United States.

this resolution was twofold: on the one hand, the resolution aimed to declare, once and for all, the laws and other legal sources that were still in effect in the territory so as to dispel any doubts that prevailed on this matter; on the other hand, the resolution proposed to prevent the governor and some of

---

John Watkins
Speaker of the House of Representatives

Jean Noel Destrehan
President of the Legislative Council

On Tuesday, June 10, 1806, the *Louisiana Gazette* published an article which accurately reflects the state of uncertainty and ignorance in which most of the Territory's inhabitants lived:

To the honorable Isaac Hebert, M. Prudhome and J. Etienne Boré!

AUGUST LEGISLATORS!
A citizen anxious for information...begs you to explain to him the merits of the law which the council...approved, and for the rejection of which our governor is esteemed so censurable. I am particularly desirous to know in which century the code of the emperor Justinian was written? of how many volumes it is composed? and whether the seven parts or partidas of the king Don Alphonso the learned can be purchased in this City?
If the Recopilacion de Castille, and Autos acordados, the laws of Toro, and the ordinance of Bilboa are in either of your libraries?
I beg you gentlemen, to furnish your constituents with a short commentary.
                                             A MERCHANT

his allies from imposing the preeminence of the common law. Faced with this formidable challenge and a determination on the part of the legislature as relentless as his own, the governor could not retreat without permanently impairing his own authority as well as that of the federal government which he represented. Therefore, on May 26, Governor Claiborne vetoed the resolution. On that same day, the Legislative Council and ten members of the House of Representatives issued the following "Manifesto":

Whereas the most essential and salutary measures taken by this Legislature have been successively rejected by the Governor of the Territory, and whereas this Legislature, whose members had accepted their office only in the hope of being useful to their fellow-citizens, must be convinced today that it can do nothing except cause them considerable expense;

"Resolved, that the General Assembly be immediately dissolved."

The Legislative Council believes that it owes to its fellow-citizens a statement of the motives which have determined it to propose the resolution copied above, and which have caused it to consider the act which confirmed it, and to which the Governor has refused his sanction, as that on which the happiness and future tranquility of this country depended most essentially. It is for the public to judge whether these motives were pure and free from any kind of private passion.

The most inestimable benefit for a people is the preservation of its laws, usages, and habits. It is only such preservation that can soften the sudden transition from one government to another and it is by having consideration for that natural attachment that even the heaviest yoke becomes endurable. The Congress of the United States apparently wished to reflect these sacred principles and render its domination still easier for the inhabitants of the Territory of Orleans by preserving to them their former laws: such at least is the natural and reasonable sense of Article 4 of the act of

March 2, 1805, which provides further for the government of the Territory of Orleans, and which is expressed in these terms: "The laws which shall be in force in the said Territory at the commencement of this act, and not inconsistent with the provisions thereof, shall continue in force, until altered, modified or repealed by the Legislature."

Now, what are the laws which Congress intended to preserve to us by this provision? What are the laws which must be subject to review and rectification by the Legislatures of this Territory? The question is not a doubtful one. It is evident that they are the old laws which were in use in this country before its cession to the United States of America. For Congress took care to apply to us all of the common law which it considered indispensable to prescribe for us to the end that our régime might not conflict with that which is in force in all the States of the Union, that is to say, the right to be judged by one's peers and the writ of habeas corpus, the two great palladiums of civil liberty.

Now, since we have the power to keep our old laws in so far as they do not conflict with the Constitution of the United States and the special acts passed for our provisional government, no one can deny the advantage to us of remaining under a system to which we are accustomed and which has nothing contrary to the affection which we owe to our Government. For it is necessary to distinguish, among the laws which govern a state, those which depend on its constitution and its government from those which only regulate contracts and agreements between private persons. The former must necessarily be common to all parts of the Republic, but the latter may differ without disadvantages. Thus the Constitution of United States and the other Federal laws being general for the whole Union, it would be absurd to claim that this Territory ought not to be subject to them; but as to the laws regarding contracts, wills and successions, what difference does it make that here such acts should be governed by the civil law while in the other States of the Union they are governed by the common law? How is it that the multiplicity of customs which is noticed in England is not prejudicial to the general harmony? Do those differences in local law prevent an Englishman from being just as good a citizen and just as loyal to the Constitution of his country? On the contrary, and it would be exposing his affection to the danger of being alienated and exciting disorder and general discontent to disturb those customs to which each province is attached by the bonds of experience and long habit.

In the United States itself there is no general civil code: the common law of England is not adopted here as an article of the Constitution - Ever since the original establishment of the New England colonies that common law has been received, in each province, only with modifications and alterations, which bring it about that the common law of Virginia is no more like that in use in South Carolina than the latter is like the common law adopted in the State of New York. At the time of the general confederation and after the war of the American Revolution, Congress had the wisdom not to do violence to those differences by laying down a general and uniform common law for all the States of the Union, and it left to each State the right to preserve or to modify that which it had seen fit to adopt of the common law and even to replace it with other laws according as it might judge to be most suitable to its special situation.

There is no doubt that it is a consequence of this prudent and judicious policy that Congress desired to grant to this Territory the privilege of keeping its old laws or of changing or modifying them according as its legislatures might find it necessary. Now, every one knows that those old laws are nothing but the civil or Roman law modified by the laws of the government under which this region existed before the latter's cession to the United States. If the title of the books in which those laws are contained is unknown, if those titles appear barbarous or ridiculous, those very circumstances are the most to their credit because they prove, by the ignorance of those who have obeyed them until now without knowing that they were doing so, how great is their mildness and their wisdom and how small is the number of disadvantages resulting from their execution. In any case it is no less true that the Roman law which formed the basis of the civil and political laws of all the civilized nations of Europe presents an ensemble of greatness and prudence which is above all criticism. What purity there is in those decisions based on natural equity; what clearness there is in the wording which is the work of the greatest jurists, encouraged by the wisest emperors; what simplicity there is in the form of those contracts and what sure and quick means there are for obtaining the remedies prescribed by the law, for the reparation of all kinds of civil wrongs.

We certainly do not attempt to draw any parallel between the civil law and the common law; but, in short, the wisdom of the civil law is recognized by all Europe; and this law is the one which nineteen-twentieths of the population of Louisiana know and are accustomed to from childhood, of which law they would not see themselves deprived without falling into despair. If the inhabitants of this Territory had never known any laws, if they had lived down to the present time without making agreements or contracts, it would perhaps be a matter of indifference to them whether to adopt one system or another system, and it is even probable that their attachment to their new mother country would cause them to prefer that system which would bring them nearest to their new fellow-citizens. But it is a question here of overthrowing received and generally known usages and the uncertainty with which they would be replaced would be as unjust as disheartening. Every one knows today and from a long experience how successions are transferred, what is the power of parents over their children and the amount of property of which they can dispose to their prejudice, what are the rights which result from marriages effected with or without contract, the manner in which one can dispose by will, the manner of selling, of exchanging or alienating one's properties with sureness and the remedies which the law accords in the case of default of payment. Each of the inhabitants dispersed over the vast expanse of this Territory, however little educated he may be, has a tincture of this general and familiar jurisprudence, necessary to the conduct of the smallest affairs, which assures the tranquility of families, he has sucked this knowledge at his mother's breast, he has received it by the tradition of his forefathers and he has perfected it by the experience of a long and laborious life. Overthrow this system all at once. Substitute new laws for the old laws; what a tremendous upset you cause! What becomes of the experience of an old man and what becomes of the facility and sureness of transfers? Who will dare to sign a contract under a new regime the effects of which will not be known to him? What will be the lot of the inhabitant who is so unfortunate as not to have received sufficient education to learn these new laws at least by reading them, even supposing that his understanding of them is facilitated by transmitting the new laws to him in his own language? Will he not shudder every time that he wishes to dispose of his properties? Will he not then be afraid lest he be throwing himself into a bottomless pit without outlet and of bringing about his total ruin? Or must he always have recourse to the knowledge of a jurist regarding the most ordinary transactions of civil law?

The first Legislature of this Territory has to be particularly interested in establishing the fundamental bases; the secondary laws, accessory laws and details should only come later, otherwise one is exposed to making parts which will be found inconsistent with the whole. Now, what is the first law, the most important law in the present situation of this country; what is the fundamental basis of the great edifice of its future legislation? It cannot be denied that it is the matter of giving to it a civil code. The present composition of the courts, the judges presiding over them and the jurists who plead before them being almost all strangers to the French language and still more so to the language in which the greater part of the laws of this country are written, the very scarcity even of the elementary authors who deal with them, everything renders indispensable the adoption of a measure which tends to place within the reach of all citizens, both in the French and the English language, a complete collection of the laws governing us. But before undertaking that work was it not necessary to determine what would be its basis and what would be the canvas on which one would do the work? For what ought to be, in the true interest of the inhabitants of this country, the basis to be adopted? It is that of keeping, of the old laws, everything which can be saved without disadvantage and without going contrary to the general system of our Government, and of not having recourse to foreign codes except in so far as the old may be found defective or prejudicial. By this measure one will not place the courts so to speak between two different codes. For all the contracts which have been made till now must necessarily be judged by the laws under which they were made; so how great would be the embarrassment of the courts if, while canceling everything which remains of the civil law, the courts should nevertheless be left under the necessity of judging, under that same law, of the effects of all contracts and documents made down to today? The point should be reflected upon that during perhaps thirty years to come half the lawsuits which will be presented to the courts will arise over the execution of contracts anterior to the time in which we are speaking. Here, therefore, are new reasons which ought to strengthen the attachment of the Legislature to the maintenance of our old laws by making a code which shall be as near to them as possible; the courts will see in them a sure compass which will facilitate the decision of all the old lawsuits as well as the new without leaving anything to arbitrary opinion.

Such are the principles which determined the Legislature to place, before its act on the formation of the code, a preliminary and declaratory law regarding the laws which were to serve as a basis for that work.

Finally an act declaratory of the laws which continue to be in force in the Territory was proposed as a measure to preserve our present laws in so far as the latter are not contrary to the Constitution of the United States. The Legislature attached great importance to this bill for the purpose of clarifying our present judicial system and doing away with its uncertainty, until it should have time to draw up a civil code. The Legislature considered this provision as a safeguard against dangerous innovations, and a measure necessary to the tranquility of the citizens. This bill also has been rejected and we have returned to confusion.

Under this state of things, the Legislative Council had to consider it wise to think of putting an end to an expensive and useless session. Without doubt the executive holds his absolute veto from the special Constitution applied to this Territory, but if by means of that veto his will and nothing but his will is to constitute the supreme rule, if he is to reign alone, and openly, the Legislature ought not to be willing to serve as a plaything to amuse people. What difference does it make to the Territory that the executive should sanction laws regarding the Protestant Church, regarding hired persons and apprentices, and regarding drinking places if he stops by his veto the execution of a single law favorable to the happiness of the Territory?[72]

---

[72] *U.S. Territorial Papers*, Vol. IX, p. 642-657. French text: p. 643-650. *The Louisiana Gazette*, Friday, June 6, 1806, no. 168, p. 2. "Translated from the Telegraph, Extract from the Minutes of the Legislative Council, May 26, 1806." The Manifesto was signed by Sauvé, President of the Legislative Council.

The positions were well entrenched: the governor favored the common law, and the two houses of the Territorial legislature, representing the majority of the people of the territory, were resolved to retain the Roman law in all areas that related to the daily life of the individual, such as: successions, marriages with and without contracts, wills, obligations, property, etc.

The governor and the partisans of the common law had little time to evaluate the consequences of their original wait-and-see policy, which was beginning to resemble a form of retreat. On June 7, 1806, the two houses of the legislature made further headway with the adoption of a resolution which would permanently establish the originality and singularity of Louisiana law:

RESOLVED, by the Legislative Council and House of Representatives of the Territory of Orleans, in General Assembly convened, That both branches of the legislature shall appoint James Brown, and Moreau Lislet, lawyers, whose duty it shall be to compile and prepare, jointly, a Civil Code for the use of this territory.

Resolved, That the two jurisconsults shall make the civil law by which this territory is now governed, the ground work of said code...[73]

---

[73] *Session Laws of American States and Territories, Territory of Orleans*, 1804-1811. Legis: 1-1806, S.I. p. 215, *Le Moniteur*, Saturday, June 7, 1806: Villars, Boulegni, Boré, Watkins, Arnaud and Mahon appointed a committee to collaborate with James Brown and Moreau Lislet in order to prepare a Civil Code for this Territory.

Le Moniteur, June 3, 1807, no. 724. Act to determine the amount to be paid to the two jurisconsults appointed to prepare a civil code for the use of the Territory of Orleans...and to the

Governor Claiborne approved the resolution, to the surprise of both those who voted for and those who voted against it. This approval was nonetheless interpreted by certain individuals as a delaying tactic intended to disguise the true intentions of the governor who "will not approve the system when it is presented."[74] Was this really Claiborne's hidden intention? In January of 1807, he declared in a speech to the two houses of the Territorial Legislature that he was *"desirous to retain the principles of the Civil Law, which are in unison with the interests of a free people, or that it is essential to- the security of prosperity in this Territory; I have no disposition unnecessarily, or injuriously to innovate on the former Laws and usages of my fellow Citizens; But in my official Character, I can never approve measures, which will tend to bar the introduction of those great political and legal principles which are cherished thro'out the United States."*[75] The meaning of this message is very clear: the governor was making an overture to the legislature in the hope that a compromise could still be reached. Julien Poydras, the President of the Legislative Council, reassured the governor that the Legislative Council had honorable intentions, but informed him in no uncertain terms that the civil law would be preserved - and not solely with respect to those "principles of

---

translators of the said code...

[74] George Dargo, *Jefferson's Louisiana*, p. 146. This author cites an excerpt from a letter from Edward Livingston to his brother Robert.

[75] *Official Letter Books of W.C.C. Claiborne*, 1801-1816, vol. IV, p. 92; *The Louisiana Gazette*, Friday, January 16, 1807.

the Civil Law which are in unison with the interests of a free people."[76]

The governor capitulated; the civil law was to prevail in the Territory of Orleans. On March 31, 1808, the two houses of the Territorial Legislature acclaimed the fruits of the work of James Brown and Louis Moreau Lislet, and the governor signed the order that provided for the promulgation of "the Digest of the Civil Laws now in force in the territory of Orleans."[77] With the official seal appended to the order, the

---

[76] *The Orleans Gazette*, Thursday, February 5, 1807.

[77] Orleans Territory, Acts Passed at the First Session of the Second Legislature of the Territory of Orleans (New Orleans, 1808), p. 120 *et seq*. In his speech of March 31, 1808 to the two chambers of the Territory, Claiborne declared that "The civil code of the territory contains a number of excellent principles, which I trust will long be preserved: but there are others which should yield to those changes in the science of jurisprudence, approved by experience and sanctioned by the wisdom of the most illustrious statesmen. These just innovations will be directed by succeeding legislators; they will have a view "of the whole ground," and can best determine what part is susceptible of improvement."

In a letter Governor Claiborne wrote to the Secretary of State on October 7th 1808 he wrote that " The Secretary of the Territory, will transmit you a Copy of the "Civil Code", adopted at the last Session of the Legislature. You will find the English Text extremely incorrect; - This is attributable to the circumstance of the Work having been written in French, and the translation prepared by persons who were not well acquainted with the English Language;- So erroneous does the translation appear to be, that it will probably be necessary to declare by Law, that the French shall (solely) be considered the legal text.-... I could not do otherwise than sanction the

civil law finally emerged triumphant after a long and arduous battle. Although, officially, the Digest was the joint effort of two men, it was perhaps more the creation of Louis Moreau Lislet than of James Brown.[78] By virtue of his personal status, his education and his professional experience, Moreau Lislet was well qualified to play a predominant role in the drafting of the first Louisiana Civil Code — which turned out to be a rather unique undertaking. Yet Moreau Lislet would never have contributed to the drafting of the Code if he had not happened, by a stroke of good fortune, to be in New Orleans when the future of the civil law of the Territory was in the making.[79]

Code. My first object has been to render the Laws certain;- my next shall be to render them just, and to assimilate our system of Jurisprudence as much as possible, to that of the several States of the Union.-.." IX Territorial Papers of the United States, p.808-803.

[78] See the "Preliminary Report of the Code Commissioners" dated February 13, 1823 at p. XCIII.

[79] A book soon to be published by Professor Levasseur will include Moreau Lislet's biography and an analysis of his contribution to the Digest or Civil Code of 1808.

PART II

A "CIVIL LAW" LAWYER: LOUIS CASIMIR MOREAU LISLET

More than one hundred and fifty years after Louis Moreau Lislet's death, his life still remains something of a mystery. His true and highly deserved eulogy has yet to be written. The few attempts that have been made to present the biography of this eminent jurist have remained insufficient.[80] This insufficiency should not be considered as a failure and should not lead to the conclusion that the authors of those biographic essays failed in what they set out to do. The need for a detailed biography of Moreau Lislet was probably not

---

[80] Among the succinct or extensive biographies on Moreau Lislet which are available, one must cite:

a: *Dictionary on American Biography*, Vol. VII, Scribner's 1934, at p. 157. Very succinct and without much information.
b: *Louis Moreau Lislet, His Life and Works*, by Lloyd Boutte; based on other articles and books but not much of a biography of Moreau Lislet.
c: *Louis C. E. Moreau-Lislet*, by M. H. Herrin, in The Creole Aristocracy, Exposition Press 1952, at p. 120-121. Very short as indicated by the two pages.
d: *Louisiana, Comprising Sketches of Parishes, Towns, Events, Institutions and Persons Arranged in Cyclopedic Form*, by Alcée Fortier. On page 71 of volume II one can find some references to Moreau Lislet's life and personality.
e: *The French Colonists from St. Domingue and, In Particular, Moreau Lislet*, by René Nicaud, in XX Louisiana Bar Journal, No. 4.

strongly felt at the time when those authors published their essays.

This second Part is an attempt to meet that need to the extent possible. In the first chapter of this Part II we will describe as much as can be done Moreau Lislet's family tree in order to situate, with respect to him, a number of persons whose names are likely to appear in the following chapters. The actual life of Moreau Lislet follows, arbitrarily divided into five chapters covering five periods: Chapter II -Louis Casimir Moreau Lislet: Uncertainties Concerning the Early Years; Chapter III - From the Dondon to New Orleans; Chapter IV -The First Years of Integration; Chapter V - The Rewarding Years; Chapter VI - Poverty and Greatness.

CHAPTER I.

LOUIS CASIMIR MOREAU LISLET:
A FAMILY TREE

Through the "family tree" given in this section it will be possible to bring to light some facts regarding a number of persons who were more or less closely related to Louis Moreau Lislet and who, at various times, had social or business dealings with him. This chapter will also make it possible, subsequently, to simply mention these names as they appear in Moreau Lislet's life story.

Louis Moreau Lislet's parents and relatives can be divided into groups having six patronymic names or surnames: Moreau, Torel, Deynaut, Vallade, de Peters, and de Lagrange.

1. Moreau

a. *Jacob Vincent Moreau*[81] — father of Louis Casimir Elisabeth Moreau Lislet. Jacob Vincent Moreau was a militia officer, captain of the Limonade batallion. He lived in a place called "La Marre à la Roche", within the district and parish of Saint Martin du Dondon, jurisdiction of the city of Le Cap Français, Saint Domingue (now Haiti). On September 28,

---

[81] The data and facts reported here were found in the following documents:

Indemnité des colons de St. Domingue, Dossier Moreau Antoine No. 444. 1829 [Bibliothèque de la France d'Outre-Mer]; Liquidations des Colons de Saint Domingue. 1829, D 64; 1830, D 64 [id]. Dépôt des Papiers Publics des Colonies. Notariat. St. Domingue: Notaire Pont 1777-1782; Notaire Legrand 1780-1781, 1786-1788; [id.]. Archives Nationales. Minutier Central XCV, 413.

1758, Jacob Vincent was married to Elisabeth Torel who bore him three children: a daughter, Elisabeth Françoise Ignace Moreau, and two sons, Vincent Pierre Benjamin and Louis Casimir Elisabeth Moreau [Lislet]. Jacob Vincent Moreau passed away on April 1, 1782, in Dondon.

b. *Elisabeth Torel (Thorel) Moreau*[82] — mother of Louis Casimir Elisabeth Moreau [Lislet]. On November 9, 1749, Elisabeth Torel first married Jacques Christophe Deynaut. She had two sons from this first marriage: Louis Christophe Deynaut and Jacques Louis Deynaut. Elisabeth Torel became the widow of her first husband Jacques Christophe Deynaut in October 1755; she then married Jacob Vincent Moreau. She was apparently stricken by a disease that compelled her to go to France for treatment. She left Le Cap Français for a few months in 1764. Elisabeth Torel Moreau died tragically in 1793 when the schooner " The Delaware" was wrecked during her voyage from Le Cap Français to Philadelphia.

c. *Antoine Moreau*[83] — paternal uncle of Louis Casimir Elisabeth Moreau [Lislet]; he was a landowner in Haut du Trou, district in the parish of Dondon, in Saint Domingue. Antoine Moreau, a coffee planter, was murdered by prowlers on his coffee plantation in 1792. He died without children.

---

[82] The data and facts reported here were found in the documents cited in footnote 2 supra, and in the following additional documents: Moreau de Lislet [Bibliothèque de la France d'Outre-Mer]; Dépôt des Papiers Publics des Colonies. Notaire Colignon an 9 [id]; M.S.S. 1216 Consulat de France à Philadelphie an 4ᵉ. [Howard Tilton Library. Tulane University].

[83] The data and facts reported here were found in the documents cited in footnotes 2 and 3.

d. *Vincent Pierre Benjamin Moreau*[84] — was the older brother of Louis Casimir Elisabeth Moreau [Lislet]. A certificate recorded in the Register of Deaths states that "Moreau Junior Vincent, a resident of the district of Haut du Trou departed this life of blessed memory in this parish of Dondon in the year seventeen hundred ninety three, in the said district of Haut du Trou in this parish when he was shot with a rifle during the insurrection in this parish. . ."

e. *Elisabeth Françoise Ignace Moreau*[85] — sister of Louis Casimir Elisabeth Moreau [Lislet] and spouse of Joseph Merlhy de Lagrange. She was born in Saint Martin du Dondon in 1759 or in 1760. Elisabeth and Joseph de Lagrange lived in Philadelphia from August 1793 until they left for Paris at the turn of the century.

2. Torel or Thorel

a. *Elisabeth Torel/Thorel* — see above section 1b Elisabeth Torel (Thorel) Moreau.

---

[84] The data and facts reported here were found in the following documents:
Dom. C. 39 - D.4 [Bibliothèque de la France d'Outre-Mer]; Consulat de France à Philadelphie an IV n° 12 arch. et n° 262 [id].

[85] The data and facts reported here were found in the documents cited in footnotes 2 and 3 supra.

b. *Marie Anne Torel*[86] — maternal aunt of Louis Casimir Elisabeth Moreau [Lislet], inhabitant of the district and parish of Dondon in Saint Domingue. She perished in a fire in the town of Le Cap Français.

3. Deynaut (and Vallade)

a. *Jacques Christophe Deynaut*[87] — resided in the district of Dondon. He married *Elisabeth Torel* on November 9, 1749, under a community property regime. They had two sons: Jacques Louis and Louis Christophe. Jacques Christophe Deynaut passed away in October, 1755.

b. *Louis Christophe and Jacques Louis Deynaut*[88] — half-

---

[86] Some references to Marie Anne Thorel can be found in the following documents:
Dom. C. 39 - D. 4 in note 5 supra; Notaire Pont (actes du 24 octobre 1777, du 26 avril 1779) in note 2 supra; Notaire Collignon, in note 3 supra.

[87] Some references to Jacques Christophe Deynaut can be found in:
Notaire Legrand (actes du 12 avril 1784, du 2 juin 1781) in note 2 supra.

[88] Some references can be found in the following documents: Notaire Roard (acte du 23 vendemiaire an 14) [Minutier Central Archives Nationales]; Fichier du cimetière Saint Louis n. 1 [Louisiana State Museum Library]; Archives Nationales, Colonies F 5^b 17; D. no. 33 Deynaut père et fils [Bibliothèque de la France d'Outre-Mer]; Notaire Pont (actes du 21 avril 1779, du 26 avril 1779), see note 2 supra; Notaire Legrand (acte du 16 août 1781) see note 2 supra; Deynaut, actes de l'état civil [Bibliothèque de la France d'Outre-Mer].

brothers of Louis Casimir Elisabeth Moreau [Lislet]. Both Deynaut brothers lived in the district of la Marre à la Roche, parish of Dondon. Louis Christophe, the younger brother, married, in April 1779, Marie Thérèse Lucille Vallade, native of Dondon, daughter of Antoine Vallade and Marie Anne Beyrac. She bore him two daughters: Marie Joséphine Louise Lucille, born on April 27, 1781, and Marie Elisabeth Antoinette Céleste, born on July 4, 1782. Marie Thérèse Lucille Vallade died in New Orleans on January 2, 1832, at the age of 68. Jacques Louis Deynaut - a militia officer- never married. He died several years before his brother Louis Christophe.

c. *Pierre Vallade*,[89] officer of La Légion du Nord of Saint Domingue, son of Antoine Vallade and Marie Anne Beyrac, brother of Marie Thérèse Lucille Vallade, the spouse of Louis Christophe Deynaut. Pierre Vallade died in Paris in November of 1805.

---

[89] Some references can be found in the following documents: Notaire Augustin Roard (actes du 14 Brumaire an 14, du 23 Vendemiaire an 14) see note 9 supra.

4. de Peters

a. *Jean Antoine de Peters*[90] — father of Anne Elisabeth Philippine de Peters who was to become Louis Casimir Elisabeth Moreau [Lislet]'s wife. Jean Antoine de Peters was the official painter of the King of Denmark, a member of the Copenhagen Academy of Sciences and the favorite painter of Prince Charles of Lorraine. Jean Antoine de Peters married Elisabeth Marie Gouel de Villebrune on April 29, 1756. They established their residence in Paris, at 4 rue du Hazard Richelieu, Saint Roch Parish, where Elisabeth de Villebrune de Peters died on May 1, 1785. Jean Antoine and Elisabeth de Peters had four children: Marie Louise de Peters, Marie Jeanne de Peters, Augustin Antoine de Peters and Anne Elisabeth Phillippine de Peters.

b. *Augustin Antoine de Peters*[91] — a law student in Paris

---

[90] The references here given on Antoine de Peters and Elisabeth Gouel de Villebrune were found in the following documents: Notaire Deherain (actes du 12 août 1789, 10 septembre 1789, 29 septembre 1789) [Minutier Central]. Notaire Garcerand (acte du 12 mai 1789) [Minutier Central]. Notaire Morin (acte du 22 Octobre 1790) [Minutier Central]. de Peters (acte du 20 Juin 1789) [Archives de la ville de Paris].

[91] Some references were found in the following documents:

Notaire Morin (acte du 15 octobre 1790) [Minutier Central]. Serie MM n° 1109 Regestum Supplicum et Serie MM n° 1136 Regestum Examinum [Archives Nationales Salle Clisson]. Notaire Morin (actes du 19 septembre 1790, du 7 octobre 1790) [Minutier Central].

in 1787, Augustin became a lawyer at the Parliament of Paris in 1790.

5. De Lagrange[92] — de La Grange — Delagrange

a. *Joseph Elisabeth George Merlhie Delagrange* — husband of Louis Casimir Elisabeth Moreau Lislet's sister Elisabeth. Joseph Delagrange was a jurisconsult like Louis Casimir. It appears from the minutes of Saint Domingue's general assembly session in 1791 that Joseph Delagrange was an outstanding lawyer: "Reading of a petition from Mr. La Grange, lawyer appointed by the Provincial Assembly of the North to replace temporarily Mr. Chesneau de la Megrière, lawyer of the Superior Council of the Cap, soliciting from the Assembly permission to practice law under the age required in order to occupy his position as a lawyer for which he was appointed by the Provincial Assembly of the North. The Assembly...agreed to waive the age requirement and authorized him to occupy his position as a lawyer for the Superior Council of the Cap but he may not, in any way, exercise the functions of a judge until he reaches majority."[93]

In 1793, hardly two years after his appointment as a lawyer to the Superior Council of Saint Domingue, Joseph de Lagrange and his wife, Elisabeth Ignace Moreau, settled in

---

[92] The spelling of this family name takes on several different forms depending on the documents.

[93] Extracted from: Assemblée Générale de la Partie Française de Saint Domingue Procés Verbaux des Séances et Journal des débats du Lundi 3 Oct. 1791 p. 194 [Bibliothèque Nationale].

Philadelphia, where he worked as an interpreter.[94] During the first three or four years of the nineteenth century, the couple lived in Paris, at "Boulevard des Italiens N° 27 in the corner of rue de la Michaudière," where Joseph de Lagrange again took up his profession as a lawyer. A few years later, Louis Casimir Moreau [Lislet], established at the time in New Orleans, called on his brother-in-law to address the French government regarding the claims for compensation presented by the French immigrants from Saint Domingue who lived in Louisiana.[95]

---

[94] In Archives Nationales, Registers of French Consulates in America, M.S.S. 1215, 1216, 1217. [Howard Tilton Library].

[95] Besides the documents cited in footnotes 14 and 15 supra, the following documents were consulted: Notaire Roard (actes du 23 Vendemiaire an 14, du 15 Brumaire an 14) [Minutier Central]; Dossier Moreau Antoine (voir ci-dessus note 4); Dossier Delagrange Joseph n° 78 [Bibliothèque de la France d'Outre-Mer].

CHAPTER II.

LOUIS CASIMIR MOREAU LISLET: UNCERTAINTIES OF THE EARLY YEARS

Louis Casimir Moreau Lislet's biography during the first period of his life, from his birth until his arrival in New Orleans, is something of a mystery. These thirty-seven years, which are very difficult to recreate retrospectively,[96] are full of uncertainties that jurists and historians alike have used, often skillfully, either to lend credibility to certain personal political and legal theses they were advocating or to flesh out their portraits of a man about whom they in fact knew very little. Before taking up the narrative of Moreau Lislet's life, it is important to try to weigh the value of some of these assertions and to shed light on some of the uncertainties which remain.

1. Established Facts

The facts that can now be established with some degree of certainty are the year of birth and the physical appearance of Louis Moreau Lislet.

---

[96] The difficulty of this task is due mainly to two reasons: first, the documents concerning Moreau Lislet are as scattered as the many residences he had in his life of some sixty years; therefore one has to consult archives in several cities such a Paris (and several different libraries and archives in that city), Bordeaux, New Orleans (several different libraries and archives in that city), Philadelphia...The second reason, as explained by several archivists, is that the archives in what is now Haiti, and was formerly Saint Domingue, are non-existent; revolutions, fires and weather conditions have resulted in the destruction of the archives of the time Moreau Lislet lived in Saint Domingue.

a. Year of Birth

Because there is a difference of one year between the date of Moreau Lislet's birth that is generally agreed upon in all sources known to date and the date that appears in a notarized document discovered in our research, it is appropriate to establish the historical truth of this event, even though it is a fact of only secondary importance.

In his olographic testament, Moreau Lislet did not mention his date of birth at all, and it would in fact have been quite difficult to have been any more ambiguous than he was:

I was born in Saint Domingue in the district of Dondon, dependency of le Cap Français. My father and my mother died a long time ago.

All the biographical essays available to us agree on the same year of birth: 1767. For instance, Moreau-Lislet's entry in the Dictionary of American Biography is headed as follows: "Moreau Lislet, Louis Casimir Elisabeth (1767 Dec. 3)."[97] In the article he published on the French immigrants of Saint Domingue, René Nicaud wrote: "[Moreau Lislet] was born on October 7, 1767 in Cap Français, Saint Domingue. . .".[98] Although Nicaud did not mention the source of his positive statement, there is some reason to believe that he took the date of October 7, 1767, from Moreau Lislet's tombstone inscription. This date carries the aura of truth by its very precision and by virtue of the fact that it was

---

[97] Dictionary on American Biography Vol. VII p. 157, Charles Scribner's 1934.

[98] *The French Colonists from St. Domingue and, In Particular Louis Moreau Lislet*, XX Louisiana Bar Journal, p. 285.

probably engraved according to birth certificates kept by the church. These certificates are no longer available for consultation because most of them were destroyed in the numerous fires that occurred in the city of New Orleans in the past.

Despite this apparently settled agreement on the year 1767 as being that of Moreau Lislet's birth, it is possible to say, on the basis of other documents the authenticity of which cannot be challenged, that Moreau Lislet was not born in 1767 but in 1768, or in 1769 or even in 1766. A marriage certificate witnessed by Moreau Lislet in Cuba in Fructidor, year 12 (August 1804), suggests that 1768 was the year of birth of Moreau Lislet. That certificate reads as follows:

Marriage Certificate of D^{lle} Rose Henriette Schomberg and Louis Auguste de Northe des Marais. . .drawn up in duplicate for both parties in Santiago, Cuba, on August 9, 1804, in the presence of Joseph Bruno Dalson 44 years of age and Louis Casimir Moreau de Lislet 36 years of age. . ..[99]

The subtraction of 36 years from the year 1804 gives us 1768 as the year of the presumed birth of Louis Moreau Lislet.

Another certificate from the 12th year of the Republic and dated Floreal 13 (May 1804) states the following:

. . . Louis Casimir Elisabeth Moreau . . . description, 35 years of age . . .[100]

---

[99] MSS film 1206 France Archives Nationales [Howard Tilton Library].

[100] Certificate or affidavit of Mr. Moreau's residence: in French as follows:

The same mathematic formula in this case leads to the conclusion that the year 1769 was the year of Moreau Lislet's birth.

We believe that we must set aside these years 1767, 1768, and 1769 and acknowledge that Moreau Lislet was actually born in 1766. Two certificates, one whose legal value is equivalent to the above-mentioned certificates and the other which is of greater legal value, lead to this conclusion. The first certificate is extracted from the official records of Port Républicain, Saint Domingue, and dated Fructidor 28, 8th year (September 1800). It attests to this:

Louis Casimir Elisabeth Moreau, thirty four years of age, native of Dondon...[101]

According to this document the year 1766 was the year of birth of Moreau Lislet. This certificate carries more weight than the previously mentioned documents for the simple reason that it was issued in Port Républicain where Moreau Lislet had lived for several years, whereas he spent only a short time in Santiago, Cuba, where he was hardly known.

Even if we did not attach much weight to the above certificate, it would be more difficult to dispute the truthfulness of the following statement made in a marriage certificate issued in the presence of Denis François Angran d'Ailleray, Chevalier Comte des Maillis and a state counsellor, a civil lieutenant at the Châtelet of Paris:

Certificat de Résidence de M. Moreau - Archives Coloniales, St. Domingue, St. Yago de Cuba 10 Pluviose an XII - 12 avril 1809 [Bibliothèque de la France d'outre-mer]. Most documents in French were translated by the author.

[101] Dom C 39 - D.4 [Bibliothèque de la France d'outre-mer].

Appeared Mr. Louis Casimir Elisabeth Moreau, Lawyer at the Parliament, a minor, 23 years of age according to his baptism certificate dated October 29, 1766, taken from the records of St. Martin du Dondon Parish, dependency of the French Cap...[102]

If Moreau Lislet was baptized on October 29, 1766, he was born either several months before or, more probably, in the first days of October of the same year. This suggests that an error was made on the tombstone, which should state: Louis Moreau Lislet, born in St. Domingue October 7, 1766. Died December 3, 1832.

b. *Physical Appearance of Louis Moreau Lislet*

Some years ago, a professor of law at Tulane University suggested that Louis Casimir Moreau Lislet was black. It is rather difficult to tell whether Professor Franklin was serious in that assertion. At the time Professor Mitchell Franklin was lecturing at Tulane, there was no positive evidence as to Moreau Lislet's racial identity. The picture appearing at the beginning of this book is sufficient to lay to rest any question as to Moreau Lislet's race, and identity certificates issued by officials of the French government are additional evidence to the same effect:

Certificate of 13 Floréal 12th year. Description 35 years of age, five feet and four inches high, dark hair and eyebrows,

---

[102] Act of August 12, 1789; in French:

Acte du 12 août 1789 Archives Nationales. Minutier Central XCV 413.

blue eyes, large nose, large lips, sharp chin, high forehead, full face...[103]

Certificate of 28 Fructidor 8th year:

Louis Casimir Elisabeth Moreau, thirty four years of age, five feet ____ inches high, chestnut-brown hair, average nose, large mouth, rounded chin, tanned complexion...[104]

Even if Moreau Lislet's physical descriptions may vary from document to document, one can nevertheless positively conclude from these documents that Moreau Lislet was a caucasian man as is confirmed by the physical description given by Charles Gayarré in 1823:

Moreau Lislet ... was a plump Frenchman ... his eyes sparkled good--naturedly under his large spectacles that rode a small nose. He was gentle through and through. His flesh was soft, like blancmange or jam, sinking in to the touch. His hands were small and plump ...[105]

2. Questions Without Answers

Two questions regarding Moreau Lislet still remain unanswered. The first one concerns the insertion, in a petition presented by Louis de Clouet to the Spanish government, of a comment regarding a position that Louis Moreau Lislet supposedly had held with General Toussaint Louverture during

---

[103] See note 5 supra.

[104] See note 6 supra.

[105] The New Orleans Bench and Bar in 1823 by Charles Gayarré in *The Louisiana Book: Selections from the Literature of the State*. Thomas McCaleb 1894.

the Saint Domingue revolution. The second enigma is suggested by Moreau Lislet himself in his testament.

a. de Clouet's Petition

Louis Bronier de Clouet had been an officer in the Spanish army and had worked out a daring and somewhat utopian plan to take over Louisiana and return it to Spain. He then had been appointed governor of a province in Cuba as a reward for his good and faithful services to the crown of Spain. In a petition he addressed to the Spanish government on December 7, 1814, de Clouet had this to say concerning Louis Moreau Lislet:

Moreau Lislet was the secretary of Toussaint, a coloured man, in the Isle of Saint Domingue. He settled in Louisiana following the takeover. A meritorious Colleague of the preceding [Mazureau] without any distinction.[106]

This assertion regarding Moreau Lislet's association with Toussaint Louverture as his secretary is supported in no other document as far as we know. It cannot be denied that this statement was written by a contemporary of Moreau Lislet. Its brevity, however, is tinged with contempt; furthermore, it fails to include any specific information and the absence of date or facts make it hard to attach any weight to its contents. After a survey of many historical essays on Saint Domingue and most biographies of Toussaint Louverture, it appears to be impossible to subscribe to this assumption. A number of detailed works, such as *Vie de Toussaint Louverture* by Victor Schoelcher, *Histoire de la Révolution de Saint Domingue* by

---

[106] Louis Declouet's Memorial to the Spanish Government, December 7, 1814, in 22 Louisiana Historical Quarterly p. 813.

Dalmas and *Études sur l'Histoire d'Haiti* by Ardouin,[107] do not mention the name of Moreau Lislet at all, not even as a lawyer, and definitely not as the secretary of Toussaint Louverture. In his book entitled *Histoire d'Haiti*, Thomas Madiou refers, here and there, to "Moreau", but none of those "Moreaus" is represented as the secretary of Toussaint Louverture.[108] The only piece of information that seems to constitute evidence for the truth of de Clouet's assertion can be found in a report written in Brumaire, year 10 (October 1801) and addressed by a high ranking officer to the "général en chef de l'armée expéditionnaire." In this report, the officer wrote the following:

---

[107] Vie de Toussaint Louverture by Victor Schoelcher (1804-1893) 1889; Histoire de la Révolution de Saint Domingue by Dalmas 2 Vol. 1814; Etudes sur l'Histoire d'Haiti by Ardouin 1853.

[108] Translations by the author. In Histoire d'Haiti by Thomas Madiou fils - Port au Prince 1847: on page 361 one can read "...*Moreau the African at the head of 200 men of the 8th colonial...*"; on page 387: "*A short time after the following were drowned in the bay of the Cayes: they were named Moreau (a colored man), Doudou (a colored man), Viart (a colored man)...*"; on page 429: "*General Pageot had twenty noble citizens arrested, black and yellow, and among them were those known as Michel Bayard, Jean François et Moreau (a colored man)...*"; on page 415: "*With respect to Rochambeau...he knew that Labatut, a seventy year old man, to save his head, did not hesitate to sacrifice a large part of his wealth. An act of sale of 200 squares was entered into before the notaries Cormand and Moreau of the Cap...*" This Moreau was most likely not Moreau Lislet since, in 1803, the latter was residing in Port Républicain.

> *I forgot, Citizen General, to mention in my notes a white man by the name of M. . .Secretary of the General-in-Chief. This peculiar man is very opinionated; he seems, at the present time, to exult a certain confidence and could possibly follow, perhaps everywhere, Toussaint. . ..*[109]

Does the letter "M" stand for the initial letter of a last name or a first name? Is it the first letter of the name "Moreau"? If so, could it be Louis Casimir Moreau Lislet?

Notarial acts issued in the years 9, 10, and 11 of the Republic place Louis Casimir Moreau Lislet in Port Républicain, Saint Domingue, during those years, where he held various positions. Some of those positions were official but none seems to have coincided in any way with the position of secretary to Toussaint Louverture. We are therefore inclined to think that Louis de Clouet made his declaration about Moreau Lislet simply for personal or political reasons. It is important to know the background of de Clouet's petition in order to understand the spirit in which it was drafted and so as to avoid taking literally all the accusations put forward by the author. Toussard, the French Counsul to New Orleans from 1806 to 1816, had submitted to de Clouet a list of people, one of whom was Moreau Lislet, who were to be appointed to specific positions. De Clouet made these comments prior to engaging in discussions on the merits of each of the proposed candidates:

> *All these candidates who were mentioned and put forward by Toussard, were men of an unparalleled corruption and*

---

[109] Colonies F³ 59. Code Historique. St. Vincent 1787. A. 1807 p. 179. One will have noticed that "M..." was a "white man".

immorality, they were all enemies of Spain and official or secret agents of Bonaparte. They were his satellites.....[110]

Such a preface does not convince the reader of the impartiality or objectivity of its author. Thus, the statement to the effect that Louis Moreau Lislet was, at a certain time, the secretary of Toussaint Louverture requires additional evidence if it is to be believed.

b. The Enigma of Louis Casimir Moreau Lislet's Name.

We have seen in chapter I above that the name of Louis Casimir's father was Jacob Vincent *Moreau*; that his mother, brother and sister bore no other name than *Moreau*. How did, then, Louis Casimir Moreau become Louis Casimir Moreau *Lislet*? We could be satisfied with the brief and elliptic explanation given by Moreau Lislet himself in his olographic testament and not try to look elsewhere for an explanation where there is perhaps none. The sentence referred to in Moreau Lislet's testament is the following:

My name is Louis Casimir Moreau. I was given the name Lislet to distinguish me from my older brother Benjamin Moreau who died.....[111]

This statement is quite intriguing. Why did Louis Casimir receive the additional name of *Lislet*? The explanation he, himself, gives us is too naive to be convincing: *"to distinguish me from my older brother Benjamin Moreau."* What is the use of christian names except to distinguish members of the same family from one another? Louis

---

[110] See supra note 11.

[111] See testament in appendix.

Christophe and Jacques Louis Deynaut, half-brothers of Moreau Lislet, were never given different surnames to distinguish one brother from the other.

One wonders whether Louis Casimir Moreau Lislet was trying to hide something. Did Vincent Pierre Benjamin Moreau and his brother Louis Casimir get along well? Or did Pierre Benjamin act in any way that might have disgraced his younger brother, who would then have tried to distinguish himself from his elder brother? Did Louis Casimir enjoy a special attention from his parents? Did they think that Louis Casimir Moreau was more suited than his brother to receive a solid secondary and university education? Could it be possible that Benjamin became very jealous of his brother? It must be noted here that, in his own testament, Benjamin Moreau did not mention his younger brother Louis Casimir at all, either as a legatee or even as an executor, but did expressly state his mother's name and particularly his sister's. Could it be possible that the two brothers did not get along and that Louis Casimir was given the nickname *Lislet* to officially mark the separation between the two brothers?[112] Nowhere, as far as we were able to determine with some certainty, is there any mention of this singular feature of Moreau Lislet's having a particularly "isolated" or unsociable personality. We must search elsewhere than in Moreau's character for the possible origin of the nickname *Lislet*.

There was a time when it was common to give some people nicknames that helped in distinguishing them easily and conferred on them a sort of additional, quasi-legal identity. The nickname thus given was drawn either from the profession the party was engaged in, or his place of geographical origin, or from his physical features or the like.

In the French language the nickname *Lislet* can be related to a place of origin and, more specifically, to a geographical

---

[112] Id.

origin dictated by the uniqueness of the island of Saint Domingue where Moreau Lislet was born. Was *Lislet* added to Louis Casimir's name simply as a way to distinguish between a "Moreau" from France and a "Moreau" from the Colonies? This assumption could certainly be made, and it could then be said that Lislet, in the name Moreau Lislet, simply meant that Louis Casimir had come from the "iles" or islands. Perhaps it is so, but then it could be said that Vincent Benjamin Moreau was also from the islands and so would also have been entitled to the nickname *Lislet*. However, the difference between Louis Casimir and his brother Vincent Benjamin is that the former, having left the island of Saint Domingue to study in France, could rightfully claim the nickname *des Ilets*, which was attached to his name while he was in France. On the other hand Vincent Benjamin never left the island and, therefore, would not have received such a mark of distinction. The "sibling distinction" theory, moreover, has two other apparent weaknesses: First, apart from the documents of the Grand Orient de France, the nickname *Lislet* (under this form) appears only in 1794, a year when reasons which could have existed at an earlier time to distinguish Louis Casimir from his brother Vincent Pierre Benjamin would no longer have existed because Vincent Pierre Benjamin had passed away the year before, in 1793. Second, during the years 1789, 1790 and 1792,[113] Louis Casimir Moreau was known only under his official last name, and this at a time when his brother Vincent was still alive and when, therefore, there could have been reasons to distinguish the two brothers from each other.

Moreau's nickname, under its form *Lislet*, represents the ultimate phase of many different versions it went through over the years. As a matter of fact, between the year 1787, when

---

[113] There exist official notarial acts for each of these years.

the nickname appeared for the first time, and the year 1806, when its form was finally fixed, that nickname had taken the following forms: *des Ilets, de Lislet, L'Islet, des Lislets, de Lislet* and, finally, *Lislet*. The first use of the nickname *des Ilets*, seems to have occurred in the year 1787, when Louis Casimir Moreau was only twenty-one. It can be found in a document of the Grand Orient de France of the Order of Free and Accepted Masons, a document in which it is stated that Louis Casimir Moreau *des Ilets*, from Saint Domingue, is a member of Sainte-Sophie's Lodge.[114] Another document, which is dated 1788, indicates that a certain "Moreau des Ilets, an officer of the colonial army" was also a member of Sainte-Sophie's Lodge.[115] Louis Casimir was not an officer of the colonial army but he certainly did live at the Paris address mentioned, rue Thomas du Louvre, as is stated also in the document dated 1788. In the absence of a more complete and detailed documentation one can only conclude, on the sole basis of the address indicated in the 1788 document, that Moreau *des Ilets*, "officer of the colonial army", was Louis Casimir Elisabeth Moreau.

Beginning in 1794, the nickname *des Ilets* was to appear under different forms. In certain official documents issued in 1794,[116] 1800,[117] and beyond, this nickname was spelled *Lislet*,

---

[114] In French: Bibliothèque Nationale. Département des Manuscrits FM² 111.

[115] In French: Bibliothèque Nationale. Département des Manuscrits FM² 111.

[116] In French: Acte du 15 germinal an 2, 4 avril 1794. (MSS 1215 Howard Tilton Library).

[117] In French: Acte du 9 Germinal an 9 (MSS 1216 Howard Tilton Library).

the final form under which Louis Casimir would sign his full name. In 1797, the nickname was spelled *de Lislet*.[118] In 1800 and 1801 it shifted to *L'Islet*.[119] A certificate dated 1802 adopted the form *des Lislets*.[120] Finally, a certificate issued in 1804 used the form *de Lislet*.[121] These different forms of the nickname appear to match a variety of geographical names and places in Saint Domingue, with which the nickname might therefore have some connection. As examples, we may cite the following geographical names:[122]

Fort de l'Islet: Situated in Cayes, near the mouth of the Lislet River, in Saint Domingue.

Fort Ilet: Fortress built by the French Colonial government on one of the small islands which was called at the time "îlet au prince" in the harbor of Port-au-Prince.

L'Ilet or L'Islet: Borough in the city of Cayes.

---

[118] In French: Etat Civil. Port au Prince. Répertoire 1793. 1803 (Bibliothèque de la France d'Outre-Mer).

[119] Acte du 9 Germinal an 9 (see supra note 22); Brumaire an X (MSS 1217 Howard Tilton Library).

[120] Supplement to the survey of habitations; in French: Supplément à l'état des habitations. Archives Nationales 135 AP3.

[121] Acte du 20 fructidor an 12 (MSS 1206. Howard Tilton Library).

[122] These examples are taken from the dictionary: Dictionnaire Géographique et Administratif Universel d'Haiti Illustré ou Guide Général en Haiti, by S. Rouzier, Paris.

Ilet: River of Anse d'Hainault; the only pleasant fresh water stream in the City of Cayes.

It is difficult, however, to establish any direct link between these different places within Saint Domingue and Louis Casimir Moreau himself. It appears that Louis Casimir Moreau did not reside in the Departments of the south and southwest of Saint Domingue at any time when the nickname first appeared. It would seem to be logical and sensible, then, to confine the assumptions which we are making to assimilations with geographical names taken from the Departments of the north and northwest of Saint Domingue.

In the Department of the north, the City of Cap Français, which became later Cap Haitien,[123] could have given us the premise of an assumption. Louis Casimir Moreau started his professional career in that city which, for strategic and military reasons, was divided into ten *islets* in the eleventh year of the Republic (1802).[124] It is possible to speculate that Louis Casimir Moreau thus became known subsequently as the "Moreau *des Islets* from the town of Cap Français". However, this speculation cannot be easily defended because in the eleventh year of the Republic, Louis Casimir Moreau had already been living for several years in Port-au-Prince or Port Républicain.

---

[123] Cap Haitien: from the Géographie de l'Ile d'Haiti by B. Ardouin, Port-au-Prince, 1832: this town was known as the Paris of Saint Domingue because of its beauty; it had been called Guarisco by the Spaniards and the French named it le Cap Français.

[124] Letter from brigadier general Claparède commanding officer of le Cap to general in Chief Rochambeau (Archives Nationales ref. 135 AP3).

The city of Port-au-Prince represents, in the Department of the West, the only possible link between Louis Casimir Moreau and the potential source of his nickname. The name of this city derives, "according to a tradition, from the ship 'Le Prince' which was anchored in this port in 1706 and, according to another tradition, from the islets (small islands) facing the port which were called *ilets* du Prince in 1680."[125] Louis Casimir Moreau lived for several years in Port-au-Prince, where he assumed numerous high positions, and therein could lie the reason why Moreau Lislet was given his nickname. Unfortunately, this hypothesis loses some of its weight if we point out that Louis Casimir Moreau did not settle in Port-au-Prince until 1794, at a time when his brother Pierre Vincent Benjamin, from whom he perhaps was to be distinguished, had already passed away. This hypothesis is like the previous ones, an easy target for criticism. The lack of documents that could have given us a conclusive explanation as to the origin of the nickname "Lislet" thus compels us to weigh all of the alternatives without accepting any one of them.

---

[125] In Géographie de l'Ile d'Haiti by B. Ardouin. "Port-au-Prince".

CHAPTER III.

FROM DONDON TO NEW ORLEANS

Louis Casimir Elisabeth Moreau was born[126] in Dondon,[127] in St. Martin Parish, Saint Domingue (Haiti today), where he was baptized on October 29, 1766. When he completed his secondary education, either in the city of Cap Français, Saint Domingue, or in France (and there either in Paris or Bordeaux), he studied law in Paris and received the title of "avocat au Parlement", probably in 1788. In order to marry, Louis Casimir Moreau had to obtain from King Louis XVI "dispensatory letters allowing him to contract marriage with Miss de Peters in France."[128] The reason for these "letters" was that, according to an edict issued in 1697, the banns of marriage should have been published at the place where Louis Casimir's father, Jacob Vincent, resided at the time of his death, which would have been in Dondon, Saint Domingue. Having obtained a marriage license from the King of France, on September the 10th, 1789, Louis Casimir Moreau married Anne Elisabeth Philippine de Peters in Paris. She was "un parti et établissement convenable et sortable" or, still,

---

[126] See supra Part II, Chapter II 1. *a. Year of birth.*

[127] Dondon: the ground where this community has been erected is about 250 fathoms above sea level; the whole area covered by this community is made up of mountains split and separated by valleys. [translated from the French in *Ile d'Haiti* by B. Ardouin 1832].

[128] Contrat de mariage du 10 Septembre 1789 [marriage contract of September 10, 1789] Me Deherain (Archives Nationales. Minutier Central).

"sortable et avantageux."[129] Louis Casimir Moreau was then a minor, 23 years of age, and in entering his marriage contract he was assisted by Sieur Moreau de Saint Méry, "Conseiller du Roy en son Conseil Supérieur de Saint Domingue," who was also Louis Casimir's guardian ad hoc.

According to the first paragraph of the marriage contract,[130]

> *les futurs époux seront communs en tous biens meubles et conquêts immeubles suivant la coutume de Paris, au désir de laquelle la dite communauté sera réglée et régie et les biens d'icelle partagés quand bien même ils viendraient par la suite à établir leur domicile ou à faire des acquisitions en des pays soumis à des lois, coutumes et usages contraires auxquels ils ont expressément dérogé et renoncé par ces présentes. . ..*

During the few weeks they spent together in Paris, before sailing back to Saint-Domingue, the young couple stayed in the house that Louis Casimir Moreau occupied, "rue Saint Thomas du Louvre paroisse Saint Germain L'Auxerois à l'hotel de la

---

[129] Avis en l'hotel, Mariage Moreau, 12 août 1789. Me. Deherain (Archives Nationales. Minutier Central). [Notice posted at City Hall, Moreau Marriage, August 12, 1789].

[130] See supra note 3. Translation from the French: "the future spouses will be married according to the matrimonial regime of the community of movables and acquired immovables according to the custom of Paris, the prescriptions of which will regulate and rule the said community and the assets to be shared even though the spouses should later on establish their domicile or acquire assets in countries governed by laws, customs and usages to which the parties expressly state that they will not be subjected and the application of which they renounce hereby... ".

princesse royale d'Angleterre". At the end of September 1789, Louis Casimir Moreau and his wife made and appointed Marie Louise de Peters, Elisabeth's sister, as their general and special mandatary or attorney. The necessity for this power of attorney suggests that Anne Philippine de Peters was in fact an advantageous match for Louis Casimir, which is confirmed if one is keen on giving a financial connotation to the expression used by Elisabeth Torel Moreau when she consented to the marriage of "her younger son who had earned her confidence through his good conduct".[131]

In 1790, Louis Casimir Moreau Lislet and Anne Philippine settled in Cap Français, where he became "Premier Substitut du Procureur Général au conseil Supérieur de' Saint Domingue", a position equivalent to that of first assistant public prosecutor or assistant district attorney.

On July 5, 1790, Anne Philippine gave birth to a girl, Julie Elisabeth Hatté, who was baptized on September 18, 1797, in Port-au-Prince.[132] In 1793, a boy named Léon was born a few weeks before the terrible fire that would heavily damage the city in June of 1793,[133] and in which Louis Casimir's maternal aunt perished. This fire and the events that followed seem to have prompted Louis Casimir Moreau to send his wife, children and mother to a safe place. "At the

---

[131] Procuration du 29 Sept. 1789. Notaire Deherain XCV 413. (Archives Nationales. Minutier Central). [Power of attorney dated September 29, 1789].

[132] Acte du 18 avril 1789 consentement de Madame Moreau. Notaire Deherain (supra note 6). [Act of consent given by Mrs. Moreau, April 18, 1789].

[133] Etat Civil. Port-au-Prince. Répertoire 1793 à 1803 (Bibliothèque de la France d'Outre-Mer). [Civil Registry, Port-au-Prince, Register 1793 to 1803].

end of June 1793, the catastrophe caused, out of necessity, a convoy of a hundred sails with thousands and thousands of white passengers on board to the Carolinas, to Savannah and to Philadelphia."[134] In August of 1793, Anne Philippine, along with her children and Elisabeth Torel Moreau, Louis Casimir's mother, boarded the schooner *La Delaware* en route to Philadelphia.[135] Unfortunately, the ship was shipwrecked and Elisabeth Thorel Moreau and Léon Moreau Lislet drowned. Anne Philippine and her daughter managed to make it to Philadelphia where the Delagranges lived and where, some months later, they were joined by Louis Casimir.

The opening of the will of Pierre Vincent Benjamin Moreau, executed before the Consul of the French Republic in the city of Philadelphia on April 4, 1794, attests to the following:

This year 2nd of the French Republic, one and indivisible, Germinal 15, have appeared before me Jean Baptiste Petry, consul of the Republic in Philadelphia, the citizens Joseph Elisabeth Georges Merlhy de LaGrange, attorney of the Superior Council of Le Cap Français, residing in this city...and Louis Elisabeth Casimir Moreau, assistant district attorney of the said council also residing in this city...[136]

The Moreau Lislets returned to Saint Domingue in 1794 and settled in Port Républicain (Port-au-Prince) where they were to reside until 1803. Louis Casimir Moreau Lislet's high

---

[134] Réfugiés de Saint-Domingue aux Etats-Unis, par G. Debien 1950 p. 3.

[135] L'ami de l'Egalité ou Annales Républicaines. Samedi 27 juillet 1793. L'an deuxième de la République Française.

[136] See supra note 21 Chapter II Part II.

intellectual and moral qualities seem to have earned him a solid reputation there, as illustrated by the fact that he was appointed to various legal positions, at times simultaneously. Among these various functions which Moreau Lislet occupied, the function of land administrator or agent reveals the extent of the confidence he inspired. The emigration of a great many colonists was one of the several repercussions of the revolutions, the fires, the wars and the massacres that devastated the Island of Saint Domingue on and after 1791. Many residents left the island with the firm intention of returning but, in the meantime, it was necessary for them to ensure the proper administration of their personal property, especially real property, which they would leave behind. This is how Louis Casimir Moreau came to be the agent or attorney of a great number of emigrants. Here are two procurations, or powers of attorney, illustrating this fact:

1. *Germinal, year 9*
   Power of attorney from Madame La Rivière
   To Citizen
   Moreau Lislet
   Before me Jean Baptiste Porée, chancellor of division for commercial relations of the French Republic [in Philadelphia], have appeared in person the citizen Marguerite widow La Riviere, resident of Saint Domingue from where she was deported...
   The said person has stated to have appointed and constituted...as her special attorney...the person of Louis Casimir Elisabeth Moreau L'Islet, lawyer, resident of Port Républicain...[137]

---

[137] MSS 1216 (Howard Tilton Library, Tulane). One will have noticed the two different spellings of the name: "Lislet" and "L'Islet".

2. *Brumaire, year 10*
   Power of attorney
   To
   Moreau Lislet
   Before me Jean Baptiste Porée...have appeared in person Benigne Charles de St. Memin and Victoire de Motmans his wife...both owners in St Domingue, ordinarily residents of Burlington, New Jersey...
   The said parties have stated to have appointed and constituted...as their general and special attorney...the person of Louis Casimir Elisabeth Moreau L'Islet, lawyer, resident of Port Républicain...[138]

As a practicing lawyer Louis Casimir Moreau Lislet argued many cases, one of which dealt with a problem of private international law and was recorded with the clerk's office of the tribunal de Commerce of the Department of the West of Saint Domingue, sitting in Port Républicain:

Session of 23 Floréal year nine

To all present and to come, greetings... Considering the claim before the court opposing Mr. Zephiria Kingsley, American businessman from Charleston present in Port Républicain... represented by the citizen Jean Jacques Daulhième, his counsellor, on the one hand, against the citizen Thomas Mierre, ship captain in command of the brig "La Lucy" under Danish flag, defendant represented by the citizen Moreau Lislet his counsellor, on the other hand...

---

[138] MSS 1217 (Howard Tilton Library, Tulane).

The court decides...that within a time frame of four months, Mr. Kingsley is required to justify his ownership of the brig "La Lucy"...[139]

Because of the high esteem in which he was held by his colleagues and on account of his competence and dedication acknowledged on many occasions by the public authorities, Moreau Lislet was called to exercise the functions of judge during several months of the year 10 of the republic (1801-1802). This is confirmed by the following excerpt:

Messidor 16, Year 10
Adjudication

Today, Messidor 2, Year 10 of the French Republic one and indivisible, before us Louis Casimir Elisabeth Moreau Lislet, public defender, sitting as judge in the absence and impediment of the judges of the court of original jurisdiction of Port Républicain, in the presence of citizen Cotelle, Government Prosecutor with the said court...[140]

---

[139] Huard, notaire au Port au Prince. An 9, an 10; jugement du tribunal 23 floréal an neuf; see also, jugement du tribunal 2 floréal and dix. [Bibliothèque de la France d'Outre-Mer]. Moreau Lislet is referred to in many juridical acts as a "defenseur", a public defender. See also, Dépôt des papiers publics des Colonies de St. Domingue. Greffe de Port au Prince: GAC. H.I. J. Kir.: G2. 56. 5: p.290, 304, 306, 307, 430...See also, Acte du 9 Nivose an 10, Guieu, notaire Républicain [Bibliothèque de la France d'Outre-Mer].

[140] Dépôt des papiers publics des Colonies St. Domingue. Greffe de Port au Prince. G2.56.5 p. 258. See pages 284, 307. See also: 3 prairial an X, 6 prairial an X et 29 Messidor an X dans Huard. notaire au Port-au-Prince an 10. See also:

According to an act issued on Pluviose 9, year 11, Moreau Lislet was acting also as an attorney-at-law[141] and, as reported in other acts, he was an executor of successions in abeyance.[142]

Although Louis Casimir Moreau was a jurist fully dedicated to the obligations and the duties of his positions, he also had to look after his personal affairs. The precarious and troubled times he went through with his family probably incited him to look for new sources of revenue in addition to the income he earned as a lawyer. This is why in the year 9 he claimed ownership of several immovables and attempted to manage his personal properties and those of his wife to the best of their common interests. On Frimaire 9, year 9, (November 1800) Louis Casimir Moreau Lislet was able to obtain a certificate of identification establishing his ownership of certain immovables, as follows:

Frimaire, year 9
In the name of the French Republic
Before the public notaries for the district of western Saint Domingue at the city hall of Port Républicain, where the undersigned parties reside, have appeared in person the citizens Jacques Duviella, Jean-Paul Carouge, Jean

---

1er 7C^{re} an X et 6e 7C^{re} an X dans G2.58.7.

[141] Acte du 9 Pluviose an 11 No. 6508. Me Hacquet. Notaire 1er au 20 pluviose an 11. Port Républicain. Port au Prince [Archives de la France d'Outre-Mer].

[142] Acte du 29 germinal an 11 [19 avril 1803] Me Loreilhe Notaire. Juillet 1787 au 29 Germinal an 11. [Bibliothèque de la France d'Outre-Mer]. Acte du 2 thermidor an 11, Me Huard notaire Port-au-Prince an 11 [Bibliothèque de la France d'Outre-Mer].

Chrisostome and Francois de Salles Conigliano, all residents of this parish, who have sworn and stated by act of notoriety as having seen and read deeds before they were lost, that the citizen Louis Casimir Elisabeth Moreau, previously resident of Dondon, dependency of Le Cap, and currently residing in this city, is the sole and unique owner,

1-of one estate established as a coffee plantation in the locality of La Mare-à-La-Roche, parish of Dondon, known under the name of Moreau and coming from the succession of his father and mother.

2-of another estate established as a coffeee plantation in the locality of Le-Haut-du-Trou, district of Dondon, known under the name of Moreau and coming from the succession of the late Antoine Moreau, his paternal uncle, who died without children.

3-of a house, not burned down and located in Le Cap, street de la Pointe (formerly du Marché aux Blancs) n__ and presently rented out to citizen Dubertet, as coming from the succession of his aunt and his mother, who were indivisible owners as heirs of the succession of the late Thorel, their father, and maternal grandfather of the said citizen Moreau.

And the citizens Duviella and Conigliano further stated in particular as having known for certain that the late citizen Antoine Moreau resident of Le Haut-du-Trou, paternal uncle of said citizen Moreau, died there in the year 1792, murdered by some marauders not long after the retaking of Dondon by commander de Neuilly; [they stated] as well that citizen Thorel... his maternal aunt, has unfortunately perished in the fire of Le Cap; and finally that the citizen widow Moreau, his mother, died during the crossing from Le Cap to Philadelphia aboard the schooner "Delaware", captain Davis,...on which they were passengers themselves.

In testimony whereof they have made the present statement to stand as a substitute for the citizen Moreau's deeds lost in the events of the Revolution...[143]

Upon reading this document we are led to make two statements. It is remarkable, first of all, that the death of Vincent Pierre Benjamin Moreau, Louis Casimir's brother, is not mentioned at all. Yet, according to other documents, Vincent Benjamin Moreau had died in 1793. Was this an intentional omission? Would there have been any legal purpose in referring to Vincent Benjamin Pierre Moreau's death? One may only speculate at this time, but from a legal standpoint a reference to Vincent's death would have clarified the line of succession to the properties involved. An additional important fact that was not stated was the existence of Elisabeth Françoise Ignace Moreau, Mrs. de Lagrange and Louis Casimir's sister, who was still alive in the year 9 and who was also an heir in the same manner as Louis Casimir to the properties mentioned in the certificate of identity. Was Moreau Lislet trying to cheat his sister of her rights of inheritance by relying on the fact that she lived in Philadelphia, thus very far from Port Républicain, and that, therefore, it would be easy for him, perhaps in connivance with some witnesses, to claim that he was the only heir? We will be in a better position to pass judgment on the state of mind of Louis Casimir Moreau after we take cognizance of the following petition that he addressed to General Toussaint Louverture concerning the ownership of two houses:

To citizen Toussaint L'Ouverture, commander general of the colony of Saint Domingue;

---

[143] Acte du 9 frimaire an 9, Collignon notaire au Port au Prince [Archives de la France d'Outre-Mer].

> *Louis Casimir Moreau, defender before the courts of Port Républicain,*
>
> *Hereby discloses to you, Citizen General, that as sole heir of his mother, father and uncle, he is the owner of two estates in Dondon and a house in the city of Le Cap which have been sequestrated while he was in residence at Port Républicain;*
>
> *Just and generous, you have stated, Citizen General, that you would reconvey their properties to the owners who meet the legal requirements;*
>
> *Here are three documents in justification of my claim:*
> *1- of my residence under the terms of the statute,*
> *2- of my ownership and of the death of my ancestors,*
> *3- of the death of my brother;*
>
> *May it please you, Citizen General, on account of these justifications, to order the cancellation of the order of sequestration that was placed on the following properties...*[144]

On Frimaire 29, year 9, (November 1800) a decree was passed granting Louis Casimir the cancellation of the sequestration of his properties as he had petitioned Toussaint Louverture.[145] Subsequently, on Nivose 9, year 9, (December 1800) his attorney, sieur Bourget, took possession of the properties on his behalf.[146] However the decree in question contained a restriction that must have caught Louis Casimir Moreau's attention. That decree stipulated that Toussaint Louverture, the general-in-chief of the troops in Saint Domingue,

> *...decides that the order placing under sequestration the said estates located in Dondon and a house located at 86 street*

---

[144] Document. Dom. C 39:D4.

[145] See text in Dom. C 39: D4, supra note 19.

[146] Id.

de la pointe in Le Cap is withdrawn, without prejudice to the rights of any other party, should any be existence...[147]

   One may wonder whether it had been impossible for Elisabeth Françoise Ignace Moreau, Mr. de Lagrange's wife and Louis Casimir Moreau's sister, to claim her rights of inheritance despite the several steps taken by her husband, Joseph de Lagrange to do so? The latter had, on two occasions, in 1796[148] and in 1799,[149] sent out powers of attorney, one of which had been addressed to the Sieur Durainé and the other to the Sieur Laplace, giving them the:

   power to...administer the quarter of ownership of a building belonging to him, in his said quality, located in Le Cap and known as habitation Moreau located in an area known as La Mare, district of Dondon...
   Subsequent events seem to indicate that the above-mentioned agents never acted as instructed to do. Indeed, on vendémiaire, year 13, (September 1804) several years later, Joseph de Lagrange, then a resident in Paris, addressed to the Minister of the Navy the following correspondence:

3- Your Excellency,

   I am respectfully requesting that your Excellency accede to my request to deliver to my wife Elisabeth Françoise Ignace Moreau a certificate declaring her ownership of estates and

---

[147] Id.

[148] MSS 1216. Consulat de France à Philadelphie An 4e, Thermidor [Howard Tilton Library, Tulane].

[149] Id. Power of attorney dated 14 Brumaire year 8.

buildings located in Saint Domingue in the city of Le Cap Français and the district of Dondon.

I must confess that I may owe to my honesty to inform you that my intentions are not to benefit from the relief efforts that are being extended to the native settlers. Although, like them, I have lost everything, I still have a State, and I would be ashamed to worsen their misfortune by diminishing the relief such a paternal government grants them... [150]

On the basis of all these documents can it be said, on hindsight, that Louis Casimir Moreau Lislet had acted in bad faith and attempted to deprive his sister of her rights of inheritance? We believe that we can answer this question in the negative. The only reason for this apparent "disguise", if it was one, would have been to facilitate and expedite the handling of a succession which, because of political and social events, had become complicated. Having remained in Saint Domingue presented a great advantage for Louis Casimir as compared to the almost insurmountable obstacle that emigration created at the time. As the means of communications were slow and not very reliable, official records and other important documents could easily be destroyed or be lost in transit. In short, it was often quite difficult to claim one's right from a distance. Whatever guess or speculation we might be tempted to make, the fact remains that Louis Casimir Moreau was always on good terms with his sister and his brother-in-law, as illustrated by the business relationship they were involved in after Louis Casimir Moreau had moved to New Orleans. It can fairly be said that Louis Casimir Moreau may have acted the way he did simply in order to expedite the cancellation of the sequestration of the properties for fear that some intruders would illegally take

---

[150] Dossier Delagrange (Joseph) [Archives de la France d'Outre-Mer].

possession of these assets. Louis Casimir could have done this with the intention of paying his sister her share of the profits he might have made from the administration and sale of these immovable properties. In fact, Louis Casimir Moreau's administration of these assets was more a source of trouble than of satisfaction to him. As he did not live in Cap Français, to manage the property there he appointed someone as his agent. On Nivose, year 9, in an official certificate[151] he appointed "Mr. Bourget, a merchant in Cap Français, as his general and special attorney" to whom he gave full powers:

to take possession of two estates established as coffee plantations and both known under the name Moreau and located in Dondon...to receive the accrued and future revenues...to rent out the house located 86 Rue de la Pointe, belonging to him...to file any claim...to exercise all the rights belonging to the principal and grantor of this power...

On Vendémiaire 20, year 10[152] he appointed "Mr. Prevot, civil judge and Mr. Bourget, merchant in Cap", with full power to act jointly. The following day, Vendémiaire 21,[153] however, he appointed Mr. Prevot, civil judge in Cap, as "his general and honorary attorney" with the mission of "keeping a close eye on the administration conducted by Mr. Bourget, and even to revoke his power if need be. . ." Moreau Lislet was apparently a candid, meticulous and firm businessman as indicated by the fact that, on ventose 6, year 10, he revoked

---

[151] Me Hacquet, notaire, St. Domingue [Archives de la France d'Outre-Mer].

[152] Acte No. 5033 Me Guieu, notaire. St. Domingue, Port Républicain [Archives de la France d'Outre-Mer].

[153] Acte No. 5040, id.

the procuration he had given Mr. Bourget because the latter had:

...openly violated the instructions consigned in the letters sent to him, acted without authorization and exceeded the powers that had been given to him...[154]

The events that occurred during the summer of 1803 in Saint Domingue prevented Moreau Lislet from enjoying for very long the benefit of the inheritance he had eventually acquired, or even from drawing any profit from the sale of those assets. This assertion is confirmed by some documents dated 1829,[155] according to which Joseph Merlhy de Lagrange was still trying, at that time, to establish the rights of inheritance of the Moreau heirs with respect to the succession to the above-mentioned properties.

At the same time Moreau Lislet was managing his personal properties he was keeping a close eye on the administration of his wife's assets. That administration was put in the hands of Joseph Merlhy de Lagrange which, in a way, shows that both families were on good terms and that the two brothers-in-law trusted each other. On Prairial 26, year 11 (1803), Louis Moreau Lislet and Anne Philippine, before a notary:

---

[154] Acte no. 5441, Me Hacquet, notaire, Port Républicain [Archives de la France d'Outre-Mer]. In this same juridical act, Moreau Lislet gives a power of attorney to the citizen Pierre Chauveau, merchant in le Cap, to bring an action in nullity of all the leases negotiated by the citizen Bourget on all houses owned by Moreau Lislet. It is argued that the citizen Bourget had acted without any authority.

[155] Marine et Colonie. Archives Coloniales. Dépôt des Papiers Publics des Colonies. Renseignement d'intérêt privé et pièces déposées. Dossier Moreau Antoine no. 444 [Archives de la France d'Outre-Mer].

Have said and stated to give by the present, general and special powers of attorney to citizen Merly Delagrange, public defender and in case of default, to citizen De Petters, brother of the appearing party (Anne Philippine), both residents of Paris;

To whom they give power, for them and in their names, to file any claim for the cancellation, nullity or for any other ground against the transfer of a house located in Paris, rue du Hazard Richelieu; the said house being indivisibly owned by the person appearing before us and her brother and sister...the whole on account of the lesionary price of the sale of the said house...[156]

Such was, in 1803 in Port Républicain, the social condition and more or less comfortable financial situation of the Moreau Lislets. Nothing in their attitude, and Louis Casimir himself will confirm it later, could then have suggested that they had any intention of leaving the island of Saint Domingue, even though the political climate was becoming quite tense and even hostile. An unforeseeable event, combined with a sense of duty, ultimately led the couple into a forced exile, causing them to break forever the bonds that tied them to Saint Domingue and setting them off into a new adventure on the North American continent.

In August of 1803 the Moreau Lislets were sailing towards Cap Français from Port Républicain. This voyage had nothing to do with "the last great departure of those who had escaped in the south from the vengeance of Rigaud, or in the West and the North from the vengeance of Dessalines. .. "[157] On the

---

[156] Acte du 26 Prairial an 11 no. 6959, Me Hacquet notaire, Port-au-Prince [Archives de la France d'Outre-Mer].

[157] G. Debien. "Réfugiés de Saint Domingue aux Etats-Unis" 1950 p. 6 & 7.

contrary, Louis Casimir Moreau Lislet had been appointed to serve on an official assignment in Cap Français. As fate would have it, and as it appears from a declaration Moreau Lislet made on Floréal 13, year 12, he never made it to the Town of Cap Français:

On Floreal 13, year 12, before noon, has appeared at the Secretary's office of the Agency of the French Government located in Santiago de Cuba and before the undersigned Secretary of the said Agency...the Citizen Moreau Lislet, curator of estates in abeyance (unclaimed inheritances) in Port Républicain, Island of Saint Domingue, now a refugee and resident of Santiago de Cuba;

who said and declared that he left Port Républicain around the middle of last August on the ship "L'Alexandrine", Captain de Boyner, in order to take up his assignment at Le Cap to be under the orders of Mr. Lulot, Higher Judge of Saint Domingue who had requested him in writing to do so at the time of his departure from Port Républicain with the military headquarters and had provided him with a passport issued by General Rochambeau and stamped by General Lavalette, commander in chief of Port Républicain and registered at the Court of Appeals of the department (Parish) of L'Artibonite, who had approved of his departure; that the ship l'Alexandrine was carrying official documents and correspondence of the government and that she was to stop at Mole before heading for Le Cap, that the ship met with strong head winds and was forced into the canal where she encountered enemy ships so that she was forced to find refuge in Santiago where the person appearing before us arrived on August 25 and where he stayed waiting for a favorable opportunity to reach his destination, after having given notice of his forced stay in Santiago to the Captain General and citizen Minutti, temporary High Judge who invited him to seize upon the first opportunity to return to Port-au-Prince;

but as this letter was received, news had spread that Port-au-Prince had been evacuated on October 18, preventing the person appearing before us to comply with the new orders he had received and he continued to reside in this city...[158]

It was under these extremely difficult circumstances that Louis Moreau Lislet started his second career, one that was to make him a highly distinguished man, cast his name in history and raise him from the likely obscurity where he would have been forgotten had he remained in Saint-Domingue. He lost everything in this adventure:

On Floreal 13, year 12, in the afternoon, has appeared at the Secretary's office of the Agency of the French Government in Santiago de Cuba, the Citizen Moreau Lislet...;
who declared...that citizen Canbonne whom he had empowered to take care of his affairs and his law office, had been forced to abandon all the documents in the said office...along with all the furniture and effects left by the person appearing before us, who hereby declares the above losses...[159]

There are other official documents from the Agency of the French government in Santiago, Cuba, which attest to the fact that the Moreau Lislets spent approximately a year in that city before they emigrated to Louisiana. The last official certificate providing evidence of the presence of Louis Moreau

---

[158] Archives Coloniales. St. Domingue, St. Yago de Cuba, 10 Pluviose an XII, 12 avril 1809 [Archives de la France d'Outre-Mer].

[159] Id.

Lislet in Santiago is dated Fructidor 20, year 12, which would correspond to August 9, 1804.[160]

It was between August of 1804 and the beginning of the month of February, 1805 that the Moreau Lislets shared the same fate as the great number of colonists who settled in Louisiana after they were expelled from Saint Domingue. Louisiana would welcome a brilliant man, a true scholar, a dedicated citizen and, unbeknownst to the new land in which he would settle, the hand that would carve a legal system out of confusion, chaos and bequeath it to history.

---

[160] MSS 1206 [Howard Tilton Library, Tulane]. Acte de mariage (written act of marriage) dated 20 fructidor an 12. Many other acts testify to Moreau Lislet's presence in Santiago; examples are: an act of 2 floréal an 12, Archives Coloniales St. Domingue. Réfugiés-Consulats Norfolk An IV, 1814, Nouvelle Orléans An XII [Archives de la France d'Outre-Mer]; acts of 2 floréal, 13 floréal (3 acts bear that date), 20 ventose and 10 messidor an 12. Archives Coloniales St. Domingue. St. Yago de Cuba 10 pluviose an XII, 12 avril 1809. [Archives de la France d'Outre-Mer].

CHAPTER IV.

THE FIRST YEARS OF INTEGRATION

Louis Casimir Moreau Lislet was not the kind of man to let himself be dominated by events. He proved it later in many instances. Moreau Lislet seemed always to have been driven by a very strong will power and an unwavering determination. No sooner had he set foot in Louisiana[161] that it was almost certain that he would adapt to this new environment and contribute efficiently to the building and well-being of this newly-acquired territory of the young country of the United States. Two factors of undeniable importance worked in his favor. First of all, he was a man of law, educated and raised in a country whose legal system was almost the twin brother of the one in place in the territory where he had decided to settle, and he had shown, in other respects, that he was capable of filling positions of responsibility. The second factor upon which Louis Moreau Lislet could certainly count was his knowledge of French, English and Spanish. His short stay in Philadelphia and his American "patrons" in Port Républicain had made it possible for Louis Casimir to have a good command of the English language; furthermore, having spent a whole year in Cuba had given him the opportunity to learn Spanish. Is it not an extraordinary and happy coincidence that, later on, he would find these three languages in use in his new and last home, New Orleans?

Moreau Lislet took advantage of the situation and made a name for himself. The first manifestation of his presence in

---

[161] Moreau Lislet and his family settled in New Orleans some time between August 1804 and February 1805.

New Orleans[162] clearly shows the unique position he was enjoying. On February 4, 1805, his name appeared at the bottom of a joint resolution of the two legislative chambers of the Orleans Territory:[163]

I certify this translation
Moreau Lislet
Translator

Other resolutions from the city council of New Orleans,[164] dated July 20, 1805, and most probably drafted in French, are also signed by Moreau Lislet, translator, who certified their translation into English.

After having worked as a translator for a few months, which he found somewhat unrewarding, but through which he made himself known among his peers, Louis Casimir Moreau

---

[162] Although the New Orleans directory of 1805 did not list Moreau Lislet, it is a fact that he lived in the city at least since February 1805. The same directory refers to Pierre Derbigny, 14 Carondelet Street, Edward Livingston, 22 Condé Street...[New Orleans in 1805, A Directory and A Census]. Howard Tilton Library, Tulane, 976-31, 917 N 531.

[163] Joint resolution of the two chambers, signed by J. Poydras, President of the Council and approved by the governor, W. C. C. Claiborne on February the 4th 1805.

[164] Territorial Papers of the United States, Vol. 9. S.1.36.9 p. 482 and 483: "I do Certify the above translation Moreau Lislet interpreter." In July-August 1805 Moreau Lislet certified that some letters in Spanish by The Marquis of Casa Calvo to Governor Claiborne had been accurately translated into English. Id. at p., 484-487.

resigned from his position[165] and established himself as a lawyer in a partnership with another French jurist, Pierre Derbigny, as it appeared from a notice in the *Louisiana Gazette* dated October 29, 1805.[166] This partnership did not last very long, as indicated by notices which were published at the start of the month of April, 1806, and which bore only the signature of Moreau Lislet.[167] Perhaps Moreau Lislet was not easy to get along with. He was certainly very demanding, meticulous and hard-working; these were qualities that certain "partners" might have viewed as defects when they were stretched to the extreme. In any case, he was not the kind of man who took an insult or a calumny lightly as he valued very highly his moral integrity and his intellectual honesty. Following the publication of an article entitled "*Subtilité et ruse d'avocat*"[168] that appeared in a local newspaper, in which

---

[165] In the same Territorial Papers of the United States, at p. 603, under the year 1806, it is reported that "Moreau De Lisle" (sic), Interpreter had resigned in June, 1805.

[166] The Louisiana Gazette: Tuesday, October 29, 1805: "Notice
Stephen Zacharie....by public instrument of writing, lodged in the office of Messrs. Moreau de Lislet et Derbigny, Counselors at Law, in this city..." [It is worth pointing out that the French version of this same Notice or Avis refers to Moreau Lislet as "Moreau de
Lislet".

[167] See Le Moniteur April 12, 1806 #605; Le Moniteur July 16, 1806 #632; Le Moniteur September 24, 1806 #652. (in French).

[168] "Le Moniteur" de la Louisiane, No 693, Samedi 14 février 1807.

Jacques Nadaud leveled criticisms at him, Moreau Lislet responded vehemently:

To the editor of the Louisiana Monitor.
Sir,
I have read the contemptible pamphlet that Jacques Nadaud was proud to have printed in your last edition. Fifteen years of an honorable profession, the public respect that I believe I have earned and that I will always strive to deserve, would probably have given me the right to look upon this writing with contempt which is its proper destiny; but I thought that I owed it to myself and to the Bar of which I am proud to be a member, to deny vehemently the statements made by Mr. Nadaud as false, nasty and slanderous as I hope to prove before the court where I intend to challenge him.

The qualities and talents that Moreau Lislet displayed apparently earned him the respect of the local authorities. Already in June of 1806, the Legislative Council and the House of Representatives of the Territory of Orleans had named him, along with James Brown, *"to draft and organize an adequate Civil Code for this territory"*.[169] In the month of

---

[169] Session Laws of American States and Territories. Territory of Orleans 1804, 1811. Moreau Lislet was apparently neither the first choice nor the second one if this excerpt from a letter by James Brown to John Breckinridge is indicative of the events that took place:
"New Orleans January 22nd 1805
DEAR SIR,....It is generally expected here that the Memorial will only succeed so far as to obtain us the second grade of Territorial Government. ...much good might be done by availing ourselves of the assistance of the Council to adopt a good code of Laws for the Government of the Territory. We possess all the materials for the able execution of such a work.

March of the year 1807, the Governor of the Territory of New Orleans, William C. C. Claiborne, appointed him judge of the city and parish of Orleans to replace James Workman who had resigned.[170] At the end of the term of Workman's former appointment, in May of 1807, Louis Moreau Lislet was appointed again but, this time in his own name.[171] In his capacity as judge, he was involved in numerous activities: to

---

The Civil Law- the Spanish Ordinances-the British Statute and Common Laws, and the codes of all the States are spread before us, and the people are prepared for the reception of a code ably compiled from these several systems....Should a good system be adopted it will probably long remain unchanged... Impressed with these ideas the Council appear disposed to engage Mr Livingston and myself to digest a Code; but such is the unfortunate dislike of the Governor towards the only man in whom the Council seems disposed to confide as my assistant, that it is believed the measure will fail and the Country be left without any laws except a few unimportant ones..." IX Territorial Papers of the United States, The Territory of Orleans 1803-1812, at p.378-379. One will have noticed that Brown was going to consider Livingston as his assistant! Compare this statement to the statement made by the three reporters of the 1825 Louisiana Civil Code!

[170] The Louisiana Gazette, Tuesday March 17, 1807
New Orleans March 17
Appointment by the Governor
Moreau Lislet, judge of the County of Orleans,

[171] The Louisiana Gazette, Friday May 8, 1807
Appointments by the Governor of the Territory of Orleans Moreau Lislet, judge of the Parish of New Orleans; See also Territorial Papers of the United States at p. 749.

pass judgment, of course, but also to issue orders,[172] approve resolutions of the city council,[173] enact regulations,[174] issue notices of all sorts,[175] inform the city about its obligations,[176] etc.

Despite the importance and the burden of his professional duties, Moreau Lislet did not give up the other activities that were dear to him. There was one in particular to which he always dedicated and would dedicate for a long time his energy and many talents — freemasonry. Among the refugees from Saint Domingue who had settled in Louisiana, a great number belonged to the order of the free masons, in particular to the *Lodge La Réunion Désirée No. 3073*. On February 15, 1806, they had a meeting and a lodge was formed by the former officers: with Louis Casimir Elisabeth Moreau Lislet as Master . . . they took the resolution of resuming their activities in New Orleans until they could return to their homeland. . ., requesting from the great orient of France a copy of their Charter and declaring their activities as valid until they received their charter. A temporary election of the officers took place at that time and these were the results:

---

[172] Le Moniteur, May 6, 1807 #716 (in French).

[173] Le Moniteur, May 13, 1807 #718 (in French).

[174] Le Moniteur, May 27, 1807 #722; Le Moniteur, May 30, 1807 #723 (in French).

[175] Le Moniteur, May 13, 1807 #718; Le Moniteur May 30, 1807 #759; Le Moniteur, October 7, 1807 #760 (in French).

[176] Private Papers #41. J. M. Wisdom Collection [Howard Tilton Special Collections]. Letter from Moreau Lislet to the Mayor of New Orleans dated August 8, 1807.

Moreau Lislet, G.M.; J. Rice Fitzgerald, G.S. and Jean Zanico, D.G.S. The official election took place on the next June 17, and Moreau was reelected. . . The attendance at the meetings of the lodge started decreasing and during the meeting of November 27, 1808, Moreau Lislet, in his capacities as G.M. administered a reprimand to his brothers for their lack of masonic zeal. . .[177]

In February of 1808, Moreau Lislet was appointed a judge of the Superior Court of the Orleans Territory by the President of the United States. For reasons that he expressed in a letter of May 7, 1808, Moreau Lislet turned down this appointment:

New Orleans May 1st 1808
JAMES MADISON Esq. Secretary of State

Sir I have duly received your letter of the 18th of March last, including the Commission of Judge of the Superior Court of the Territory of Orleans, which the President of the United States has been pleased to bestow on me. It is with sincere regret that I Feel under the necessity of Declining to accept that honourable station, my situation in life being such as to make it impossible for me to maintain my family with the salary attached to that office. I pray you to assure the President that I value, as I ought, that token of his Esteem and would have been happy to accept the Commission if so insuperable an obstacle had not forbidden it.

---

[177] James B. Scot: Outline of the Rise and Progress of Freemasonry in Louisiana. New Orleans 1912 at p. 6-7. The picture of Moreau Lislet that appears at the beginning of this book was taken by the author at the Masonic Temple, the Grand Lodge of the State of Louisiana, New Orleans, LA.

Permit me to avail myself of this opportunity to express the almost General wish of the inhabitants of this Territory and my own sanguine expectation that you may be the successor of our worthy President.

I am with Great respect Sir your most humble and obedient Servant.

J. Moreau Lislet[178]

Thus Moreau Lislet continued to be judge for the city and parish of Orleans. But was it really financial reasons that incited him to turn down an appointment to a prestigious position for a jurist who had just immigrated in the country? Perhaps Moreau Lislet replied in the negative because he had political ambitions. The Wednesday, June 24, 1808, issue of *La Gazette de la Louisiane* contained the following handout:[179]

"There are all reasons to believe that the candidates whose names appear hereunder will obtain the majority of the votes at the next election:
Senator
Mr. Michel de Armas
Repesentatives
MM. Louis Moreau Lislet
Louis B. Macarty"

If such was the ambition of Moreau Lislet, he must have been certainly very disappointed, and perhaps humiliated, for he was not elected. He continued to be judge for the city and

---

[178] Territorial Papers of the United States, at p. 785.

[179] Author's translation from the French.

parish during 1808 and 1809,[180] perhaps regretting the fact that he had not accepted the honor extended to him by the President of the United States. Nevertheless, there was certainly some truth in the reason Moreau Lislet gave for his refusal; for even though he was the judge of the parish, he was also allowed to act as an attorney.[181] The fees that he received from his clients added to his salary as judge of the parish and constituted, very likely, a much bigger income than that which he would have received as a judge of the Superior Court.

In the month of April of 1809, Moreau Lislet was severely affected by the death of his wife, Elisabeth de Peters, who

---

[180] See: Le Moniteur, April 26, 1809 #922 (in French); Le Moniteur, July 1, 1809 #941 (in French); Le Moniteur, December 20, 1809 #990 (in French). The Louisiana Gazette, Wednesday June 6, 1809: "Resolve of the City Council, Providing for the forming of a committee of benevolence for the purpose of relieving the refugees from the Island of Cuba,...the committee formed...& composed of his excellency Wm. C.C. Claiborne,...the honorable Moreau Lislet, judge of the parish of New Orleans...".

[181] Le Moniteur, February 22, 1809 #904: "We the undersigned, members of the jury to whom was submitted the case of Pascal de la Barre vs Lalonde Ferrière and Claude Colon, for damages claimed of the
defendants, for inhuman treatment of one of the plaintiff's negro slaves, do certify, that Mr. Moreau Lislet council for the plaintiff, did not say in his argument that "when a white man beats a negro unjustly, the slave has a right to repel force by force, nor make use of any expressions conveying such a sense".

Signed Dejean Cade, Mazureau...

passed away on the 19th of that month.[182] After the death of his parents, his brother, his uncle and aunt, and his son, the only close relative Moreau Lislet had left was his daughter Julie, who stayed close by in New Orleans, and his sister Elisabeth Françoise Delagrange, who lived in Paris. On November 25, 1809, Louis Moreau Lislet and his daughter moved into a big house located on Condé street (today 1027-1029 Chartres Street), which they bought from François Lalonde Dalcour.[183] It was in this house that Moreau Lislet would live until he died.

In the year 1810, Moreau Lislet was still the judge of the parish of Orleans[184] putting all his energies into his work. His zealous attitude brought him criticism from some of his fellow citizens, as illustrated by the following letter addressed to:

LOUISIANA GAZETTE, Tuesday October 2, 1810[185]

To the Honorable Moreau Lislet, Parish Judge of New Orleans

---

[182] Le Moniteur de la Louisiane, Saturday April 22, 1809 #921 (translated from the French):
Obituary Notice

[183] Notarial Archives. S. de Quinones Notaire, Acte du 25 novembre 1809 11/220. (Act of November 25, 1809).

[184] Le Moniteur de la Louisiane: (in French) Saturday January 13, 1810; Wednesday February 7, 1810; August 4, 1810; (in French) Le Courrier de la Louisiane, July 16, 1810; October 1st, 1810 (strangely enough, Moreau Lislet's name appears as "L. Moreau Lillets, Judge".

[185] Louisiana Gazette, Tuesday October 2, 1810.

The regulations which you have published, relative to patrols, makes it the duty of every free white individual, from 16 to 50 years of age to inquire where, how and by what authority, you have assumed to yourself the right of commanding the militia of the city and parish of New Orleans.

In your preamble to those very extraordinary regulations you say "Considering that in several unprovided and urgent cases it is impossible to resort to the assistance of the militia in so prompt a manner as to prevent the disorders with which the public tranquility is threatened." If any danger presents itself where the service of the militia is necessary, the law provides for calling them out and it also provides how and by whom it shall be done [act of the legislature passed the 31st March 1807].

It will now be necessary to enquire of you by what authority you have attempted to encroach on the powers of the Governor? You cannot be so ignorant of the laws of our country as to suppose that any regulations you could make, aided by the justices of the parish and twelve freeholders, would be paramount to the laws of the territory; yet your regulations are in direct opposition to them...The law puts it in the power of the governor when "he deems it necessary" to order patriots; but, pray Sir, where do you find the law by which you are authorised to command all the free white individuals in this country? Where do you find your authority to oblige me and every other man to purchase within three months a musket and its accoutrements - powder and bullet? Pure as the motives may be that urged you to assume powers not delegated to you by law, still it is evident that you cannot ever expect to enforce your regulations. The people are too well acquainted with their rights to be forced into the obedience of illegal regulations, much as they may be taught to respect the ermine of justice when acting in its proper sphere.

Love of power appears to be an innate principle in many; this principle must have stimulated you and your advisors, or you would not under any pretext have assumed the right of regulating the police of our corporation, you would not, Atlas like, have taken the world on your back as you have done. What will the people of the United States say, who read your regulations? Will it not be reasonable for them to conclude that you have assumed the whole command of the militia of the city and county of New Orleans; that you have taken proper measures to have them armed and equipped for the field, etc...It would not perhaps be improper to enquire whether the hand of Napoléon is not at the bottom of the regulations, although you may not have discovered it.

I shall again, if I find it necessary, address you fully on this last point, and close with advising you to reconsider what you have been doing. Call your justices and freeholders, together - consult the laws - take the opinion of the best informed members of society, before you attempt to enforce your regulations.

Zeno

The day after this article, in which his integrity was questioned, appeared, Moreau Lislet replied by writing a letter to the editor of the *Courrier de la Louisiane*[186]. Moreau

---

[186] Courrier de la Louisiane, Mercredi 3 October 1810. [author's translation].

" Mr Editor,

Some persons having raised some questions regarding the right that the Assemblies of the Parish, and each one of them in its domain, have to issue regulations dealing with the creation and organisation of patrols, I beg you...to be kind enough to print, after this letter, the act passed by the third legislative assembly of this territory on March 20, 1810. This act having been approved by his Excellency Governor Claiborne, it will appear to have abrogated the powers granted to the executive branch by the previous act of March 31,

Lislet's short but forceful reply did not calm the ire of Zeno. Feeling that he had been beaten on his own turf, he decided to push the controversy further by invoking the authority of the Constitution of the United States:

To the Honorable Judge Moreau Lislet

I have read the explanations you have published in the Courrier...If I am not very wrong in my logic the militia of every state and territory in the Union are under the control of Congress; they alone possess the power to call them forth to execute the laws of the nation...With this view of the subject, I conceive it is not in the power of any governor of any territory to transfer the militia of it to any parish judge, or for any local or menial purposes...Now I contend that you cannot have any control over my person in consequence of any act of the legislature, even after its being sanctionned by the governor when the act is in direct violation of the constitution of the United States....and I declare that I never will purchase a musket in consequence of your mandate; because you do not possess the right to order it, no more than you do possess the right of ordering conscripts...

Zeno[187]

In 1811 and 1812, other than his functions as judge for the parish of Orleans,[188] a position to which he was once again

---

1807...."

[187] The Louisiana Gazette Friday October 5, 1810.

[188] Le Moniteur, mardi, 8 janvier 1811; 29 janvier 1811; 23 avril 1811; etc...See also, Le Moniteur, 30 janvier 1812;

reappointed on April 3, 1811,[189] Moreau Lislet was called upon to carry out other duties; he even sought to be involved in yet more activities. Thus, for example, on May 18, 1811, the New Orleans City Council resolved "that Mr. Moreau Lislet, one of the attorneys of the corporation, will be invited to draft a memorandum of law whose purpose is to certify the rights of the City over lands for which it claims ownership..."[190] During the month of May, Moreau Lislet was also appointed by the Council of Regents of the University of New Orleans to join a commission charged with receiving, from architects and entrepreneurs, plans for the building of a new college.[191] In July of the same year, for participation at the meeting of the convention that was to establish the first constitution of the state of Louisiana, a leading article of the *Gazette de la Louisiane* recommended to

---

22 septembre 1812; 14 novembre 1812, etc.

[189] Territorial Papers of the U.S. vol. 9, p. 984.

[190] "Conseil de Ville de la Nouvelle Orléans
Résolu que M. Moreau Lislet l'un des avocats de la Corporation sera invité à rédiger un mémoire à l'effet de constater les droits de la ville sur les terres dont elle réclame la propriété..." Délibération du Conseil en sa séance du 18 mai 1811. J. M. Wisdom Collection #46.

[191] Le Moniteur: 18 mai 1811: " Notice To the Architects and Undertakers. The Architects and Undertakers of buildings are informed that Messieurs R. Dow, Charles Turdeau and Moreau Lislet, have been appointed by the Council of the Regents of the University of Orleans to receive the Plans which they might offer for the Establishment of a college on the plantation formerly belonging to Mr Treme near this town..."

its readers a certain number of persons reputed for "their honesty, their integrity, and their love for their country".[192] The name of Moreau Lislet was cited with those of Edward Livingston, John Watkins, and Pierre Derbigny... Unfortunately, Moreau Lislet was once again disappointed, as he did not receive the privilege of being appointed as one of the members of the convention.[193] On the other hand, on March 7, 1812, along with Derbigny and Mazureau, Moreau Lislet was elected as a member of the board of directors of the New Orleans library, of which he was to become the president at a later date.[194]

During the years 1810, 1811 and 1812 Moreau Lislet continued to work hard for the development of freemasonry in the territory. For example, on December 23, 1810, he instituted the *Perseverance Lodge No. 118*, provided for

---

[192] The Louisiana Gazette and daily advertiser, Saturday evening, July 27, 1811. "It is of primary importance that the Convention, who are to form a state Constitution for this Territory should not only be men of sense, but that their fellow citizens should place full confidence in their honesty, probity, integrity and love of country; and that they are decidedly in favour of becoming a State. It is believed that the following gentlemen will meet the support of the best informed members of society:

Moreau Lislet	John Watkins
E. Livingston	Pierre Derbigny
J. E. Boré	

[193] The Louisiana Gazette, Friday morning, November 5, 1811: Moreau Lislet's name does not appear among the elected members.

[194] Le Moniteur, Samedi 9 janvier 1813.

officers thereof and, during the fall of 1811, instituted another lodge, *Etoile Polaire No. 129*, which was later absorbed by the *Etoile Polaire Lodge No. 4263*, to which he belonged.[195]

At the close of 1812, when Moreau Lislet had been a judge for the parish of Orleans since March of 1807, a number of citizens, among them some of the most famous, published the following notice in *Le Moniteur*:

Mr. Moreau Lislet is recommended to the Governor and the Senate to be continued in his functions of Parish Judge or Judge of first instance in New Orleans...[196]

Among the signatories, there were names like Mazureau, Gayarré, Derbigny, Bruslé and some others. Despite this public demonstration of the trust accorded him by his peers and the esteem in which he was held, Moreau Lislet was to ask the mayor of New Orleans not to renew his appointment as judge:

Mr. Mayor,

I have been assured that I have been appointed judge for the city and the parish of Orleans. Although I would very much like to accept this appointment as proof of the fact that I have not become unworthy of the position I have held for six years, it is likely that I will decline the offer of this judgeship or that I will resign within twenty four hours.

Consequently, Mr. Mayor, I beg you to make sure that the position of city attorney that I have occupied until this day is

---

[195] James B. Scot, outline of the Rise and Progress of Freemasonry in Louisiana, New Orleans, 1912, p. 9 et seq.

[196] Le Moniteur, Mardi 8 décembre 1812.

not granted to another if the City Council intends to preserve it for me, and this until I am in a position to inform you of my ultimate decision regarding the judgeship.

I hope that the interest you have always showed in me will easily lead you to grant me this favor.[197]

From the month of April of 1813 onward, James Pitot replaced Louis Moreau Lislet in his functions as judge of Orleans parish.[198] This allowed Moreau Lislet more time to pursue an immense work that he had undertaken, the translation from the Spanish into French of *Las Siete Partidas*,[199] as well as to concentrate on his practice as an

---

[197] Lettre du 22 mars 1813. [Letter of March 22, 1813 addressed to the Honorable M. Girod, Mayor of New Orleans]. [J. M. Wisdom Collection, #60. Howard Tilton Library].

[198] Le Moniteur, mardi 20 avril 1813.

[199] Louisiana Courrier, April 28, 1813.
PROPOSALS
FOR THE PRINTING OF A FRENCH
TRANSLATION OF THE LAWS OF THE

SIETE PARTIDAS
It is proposed to undertake by subscription a French translation of the Code of Spanish laws, known under the title of *"Las Siete Partidas del Sabieo Rey don Alfonso el Nono"* or the seven parts of the wise king Don Alfonso the ninth....No one is ignorant of the absolute necessity of a study of the Spanish laws, for the decision of causes which are brought before the tribunals of this state where the authority of these laws subsists in civil cases, in all that is not incompatible, with

attorney. It might also have been his intention, however, to better prepare himself for the political career which he had failed to achieve in his first attempts, but which he was determined to try for again — this time perhaps with more vigor and confidence.

---

our constitutions or has not been altered or abrogated by our several legislatures. It is well known that the Civil Code which has been digested for this state contains in some measure, only the primitive and abstract principles of that law, the developments, examples, consequences and limitations of which are to be perceived in the ancient laws of the country, which formed its basis. The study of the Spanish laws may be the more useful,...that study cannot be without interest, when we consider that the Spanish laws are almost entirely derived from the Roman law, a code, which on account of its wisdom, has excited the admiration of modern nations,...At the head of each title, the translation of which will be given, will be placed a list of the several titles of the institutes of the pandects, of the code and the novels of Justinian, of the different Spanish codes, and of the canonical law, as well as the several works treating of the same matter such as Domat's civil laws, Pothier's writings, Febrero's library, and the Curia philipica. In fine at the end of each law will be placed a note showing all such laws of the civil code of this state, and of the recopilation de castilla, which contain provisions on the same subject, in such manner that it will be easy to verify what alterations the ancient law contained in the seven *Partidas*, may have experienced in modern or actual legislation....The said translation has been made by Mr. Moreau Lislet, counsellor at law of this city,...Mr. Moreau Lislet hopes to be seconded in his undertaking, by Mr. Mazureau, another jurisconsult of this city, well versed in the Spanish language, and known by his talents in jurisprudence...."

During the month of June of 1814 and the first week of July, *the Gazette de la Louisiane*[200] published in several issues the following statement:

The list of persons with the following names will be strongly supported for the next election by numerous electors

Congress -- Prevot
Senator -- Thomas Urquhart
Representatives at the General Assembly
    J. R. Grymes
    Moreau Listel [sic]
    J. Blanque
    B. Marigny

Despite all the efforts made by Moreau Lislet, and although he was accorded the support of a number of prominent electors, the verdict of the people was disappointing to the political ambitions of the former judge. He placed sixth on a list of seven candidates and he was very far from the first four.[201] Luckily, Moreau Lislet had not resigned the post he

---

[200] The Louisiana Gazette, Saturday July 2, 1814.

[201] The Louisiana Gazette, Thursday July 7, 1814.

Results of the elections to the House of Representatives:
    J. Blanque   662 votes
    D. Rouquette   615 votes
    J. Ro...   536 votes
    B. Marigny   515 votes
    J. R. Grymes   162 votes
    Moreau Lislet   138 votes
    Ducros   132 votes

held as the attorney[202] of the city of New Orleans; he was thus able to keep a certain public image and to continue to see frequently the influential personalities of the city council and the legislature.

---

[202] See three letters of May 7, August 6 and August 27, 1814, in J. M. Wisdom Collection.

CHAPTER V.

THE REWARDING YEARS

The year 1815 was to bring Moreau Lislet the consecration that he had been looking for and had not yet obtained. In September of that year senator Thomas Urquhart resigned from the senate of the state of Louisiana and Moreau Lislet ran as a candidate to replace him.[203] Once elected, one might have thought that Moreau Lislet would have effectively participated in the debates of the commissions and would have tried to give his point of view on all matters taken up by those commissions. But, according to the reports of the debates which were published in the *Senate Journal* and the newspapers of that time, it does not seem that Moreau Lislet was very active[204] or, at least, that he showed much of the initiative that he would show later. In fact, Moreau Lislet resigned from the state senate on February 17, 1817, after a year and a few months in that office.[205] As soon as he

---

[203] La Gazette de la Louisiane, Samedi matin 23 septembre 1815. See also, Journal of the Senate, First Session, Third Legislature.

[204] The Louisiana Courier: Monday, January 20, 1817.
Under the title "Senate Journal", Tuesday December 17, 1916 it is written that Moreau Lislet approved the bill to authorize the governor of the state to purchase for the use of the state, 50 copies of Martin's reports of the supreme court of the state.

[205] The Louisiana Courier: Wednesday, April 9, 1817.

James Villere
Governor of the State of Louisiana

renounced his senatorial functions, Moreau-Lislet became Attorney-General of the state of Louisiana.[206] The availability of the appointment to this position was perhaps the reason why Moreau Lislet had given up his senate seat so quickly.

Even as attorney general of the state, Moreau Lislet did not restrict himself to one job. During the same year of 1817, he acted as an attorney for the absent heirs of a decedent[207] and as a surrogate guardian of the minor Thierry.[208]

---

to James Pitot
Judge of the Parish of New Orleans

....having been officially informed of the resignation of Mr. Louis Moreau Lislet, Senator of the general assembly of the state for the 2nd district of Orleans County, it is my duty to issue a proclamation, ordering that an election be called...to fill the vacancy left by the resignation of Louis Moreau Lislet.
The 25th day of March, 1817.

[206] The Louisiana Courier: Monday, May 5, 1917; id. Friday, May 9, 1817. Parish Court April 26, 1817. Present the Honorable James Pitot. Toussaint Mossy versus L. Moreau Lislet, Attorney-General of the state of Louisiana.

[207] The Louisiana Courier: Friday, October 3, 1817.

Notice — The creditors of the late Mr. Henry Boneval Latrobe...Moreau Lislet, Attorney of the absent heirs of the deceased.

[208] The Louisiana Courier: Monday, August 25, 1817.

Notice — Several persons remaining still indebted to the estate of the late Jean Baptiste Thierry...Moreau Lislet. Co-tutor of the minor Thierry.

Moreover, Moreau Lislet still held his position as an attorney for the city of New Orleans.[209]

The year 1818 was a year of reflection and achievement for Moreau Lislet. His position as attorney general gave him a sense of security, and prestige, as well as the possibility to be in close touch with the members of the government and of the legislature.

Moreau Lislet kept this position for only about two years, as is indicated in two documents, one of February 1818[210] and the other, most probably, of late October or the beginning of November 1818.[211] One may wonder if, despite his decision

---

[209] Le Courrier de la Louisiane, Vendredi 10 octobre 1817; [author's translation]: Notice. The City Council having instructed its attorney to defend...

    Moreau Lislet, Attorney for the Corporation.

[210] Cabildo Archives. English Documents 1818.

"Received by Felix Arnaud, Esq. Treasurer of the State of Louisiana....

"....New Orleans February 19th 1818
    Moreau Lislet
    Procureur Général [Attorney General]

[211] Cabildo Archives. English Documents 1818.

"The State of Louisiana
    the Criminal Court
    of the City of New-Orleans

The Grand Jurors for the state of Louisiana empaneled and sworn in and for the body of the city of New Orleans...present that Jean Baptiste...feloniously did steal, take and carry away....

    L. Moreau Lislet, Attorney General.

to leave the senate in February of 1817, Moreau Lislet had not been attracted all the same by politics as practiced in the legislature and the atmosphere of the debates that he attended during his membership in the legislature. The fact is that in May of 1818, at the start of the election campaign for the July elections, Moreau Lislet was once again a candidate but, this time, for a seat in the Louisiana House of Representatives. He was backed by "a certain number of respectable people," who recommended and supported him along with other candidates for the next election.[212] He also had the support "*of an assembly of a great number of electors which did not settle its choice on a candidate to the Congress or on a senator of the district in question but which has decided to back for the next election to the House of Representatives of this State: L. Moreau Lislet, Morrel. . .*"[213] The results of these elections were to confirm the wishes of many people as Moreau Lislet headed the list of persons elected to the House of Representatives of the state of Louisiana with 808 votes, before B. Macarty with 791 votes, and Blancard with 616 votes.[214]

Moreau Lislet took his mandate as a Representative very seriously, as shown by his participation in numerous committees[215] and the fact that he ran for the position of

---

[212] Le Courrier de la Louisiane, lundi 23 mai 1818.

[213] Le Courrier de la Louisiane, jeudi 25 juin 1818.

[214] Gazette de la Louisiane, Nouvelle Orléans, jeudi 9 juillet 1818. Le Courrier de la Louisiane, vendredi 10 juillet 1818.

[215] In the January 1819 and 1819 issues of Le Courrier de la Louisiane, there are many references to Moreau Lislet as an active member of several committees of the House of

Speaker of the House. Although he was not elected, his running for that position showed nonetheless his interest in the legislative process and also, perhaps, exhibited a political ambition that he might have felt had still been only partially fulfilled.[216] In June of 1820, as the election campaign for the fifth legislature opened, Moreau Lislet asked for the renewal of his mandate as a Representative. As in June of 1818, his candidacy was once again backed by "a great number of voters".[217] It was no surprise to see him elected again in July of 1820, finishing first on the list with 481 votes, against 480 for Duralde.[218] The first task of the new assembly was to

---

Representatives.

[216] Le Courrier de la Louisiane, lundi 1 mars 1819. [author's translation]: "on a motion by Mr. Randall, the House held a vote for the election of a Speaker pro-tempore.

Mr. Beauvais	24
Mr. Moreau Lislet	2
Mr. Caldwell	1

[217] Gazette de la Louisiane, vendredi 17 juin 1820. Courrier de la Louisiane, vendredi 24 juin 1820.

[218] Courrier de la Louisiane vendredi 7 juillet 1820. [author's translation]: "...results of the election in the first district of the county of Orleans:

To the House of Representatives	
L. Moreau Lislet	481
Macarty	442
Grymes	416
Duralde	480
Blancard	427

elect its speaker. Once again Moreau Lislet stood as a candidate, but in vain. The tally was: Beauvais sixteen votes, Randall nine votes, Livingston two votes and Moreau Lislet one vote. (his own?). In any case, Moreau Lislet participated very actively in the works of the different committees to which he belonged, such as the committee on proposals and grievances.

It was during this session of the legislature that Moreau Lislet was to suffer a setback that was to have an important effect on him. In March of 1821 the two houses of the legislature of the state examined a resolution for the nomination of the person who would be charged with drafting a penal code for the state of Louisiana. Having actively contributed to the drafting of the Digest of the Civil Laws of 1808, so much so that many considered Moreau Lislet to have been, in fact, the author of the Digest, it was only natural that he would offer his services for this new project. Two other candidates, Edward Livingston and A.L. Duncan, were equally tempted by this undertaking. Out of the forty-five votes cast, thirty went to Livingston, ten to Moreau and five to Duncan.[219] As a result, Moreau Lislet was denied the

---

MM. Moreau Lislet, Duralde, Macarty, Blancard, Grymes....have been elected to represent the first district.

[219] Courrier de la Louisiane, #2104, Supplement, Monday, March 12, 1821, Journal of the House of Representatives:

"And it being now five minutes of twelve, on motion, ordered, that the clerk be ordered to inform the Senate, that the House is now ready, to receive them agreeably to the resolution for the appointment of a person to prepare a criminal code.

It being twelve o'clock, the Senate met the House, on

opportunity to do in the criminal law area what he had done for the "civil law" and frame the former in a code as he had done to the latter.

During this legislature, Moreau Lislet was a member of the committee in charge of the reprint of the Civil Code, a member of the judiciary committee and many others. Although Moreau Lislet lost to Livingston on February 13, 1821, he, on the other hand, had the great satisfaction of outvoting the same Livingston on March 14, 1822, in the election, by both the senate and the house of representatives, of a committee of three jurists who would be vested with the task of revising the Digest of 1808. Out of 48 present members, Moreau Lislet received the votes of forty-three; Livingston twenty-five; Derbigny twenty-five; Workman twenty-three; Mazureau twenty-two; Smith three; Morel two and Carleton one. Thus, Moreau Lislet, Livingston and Derbigny became the drafters of the Louisiana Civil Code of 1825.

Moreau Lislet, the attorney, was still very busy and involved in many activities during these years. It is important here to pay special attention to another essential contribution made by Moreau Lislet to the legal system of the state of

---

motion, ordered, two tellers be appointed, whereupon Mr. Clark was appointed on the part of the Senate, and Mr. Randall on the part of the House.

The ballot box having been carried round, on opening the same, it appeared, that out of 45 members present.

Mr. Livingston had obtained	30 votes
Mr. Moreau Lislet	10 votes
Mr. A. L. Duncan	5 votes
Total	45 votes

In consequence whereof, Mr. E. Livingston was proclaimed duly elected as the person to prepare a criminal code.

Louisiana. It is a fact that, for several decades, Spanish law had been the law of the territory of Orleans and that in 1806 James Brown and Moreau Lislet had been instructed to draft a code on the basis of "the civil laws which presently govern the Territory".[220] This assignment having been accomplished, there remained to be put at the disposal of jurists, be they judges or attorneys, an English version of the Spanish laws on the basis of which the Digest of 1808 had been drafted. Moreau Lislet and Carleton, therefore, took upon themselves the thankless task of translating into English several sections of Las Siete Partidas. In February 1819, the *Courrier de la Louisiane* published the following:

The first volume of the translation of the Spanish Laws of the Partidas by MM. Moreau Lislet and Carleton, attorneys, containing all matters relating to promises, obligations and contracts of sale and exchange is now on sale at MM Noche Brothers and Benjamin Levy. Price: 3 piasters per copy. The praise given to this translation by the honorable Judges of the Supreme Court and judges of the first district and of New Orleans parish, as well as by different jurisconsults, encouraging the pursuit of this work as extremely useful to the administration of justice in this state, is the best commendation this attempt could receive. We have learned with pleasure that the legislature is now working on a bill which would promote the continuation of this work.[221]

---

[220] See supra Part I.

[221] See also, Courrier de la Louisiane, lundi 8 février 1819; lundi 25 janvier 1819. The Louisiana Courier of Monday, January 8, 1821, in a supplement to # 2077, reported the following:

Journal of the House of Representatives - Wednesday,

Jan.3.1821

The report of the committee to whom had been referred the letter of the translators of the Partidas, was then taken up and read in the following words:

Your committee to whom had been referred the joint letters of Messrs Moreau Lislet and H. Carlton, translators of such part of the Partidas as are considered to have the force of law in this state, by
virtue of an article passed for that purpose, approved on the 3rd of March 1819, beg leave to report that in the opinion of your committee the said translators have discharged the duties imposed by said act with zeal and ability, except however the binding of the 2nd volume of this work, which they may be able to deliver within the time required by the said act. But your committee are of opinion that the second volume may be injured from being bound so soon after the printing and that therefore the time for the delivery of said work ought to be extended to the 10th of April 1821.

Your committee are of opinion that the labors of the translators in this invaluable work have been greater than they at first imagined: that the original Partidas is composed in about 3,000 folio pages and written in an antiquated dialect, alike unconnected with the living and dead languages, and very little aided by the common facilities for the acquirements of either; that they have bestowed more labour than necessary to comply with the provisions of the act, inasmuch as each title of the work is preceded by a list of the titles of the Roman and Spanish laws, and the civil code of this state, relative to the subject of which it treats, thereby adding to the utility of the work, and rendering it more complete and satisfactory, and which must have required uncommon

The year 1822 was an election year and Moreau Lislet was once more a candidate in July. That year, however, instead of asking for the renewal of his mandate as a representative, Moreau Lislet became a candidate for the state senate seat for the second district of the city of New Orleans.[222] Moreau Lislet was elected senator with 648 votes.[223] As soon as he settled into his new functions, Moreau Lislet introduced a resolution that would cause the local media to react most passionately, as shown by the following extract from the *Gazette D'Orleans*:

"A resolution was introduced yesterday in the Senate by Mr. Moreau Lislet stating that the three senators for the district of the State, commonly referred to as Florida, had no right to have a seat in the Senate...

---

research in traversing the immense codes of Roman jurisprudence and pausing the less expanded but more complete abstract provisions of our civil code.....

With these considerations your committee beg leave to introduce the following bill entitled "An act supplementary to the several acts authorizing and encouraging the translation of such parts of the Partidas as are considered to have the force of law in this State."

[222] Le Courrier de la Louisiane, mercredi 19 juin 1822.

[223] The Louisiana Gazette, Thursday July 4, 1822.
Result of the election
Representative to Congress
Edward Livingston   645 votes
State Legislature Senate
L. Moreau Lislet   648 votes

We find no words strong enough to express our astonishment and our indignation at the resolution introduced by Mr. Moreau Lislet. Coming from a member who, until now, has always attempted to reconcile all the parties as much by his speeches as by his example, coming from a member most respected in his private life and his political career, exhibiting so much zeal for the benefit of all, we have all reasons to fear that the greater part of his party, more passionate and obeying less to the voice of prudence, is harbouring even more dangerous thoughts, assuming it is possible to imagine anything even more dangerous...

If Mr. Moreau Lislet and his party are determined to bring down this political society to its first component parts and to lead us into the horrors of anarchy and the civil war, then let it be; the sooner they raise a huey and cry, the better it will be... "[224]

---

[224] Gazette de la Louisiane, mercredi 22 janvier 1823: [author's translation from the French]

"Une résolution a été offerte hier au Sénat par Mr. Moreau Lislet déclarant a que les trois sénateurs pour le district de l'Etat, communément appelé Floride, n'avaient aucun droit de siéger au
Sénat...

Nous ne trouvons pas de termes assez forts pour exprimer notre étonnement et notre indignation à la résolution introduite par Mr. Moreau Lislet. Venant d'un membre qui jusqu'ici n'a cherché qu'à concilier tous les partis tant par ses discours que par son exemple, d'un membre aussi respectable dans sa vie privée et dans sa carrière politique, si zélé pour le bien public, nous avons tout lieu de craindre que la masse de son parti, plus passionnée et obéissant moins à la voix de la prudence, nourisse des desseins plus dangereux, si toutefois il était possible d'en imaginer de plus dangereux....

Did this diatribe prompt Moreau Lislet to withdraw his motion? It may be so. In any case, the senator refrained from causing any further controversies and continued to accomplish his duties with devotion, energy, and intelligence.[225] The quality of the services rendered by Moreau Lislet were at last recognized by his colleagues from the senate when he was elected, on November 16, 1826, to sit as temporary President of the Senate in the place of H.S. Thibodeaux who had assumed the post of Governor following the resignation of Thomas B. Robertson.[226] Among the numerous activities of senator Moreau Lislet in 1825 and

---

Si Monsieur Moreau Lislet et son parti sont déterminés à réduire cette société politique à ses premiers éléments et nous plonger dans toutes les horreurs de l'anarchie et de la guerre civile, qu'il en soit ainsi; le plutôt qu'ils sonneront le tocsin, ce sera le mieux..."

[225] See some actions and initiatives taken by Moreau Lislet in: La Gazette de la Louisiane, samedi 25 janvier 1823; vendredi 24 janvier 1823; Journal du Sénat 6e législature 1re session, 6 janvier-26 mars; 2e session, 5 janvier-12 avril 1824. Journal du Sénat 7e législature 1ere session, 15 novembre 1824-19 février 1825; 2e session, 12 janvier-25 avril 1826.

[226] Le Courrier de la Louisiane, mercredi 17 novembre 1824;
"House of Representatives
A message from the Senate informed the House that Governor Ths. B. Robertson had sent his resignation to the Senate, that in consequence the Hon. H. S. Thibodeaux had assumed the executive functions, that Mr. L. Moreau Lislet had been elected President pro tempore of the Senate, and that the other officers of the Senate continued in office..."

1826,[227] it is particularly worthy of note that Pierre Derbigny and himself were commissioned by the legislature of the state to draft a mercantile law in order to provide the business community with a body of legal rules that would promote both the swiftness of transactions and their safety.[228] These two lawyers were also members of a committee in charge of organizing a city court of New Orleans[229] and, by a just recurrence of history, Louis Moreau Lislet, who had been denied by his colleagues of the legislature the opportunity to draft a penal code, was appointed a member of the committee in charge of examining the plan of the penal code proposed by Edward Livingston (a committee the creation of which has been attributed to Moreau Lislet himself!).[230]

---

[227] See, for example, La Gazette de la Louisiane, mercredi 1er février 1826: "Journal du Sénat" and Le Courrier de la Louisiane, jeudi 23 février 1826 (Moreau Lislet on a banking committee); Le Courrier de la Louisiane, mercredi 5 avril 1826 and La Gazette de l'Etat de la Louisiane, jeudi 6 avril 1826 (Moreau Lislet as a Regent of Schools to be created in and around New Orleans); etc....

[228] Le Courrier de la Louisiane, lundi 10 janvier 1825: House of Representatives: a letter from MM. Moreau and Derbigny, the two lawyers charged with preparing a commercial code...was read to the House.

[229] Louisiana Gazette, Friday Jan. 20, 1826; House of Representatives: Moreau Lislet and Derbigny were appointed members of a committee to organise a court for the City of New Orleans.

[230] La Gazette de la Louisiane, mardi 7 février, 1826; Senate: Moreau Lislet appointed member of a committee to evaluate the projet of the criminal code proposed by Edward

The brilliant career and future that Moreau Lislet was building for himself by earning the respect and the affection of his peers seemed even more promising when, in May and June of 1826, he sought to renew his mandate as a senator.[231] The results of the elections of July 5, 1826, show that Moreau Lislet, who won hands down, was becoming a sort of "institution", almost irremovable, and that his political aspirations had been fulfilled.

Moreau Lislet did not show very much enthusiasm or energy during the first session of the eighth legislature.[232] He did, however, take a stand against a bill that was to allot certain slaves a required time for their emancipation. That stand, among numerous others of the same nature, seem to reflect very well the philosophy of its author who did not seem to be, actually far from it, a partisan for the liberation or equality of the black people.[233]

The minutes of the sittings of the second session of the eighth legislature are filled with multiple and varied actions

---

Livingston.

[231] Le Courrier de la Louisiane, mercredi 31 mai 1826 and La Gazette de la Louisiane, samedi 17 juin 1826. The results of the elections appeared in La Gazette, vendredi 7 juillet 1826: Edward Livingston, with 597 votes, defeated Foucher in the election for the U.S. Congress; Moreau Lislet, with 684 votes, defeated C. de Armas, in the election for the Louisiana Senate.

[232] The first session lasted from January 1st to March 24, 1827. The second session went from January 7 to March 25, 1828.

[233] See, Journal of the Senate, 8th legislature, 1st session, at p. 13.

carried out by Moreau Lislet: by Act 74 of 1828 he was commissioned to draft a digest of the laws of the state;[234] he proposed a resolution suggesting that the Senators and Representatives of the state of Louisiana go before the United States Congress to lobby for a plan to build a canal linking Lake Ponchartrain to the Mississippi River;[235] he suggested that a committee be formed to consider raising a loan from a foreign country to pay for the state's debts;[236] he was charged with auditing the accounts of the treasurer of the state;[237] and he was appointed to act as a member of the committee in charge of the Code of Civil Procedure.[238] As a member of the committee in charge of reviewing the Penal Code drafted by Livingston, he contributed to the abandonment of its examination by the legislators[239] and thus, perhaps, to its failure.

---

[234] Louisiana Revised Statutes, Section 1; 1 to 5, Annex 2, p. XXL. See, also, Le Courrier de la Louisiane, 10 avril 1829, under "Le Digeste..." signed Moreau Lislet.

[235] Journal of the Senate, 8th legislature, 2nd session, p. 10.

[236] Id. at 13.

[237] Id. at 9.

[238] Id. at 41.

[239] Id. at 43, Monday March 3, 1828.

The ninth legislature[240] was to be the last one attended by Moreau Lislet and it marked at the same time the end of his political career. During the first session of this legislature, Moreau Lislet, who was a member of the judicial committee in charge of reviewing and amending the existing laws, tried, among other things, to have an amendment adopted that would have made it compulsory for circuit judges replacing district judges to speak not only English but French also. This amendment was rejected by six votes against six, six senators with French names opposing six senators with Anglo-Saxon names.[241] The second session of this ninth legislature started on January 4, 1830, under the presidency of Louis Moreau Lislet. On January 26, 1830 he asked his colleagues in the senate for permission not to participate in the sessions of the senate for the next two weeks. Moreau Lislet was excused for these two weeks. However, the minutes of the sessions and debates of the senate held from February 9 to March 16, 1830, the end of the second session, show that Moreau Lislet was absent from all the sittings that took place between these two dates and that he did not obtain formal permission from the assembly for this absence. This lack of assiduity in the performance of his duties as a senator was neither an expected feature of Moreau Lislet's political life nor a normal behaviour on his part.

The reasons for his non-performance of his obligations were due, without any doubt, to the status of his family. Before this subject is discussed, however, it is necessary to

---

[240] The 9th legislature was divided in two sessions: 1st session, November 17, 1828 to February 7, 1829; 2nd session, January 4th to March 16, 1830.

[241] Journal of the Senate, 1st session, 9th legislature, p. 39-40.

review Moreau Lislet's professional life, (as opposed to his political one), during the 1820's.

It is a fact that, in parallel with his functions as a senator, Moreau Lislet continued to be involved in a variety of professional and private activities. The reputation as an accomplished and respected attorney that he had earned brought him a great number of clients, as evidenced by the number of cases in which he appears as an attorney of record.[242] On the other hand, Moreau Lislet was to devote a good part of his time to helping his compatriots, immigrants from St. Domingue, to apply for the payment of certain allowances which they claimed were due to them.[243]

---

[242] See, for example, Le Courrier de la Louisiane, mercredi 8 janvier 1823; Le Courrier de la Louisiane, jeudi, 6 mai 1825; mardi 1er novembre 1825; La Gazette, samedi 5 novembre 1825; Le Courrier de la Louisiane, jeudi 25 mai 1826; La Gazette de la Louisiane, mardi 31 mai 1826; jeudi 14, mercredi 20 septembre 1826; Le Courrier de la Louisiane jeudi 21 août 1828; L'Abeille 29 novembre 1828;...Moreau Lislet's law office was located in different places: at 25 rue St. Louis between Chartres and Royale; at 47 rue St. Pierre; at 57 rue Toulouse between Chartres and Royale.

[243] The Louisiana Courier: Wednesday, January 8, 1823. (id. The Louisiana Gazette: Friday, January 10, 1823). [author's translations from the French].

Notice: The undersigned have removed their office to the study of Mr. Hugues Lavergne, esq., notary public, St. Louis street, No. 25, between Chartres and Royal Streets. New Orleans, january 4, 1823. Louis Moreau Lislet. John DuMoulin.

The Louisiana Courier: Thursday, May 25, 1826.

Moreover, besides being still involved with the city council of New Orleans as its attorney,[244] he was also "Master of Central and Primary Schools".[245]

In April of 1825, Louis Moreau Lislet enjoyed another moment of celebrity. The Freemasons of New Orleans were

---

Notice: Messrs. Louis Moreau Lislet and Peter Ambroise Cuvillier, lawyers in the city, have formed a partnership for the exercise of their profession... Their office is next to that of Mr. Cuvillier, No. 47, St. Peter Street. Mr. Moreau Lislet's office is still on Condé Street, near the Ursulines.

The Louisiana Courier: Thursday, August 21, 1828.

Notice: The undersigned has entrusted to his fellow member of the bar, Mr. P. Soulé, a lawyer residing in New Orleans, and partner of Mr. Louis Moreau Lislet, the unfinished files of his office. The talents of Mr. Soulet, and the great knowledge of Mr. Moreau Lislet, his partner, are the best guarantees to be expected...

The Louisiana Courier: Thursday, November 13, 1828.

Messrs. Moreau Lislet and Soulé, Attorneys at Law, now have an office at No. 57 Toulouse, between Chartres and Royal Streets.

[244] La Gazette de la Louisiane, mercredi 17 septembre 1823; Le Courrier de la Louisiane, mardi 14 juin 1825; Le Courrier de la Louisiane mardi 23 juin 1829; Le Courrier de la Louisiane, mardi 28 juillet 1829: in an article reporting on a meeting of the City Council it is stated that Moreau Lislet, as lawyer for the City, was earning 1500 piastres per year.

[245] Le Courrier de la Louisiane, mercredi 5 avril 1826.

to welcome General Lafayette and his son Georges Washington Lafayette.[246] The participation of Louis Moreau Lislet in the reception given by Gilbert du Motier, Marquis of Lafayette, was described in these terms by the *Gazette de la Louisiane*:[247]

Last Thursday, at 5 p.m., at the invitation of the Masons of the most illustrious Great Lodge of Louisiana, the most illustrious Brother Lafayette appeared at the Masonic Temple...The most illustrious brother Moreau Lislet, Great Orator, gave a speech equal to this occasion (which was qualified as grandiose).

In August of 1826, on the other hand, Moreau Lislet experienced the first of a series of painful and disturbing events that were to make smaller the family he had sought to keep around him. This first event, made public by the *Courrier de la Louisiane*, was the separation of his daughter from her husband:

Parish Court
The Honorable James Pitot presiding,

---

[246] Masonry in Louisiana. A Sesquincentennial History, 1812-1962, by Glen Lee Greene, p. 83 *et seq*.

[247] La Gazette de la Louisiane, lundi 18 avril 1825, mardi 7 juin 1825. [author's translation]: "This last Thursday at 5 p.m., on the invitation of the masons of the constituency of the Very Illustrious Grande Loge of Louisiana, the Very Illustrious brother Lafayette was greeted at the masonic temple...The Very Illustrious brother Moreau Lislet, Grand Orateur, pronounced a speech that matched the circumstances (they were described as "grandiose"...)".

E. Julie Moreau Lislet, wife of J.B. Desdunes v. J.B. Desdunes, her husband.
The Court, after having heard the parties or their counsel is convinced by the evidence that there are sufficient grounds to grant plaintiff's petition for a separation from bed and board.[248]

Some months later, in January of 1827, senator Moreau Lislet saw the Louisiana House of Representatives pass a bill for the divorce of J.B. Desdunes Leclerc and Julie Elisabeth Althée Moreau Lislet, his wife.[249]

---

[248] Le Courrier de la Louisiane, lundi 14 août 1826; [author's translation].

[249] Journal of the House of Representatives, Tuesday January the 23rd, 1827; Le Courrier de la Louisiane 24 janvier 1827. On J.B. Desdunes, see The Saint Domingue Epic, The de Rossignol des Dunes our/and Family Alliances, The Nightingale Press, 1995.

CHAPTER VI.

POVERTY AND GREATNESS

The first months of the year 1830 constituted a turning point in the life of Moreau Lislet. If, as we mentioned earlier, the senator neglected his duties during the second session of the ninth legislature, it was mainly due to family problems and perhaps also because of health problems; Moreau Lislet was now more than sixty years old. The main source of his trouble turned out to be his daughter, Elisabeth Julie. Prior to her separation and divorce, Elisabeth led a life of debauchery, as described by a contemporary[250] with a somewhat crude style:

On June 7, 1830, Mrs Dedune, born Moreau Lislet, mother of three daughters and separated from her husband for several years by reason of her misconduct and her indulging in prostitution with anyone from among the lowest, was found that evening seriously stabbed by her current lover - a lowly baker of extreme jealousy - who hit her several times in the face and elsewhere with a knife.

Her loud screams alerted the neighbors who came to her rescue and helped in the arrest of the murderer. He was sent to jail and is waiting for his day in court.

This poor woman could not articulate a single word for twenty four hours for she had been seriously injured by this worthless baker! Today, June 10, she is feeling better, but she will keep the scars on her face as a reminder of her immoral behavior.

---

[250] [Author's translation from the French] : Nouvelles Diverses, Bozé, New Orleans, to Henri Saint Gême, Saint-Gaudens, Haute Garonne. Henri Saint-Gême papers, The Historic New Orleans Collection, the Kemper and Leila Williams Foundation.

This scandalous scene, as you can expect, has deeply affected her Father with whom she was living since her separation, occupying a part of his residence on Condé Street... As to the three young ladies, they are now with their father in the Marigny district...

The worthless baker, when stabbing Mrs. Dedune, also attempted to end his own life by stabbing himself several times so that he would die with her; but he showed very little courage and his own wounds were never threatening...

The following notice, which shows both the love and despair of a father, was published in the *Courrier de la Louisiane* dated Tuesday, June 22, 1830:[251]

Notice to the public.

L. Moreau Lislet, attorney, resident of New Orleans, informs the public that, as father of his daughter, he asks anyone to whom Mrs. Julie Elizabeth Althee Moreau Lislet, his daughter, divorced from Mr. Jean Baptiste Desdunes Jr., would offer to sell any property she owns or from whom she would solicit some credit, without his written consent, to disregard these offers or requests; although Mrs Desdunes is of an age that allows her to dispose of her property and to bind herself by any kind of contracts, it is easy to prove by resorting to the testimony of numerous respectable persons that she has always drawn attention to herself by her unusual actions and her extraordinarily peculiar way of expressing herself, so much so that no one can believe that she is fully sane and sound of mind to the point of having the full capacity to enter into contracts. Furthermore it is unfortunately too well known that an individual, who is the main cause of her

---

[251] Courrier de la Louisiane, mardi 22 juin 1830: [author's translation from the French].

insanity, still has much control over her to the point that he could use threats on her life to take advantage of her property to the detriment of the three children she has from her marriage to Mr. Desdunes and who are now entrusted to his custody.

Moreau Lislet.

The fears that Moreau Lislet expressed for the life of his daughter proved, unfortunately, to be well-founded. Among the items of news that Bozé sent, on a regular basis, to Henri Saint Gême, of Saint-Gaudens (Haute Garonne, France), there was, on February 7, 1831, the following account:[252]

On this day of February 7, 1831, Mrs. Dedune's lover - a worthless baker and of foreign nationality - who had been sent to jail for several months after he had been convicted of stabbing her several times at her residence, was released after his sentence expired that day. At 7 p.m. that same day he went to her place, full of rage and vengeance and he found her alone and stabbed her with a knife and eventually cut her throat. But her maid, after entering the apartment, screamed and yelled for help at the sight of her mistress's condition. The police, timely called by some neighbors, succeeded in arresting the murderer, who still had the bloody weapon in his hand, and drove him to jail to wait for the decision of the Criminal Court.

Alas, this scoundrel, fearing the executioner's arm, was found dead after he committed suicide on the 9th day of this month, his throat cut with a razor blade. After justice had been handed down, the appropriate papers were completed and he was buried in the evening.

The deceased Mrs. Dedune was buried that same morning of the 9th; her coffin was followed only by her Father, in

---

[252] See supra, note 1, Part II, chap. VI.

tears, and a few relatives and friends, but no lady could be seen in this funeral procession.

She has left to her husband three lovely daughters, the oldest being 14 or 15 and the two others 10 to 12. They cried over the loss of their mother in spite of all her faults. They have lived for several years with their father in the Marigny district.

The deceased Mrs Dedune occupied a wing of her father's house; the latter was not at his home at the time of the murder of his daughter...

During these last years of his life, from 1830 to the end of 1832, Louis Moreau Lislet continued to practice law[253] and to give his help unsparingly to the immigrants from Saint Domingue.[254] At the same time he continued to provide legal advice to the city of New Orleans.[255] He continued to show devotion to just causes and acted with much generosity whenever he was called upon to serve, as shown by his participation in the general administration of the Jefferson Lyric, which was then a boarding school for young boys.[256] His professional ability, his intellectual gifts as an attorney and

---

[253] Le Courrier de la Louisiane, mercredi 23 juin 1830 announced that Moreau Lislet and his partner Pierre Soulé, attorneys, had transferred their office to #60 rue Saint Louis.

[254] Le Courrier de la Louisiane, mercredi 7 avril 1830; Le Courrier de la Louisiane, mercredi 5 Octobre 1831.

[255] Le Courrier de la Louisiane, vendredi 2 avril 1830; see also Moreau Lislet's letter of September 6, 1832, written in French and addressed to Edward Livingston, Secretary of State, in LSU Archives, Baton Rouge.

[256] Le Courrier de la Louisiane, vendredi 17 juin 1831 under "Lycée Jefferson".

his virtues and qualities of character brought him one last reward, which he was to enjoy for the last year of his life: he was elected, on December 19, 1831, as President of the Members of the Bar of New Orleans.[257]

On December 4, 1832, local newspapers announced the death "*last night, at eleven o'clock, after he had fallen ill for a day, of Louis Moreau Lislet, Dean of the attorneys of this City, [who] was born in the Cap François ile de St. Domingue in 1767...*"[258] The death[259] of Moreau Lislet was strongly

---

[257] Le Courrier de la Louisiane, mardi 20 décembre 1831.

[258] L'Abeille de la Nouvelle Orléans, mardi matin 4 décembre 1832; Le Courrier de la Louisiane, mardi 4 décembre 1832.

[259] The act of death of L. Moreau Lislet was written in English; it reads as follows:

Lislet Moreau Louis Casimir Elisabeth

On this day to wit: the 19th of December, in the year of our Lord one thousand eight hundred and thirty four and the fifty ninth...of
the independence...before me Vincent Ramos...personally appeared John Baptiste Desdune junior of this city aged about forty four years, a notary clerk, residing in this city, suburb Marigny, who by these presents, has declared that his father-in-law named Louis Casimir Elizabeth Moreau Lislet, a native of Dondon, north part of the Island of St. Domingo, and born on the seventh of October in the year 1767, died in this city on the 3rd of December in the year 1832, at his home situated in Condé Street between St. Philip and Ursulines Streets. The said Moreau Lislet was an attorney at law in his life time and a widower..."

felt by many people, his colleagues of the Bar and by society in general. The tributes that were paid to him are reported here to underline the fact that history never gave this man the place he rightly deserved particularly for having contributed so efficiently and passionately to anchoring the legal system of the state of Louisiana in its original roots.

The New Orleans Bar paid tribute to Moreau Lislet with the following statement:[260]

At a numerous meeting of the members of the Bar of the city of New Orleans held in the chamber of the Superior Court, for the purpose of testifying their regret at the loss of their highly respected and much lamented brother Louis Moreau Lislet. Stephen Mazureau Esq. was called to the chair, D.Augustin, Esq. was elected secretary.

On motion of H.R.Denis, Esq. seconded by F.Canonge, Esq:

RESOLVED, *that a committee be appointed in order to draft resolutions to be submitted to the meeting expressive of their regret for the loss sustained by the bar and the community in general.*

On motion of T.T.Mercier, Esq: seconded by R.Preaux, Esq.

(Source: New Orleans Health Department, Death certificates, by the Recorder of Births, Marriages and Deaths, New Orleans Public Library, mf, FF 650, 1819-1855.)

[260] Louisiana Courrier, December 6,1832. Also in French in Le Courrier de la Louisiane, jeudi 6 décembre 1832; L'Abeille de la Nouvelle Orléans, vendredi matin 7 décembre 1832.

RESOLVED, *that said committee be composed of six members, --Messrs. Canonge, Denis, Grymes, Carleton, Canon and Hoa were appointed by the President as said committee.*

After a recess of a few minutes the committee returned and reported by their Chairman J.F. Canonge, Esq. the following resolutions which were unanimously adopted, on motion of A. Pichot, Esq. seconded by E.A. Canon, Esq.

RESOLVED, *That the members of the Bar of New Orleans feel with the deepest affliction for the loss they have sustained by the death of their beloved and venerable brother Louis Moreau Lislet, Esq.*

RESOLVED, *That this Bar recollect and proclaim it with pride, that the deceased held the foremost rank [in] in this city and the state in general, and that in expressing this opinion of the high estimation in which they hold his virtues and talents, it is only adding to the credit of this bar and holding up the noblest example to the followers of their profession.*
RESOLVED,, *That the members of the bar, in order to offer a tribute of respect to the memory of the man who died without leaving an enemy, shall wear crape during thirty days.*

RESOLVED, *That the preceding resolutions be printed in French and English in the different papers of this city.*

On motion of R. Preaux, Esq. Resolved that the thanks of this meeting be voted to the President and Secretary.

On motion of E.A. Canon, Esq. the meeting was adjourned sine die.

Stephen Mazureau, Prs'nt
D. Augustin, Sec'ry.

The population of New Orleans payed him tribute, in terms vibrant with emotion, by publishing a long obituary in the *Courrier de la Louisiane* dated December 13, 1832:[261]

There are disastrous epochs in human life, when all the ties which unite the members of a community, are in a manner destroyed, and when every man's mind, absorbed by a feeling of self preservation and an anxiety at the sight of his own family exposed to imminent danger, can hardly bestow a thought of regret or a tear of sorrow, for the fate of those whom he lately delighted to call his friends, and who stood highest in the scale of his affections. At these epochs of mourning and terror, the heart is closed against mild emotions; pity is stifled by the calls of egotism, and friendship remains but a bare name. New Orleans had hardly gone through one of those violent crisis which silence the most generous feelings;-we had seen in the space of a very few days our population literally decimated; -when the destructive scourge, that originated on the remote banks of the Ganges, and which, not unlike the minister of celestial ire, seems destined to cover the globe with a sepulchral veil, seemed to abate. Already the victims were less numerous; the disease had become less intense, hope was reviving and our citizens were preparing to address the Throne of Grace in behalf of their departed friends; when at once by the death of a great citizen they were again thrown into stupor. A cry of alarm and grief is raised: MOREAU is no more; that good, that excellent man

---

[261] From The Courier, New Orleans, Dec. 13, 1832. A French version of this eulogy appears in Le Courrier de la Louisiane, lundi 10 décembre 1832. It is likely that this eulogy of Moreau Lislet was written by his friend Canonge who, like Moreau Lislet himself, was a lawyer who had emigrated from Saint Domingue (Haiti) to Louisiana. Moreau Lislet's tomb is in Saint Louis cemetery #1, New Orleans.

has ceased to live. The intelligence spreads with the rapidity of lighting, and the sympathies of the whole community become involved in the fate of one individual. Is such an effect to be attributed to the influence of power, to the prestige of wealth, to the eminence of rank? No; in a country of liberty where every power lies in the law, where no personal consideration attaches to opulence, where honors are only conferred by the people, so spontaneous an homage of the heart is bestowed to talent and to virtue alone; and in this respects who ever was more worthy of it than he whose loss creates among us a vacancy which would in vain be attempted to be filled.

LOUIS MARIE ELIZABETH MOREAU LISLET was born at Cape François, in the Island of St. Domingo, in 1767. Like most of the natives of that once rich and flourishing colony, he was in his early infancy sent to France to cultivate his mind and acquire those talents which, late in life, were to place him in the first rank among men. Nature had endowed him with the happiest dispositions; labour, application and study developed in him uncommon capacities. The Parliament of Paris, a body so capable of appreciating merit, bestowed upon him the proud title of Barrister. He was then at that time of life when pleasure possesses so many attractions, and when the world appears before our eyes under so bright and fascinating colors; he. however, knew how to resist the seduction of the great and brilliant metropolis. Like all generous souls he felt the want of seeing again his native soil. His arrival was greeted by universal esteem, and the most flattering and honorable proof of the confidence of his government soon followed him there. He was soon called to fulfill high functions in the Magistracy; and whether as an individual member of the bar, lending the assistance of his powers for the protection of the weak and the defence of the oppressed, or in the capacity of organ of the law, yielding the fate of his fellow citizens, his only guide was justice, his only aim the public good. Dreadful political convulsions forced the colonists to abandon a soil so long watered by the sweat of their brows and the blood of their *veins, and where, henceforth, their lives were threatened by the torture of the executioner and the torch of the incendiary. Moreau underwent the common fate. A fortune, the result of immense toil and labour had been engulphed in the revolutionary abyss-- he had been hurled from the eminent rank which he had occupied with so much distinction, but his talents and his virtues were still left to him-- his losses were then comparatively small. Rich in those gifts which human events could not deprive him of, he came to our shores to begin a new existence. Thirty years have elapsed since he removed to this his adopted country; and there is not one of his actions which cannot safely undergo the scrutiny of the strictest investigation. As a JUDGE, as a Barrister, as Representative, as a Senator, he found repeated opportunities of exhibiting his love of justice, his abilities, his zeal, his devotedness to the interest of the community. When our Legislature felt the necessity of giving to our legislation a character of precision and certainty, until then unknown in our sister States, they recurred to his old experience for drafting that code which was to govern a nation just born to independence-- a nation rich in prospects and favored by well founded hopes.--That work, the result of his deep meditations, is a monument that will afford to future ages a proof of the extensive acquirements of its author in that difficult science which has for its objects to provide for all wants, to satisfy all exigencies, to solve all questions and to settle all interests.*

The extent of a notice like the present does not admit of an enumeration of his numerous and useful labors. Let us hope that their results may not be lost to the community, and that those more immediately interested in preserving the remembrance of his deeds, will gratify the public by a full disclosure of them. But all those who knew him, and I among others, who loved him and felt proud to call him my countryman, there is a desire of our hearts which must be satisfied--it is to retrace his precious qualities--it is to declare that no man ever possessed in so eminent a degree, those inestimable gifts which captivate all affections. And indeed, did ever a man exist possessing at the same time more wit and greater simplicity of manners--more profound erudition, and so absolute an absence of self conceit or pride--talents of so different kinds united with so remarkable industry? What an inexhaustible stock of frank joviality, of genuine philosophy, of kindness and of benevolence!-- What a luminous and pressing logic!--What a solidity of judgment!-- Who better than him was calculated to appreciate the happiness of the fireside, to add constantly new charms to his relations, to his intercourse!-- How plain, how enticing his conversations in intimacy!-- How free and forcible his language!--How delicate the means he used, to exonerate those whom he had obliged, even of the burden of gratitude, often so heavy! Misfortune assailed him at that age when infirmities begin--when illusions vanish--when wants increase and energy diminishes; but to head the storm, he again found in himself that moral courage which at another stage of life had carried him through the toils of adversity, and that strength of mind which he had formerly evinced when, in other climes, misfortune had heaped its rigors upon him. It is true Providence afforded him on that occasion a precious consolation; for he never ceased to be surrounded by the love, regard and veneration of his fellow citizens, and calumny never dared to aim its shafts at him.

After sixty years of labour and study, he has died poor, but respected. In the absence of an inheritance, he leaves to his family honorable recollections--to the world, useful lessons-- and to Louisiana, a name which may be called national and which, when pronounced, must ever be accompanied by a concert of praise and blessings. When the fatal hour struck, numerous friends, with affected hearts and eyes filled with tears, surrounded the couch on which he breathed his last, and a numerous concourse of citizens followed his remains, in religious silence, to that last asylum where all human distinctions disappear--where all ranks are levelled.

Farewell Moreau! honest man, kind friend, Nestor of the Louisiana Bar, upright Judge, great citizen, farewell! Lie in peace! May the earth be light to thee! Heaven is just; there is another and better life, thy place must be marked there. Long wert thou a prey to misfortune; reap in another world the price of so much resignation and virtue, and may an eternity of happiness afford thee compensation for all thy sufferings in this valley of misery and sorrow. C.

One cannot add anything to this panegyric of Louis Moreau Lislet. Canonge wrote that when Moreau Lislet died, he was "poor", and this seems to have been true.[262] The

---

[262] Two inventories of Moreau Lislet's estate were made on December 19 and 31, 1832 under the direction of Louis T. Caire, notary, in the presence of J.B.Desdunes, Moreau Lislet's son in law, P.Soulé, Moreau Lislet's law partner and Félicité Foucher, "a free woman of color in whose house Moreau Lislet lived".

The first inventory listed Moreau Lislet's movable property such as his furniture and library. The total value of his furniture and other movables, such as a violin, two swords and his clothes, amounted to no more than 204 piasters. His library contained 1008 volumes for a total value of 1072 piasters. The contrast between the two sums is indicative of Moreau Lislet's interest in life and how dedicated he was to his profession. The inventory of his library is definitely impressive and instructive. One can find an abundant listing of Roman law materials: Digeste de Justinien in 7 volumes, the Institutes in 1 and in 7 volumes, the Code in 4 volumes, the Novelles in 2 volumes, the Pandectes de Justinien in 23 volumes...; many titles and volumes on Spanish law, such as: Fuero real de España in 1 volume, the Fuero Juzco (sic) in 1 volume, the Partidas-Gregorio Lopez in 4 volumes, Febrero adicionado in 7 volumes, the Libreria de Jueges in 8 volumes,

assessment that was made of his estate amounted to a total of "twelve hundred and seventy six dollars and twenty-five cents", whereas the value of his library alone was "one thousand and seventy-two dollars and fifty cents". When he died, he did not have much[263] to leave to his successors but "a name to Louisiana", a name which gained henceforth national recognition.

---

the Recopilacion de Castille in 7 volumes, the Autos accordados in 4 volumes,...; many more titles and volumes on French law or in French on Roman law and English law such as: Esprit des Institutes in 2 volumes, Code civil, Code Napoléon, Code civil des français, Maleville analyse du Code civil, Pothier (vieux) complet in 26 volumes, Toullier-droit civil français in 14 volumes, Commentaires de Blackstone in 6 volumes, nouveau Pothier in 22 volumes, Lois Civiles, Coutume de Paris in 4 volumes, Coutume de Normandie in 2 volumes...; many volumes in English on English law and the law of the states of the United States: Livermore on Agency, Chitty on Bills, Bacon's abridgment in 7 volumes, Laws of Massachusetts, Kent's Commentaries in 4 volumes, Law of Patents, Revised Code of Mississipi, Laws of the United States in 8 volumes, etc...

The second inventory of Dec.31, 1832 was made of Moreau Lislet's papers: personal papers, such as bills, invoices, promissory notes, correspondence with his brother in law, Delagrange, attorney in Paris; professional papers such as files on the cases he handled on behalf of the city or private clients.

[263] One of the last acts of sale of land and buildings recorded under Moreau Lislet's name took place on February 25, 1831; the land and the buildings located rue Condé were sold for 4,000 piastres (Notaire L.T. Caire Acte 150, Notarial Archives, New Orleans).

PART III

GRANDEUR or MOCKERY?

Although Louis Casimir Moreau Lislet's name did not reach national fame, however legitimate his own and, yet, humble expectations could have been, his masterpiece[264] may nevertheless serve as a perfect substitute. The Digest, or Code of 1808, is, without any doubt, "a testimony of his vast knowledge and mastership of a science identified with the difficulty of providing for every need to come, of meeting all the expectations, of solving all the issues and of ruling on all the interests at stake".[265] Today, it is granted that the Digest of 1808 was the work almost exclusively of Moreau Lislet who was, with James Brown, one of the two lawyers appointed by the Legislative Assembly to draft it.[266]

---

[264] Moreau Lislet's five major works can be cited as:
a. Digest of the civil laws now in force in the territory of Orleans, 1808.
b. Civil Code of the State of Louisiana, 1825.
c. A general Digest of the Acts of the Legislature of Louisiana passed from the year 1804 to 1827 Inclusive, 1828.
d. The laws of Las Siete Partidas which are still in force in the State of Louisiana, translated from Spanish by Moreau Lislet and Henry Carleton, 1820.
e. A translation of the Title of Promises and Obligations, Sale and Purchase and Exchange from Spanish, of Las Siete Partidas by Moreau Lislet and Henry Carleton, 1818.

[265] Courrier de la Louisiane, December 10, 1832.

[266] *See*: "The political career of James Brown", Thesis by Fox Lawrence Keith, LSU; See the 1823 report of the

What remains, still today, the object of some controversy is the absolute and definitive identification of the sources of law which Moreau Lislet used in drafting the Digest of 1808. Indeed, it appears that some scholars are, in a sense, raising some questions about Moreau Lislet's intellectual honesty, his good faith and his moral integrity.

One will remember that James Brown and Louis Moreau Lislet had been specifically instructed "to compile and prepare jointly, a Civil Code for the use of this territory. Resolved, that the two juriconsults shall make the civil law by which this territory is now governed, the ground work of said code...".[267] The Act of March 26, 1804 had previously defined the civil law or " civil laws" in force in the said territory as "1. The Roman Civil Code as being the foundation of the Spanish law by which this country was governed before its cession to France and to the United States, ... 2. the Spanish Law, particularly...".[268]

It is obvious from the above that James Brown and Moreau Lislet had been given some very precise and specific guidelines which left little doubt as to the sources of law they were required to use in their preparation of the 1808 Digest. And, yet, doubts have been raised and still exist in the minds of a few some 190 years later. The question still lingering is the following: did Moreau Lislet actually and faithfully follow the instructions given to him or did he *intentionally* violate these same instructions by relying on the Napoleonic Code of 1804 and the French "Projet" of the year VIII? Did he *willfully* circumvent the instructions he had been given?

---

commissioners on the project of the Code which became the Code of 1825 (page 11 of the report).

[267] *See* Part 1, Chapter IV, note 32.

[268] *See* Part I, Chapter 4, note 16.

The interest manifested in the comparative study of the law of Louisiana with the legal systems which contributed to its existence reached its climax with the controversy which pitted against each other two of the most prominent scholars of Louisiana Law, Professors Batiza and Pascal.[269] This controversy, this modern and contemporary tournament of scholars, is but the finale of a century and a half of a variety of theories advanced, first, by contemporaries of Moreau Lislet and, second, by scholars of the second half of the 19th century and of the first half of the 20th. These speculations have remained speculations and the theories elaborated have remained just that, theories. Few are those who have actually attempted to find out what Moreau Lislet did do, whether he expressed his own views on the sources of law he did consult in drafting the Digest of 1808 or whether his peers and contemporaries had anything to say about these sources of the Digest. It might be helpful, if it is not also very wise, to go beyond these speculations and theories and to look as thoroughly as possible at Moreau Lislet's work and professional life to see if he, himself, did not already give us the answer we have striven to keep in hiding, sometimes under false pretenses of scholarship.

---

[269] Professor Rodolfo Batiza, now retired, was a faculty member at Tulane University Law School. Professor Robert Pascal, now retired, was a faculty member at the Law School of the Louisiana State University Paul M. Hebert Law Center.

CHAPTER I

"THE TOURNAMENT OF SCHOLARS"[270]

In the "Foreword" of the first article written by Professor Batiza,[271] Dean J.M. Sweeney stated that: "It is fair to say, I submit, that my colleague has solved the mystery, now a century and a half long, of the sources of the Digest. There are some, it must be admitted, who suspected the truth all along and to them Professor Batiza gives due credit in his article. Still, it is one thing to foresee the answer to a riddle of history, and another to dispel it by compelling evidence and proving beyond reasonable doubt the French origin of 85 percent of the articles drafted by Moreau Lislet and James Brown."[272] In answer, and challenge, to this forceful and confident assertion, Professor Pascal, faithful to the same thesis he had been advocating since 1965, wrote that: "the Digest of 1808, though written largely in words copied from, adapted from, or suggested by the French language texts, was

---

[270] Title borrowed from the article written by Dean Joseph Sweeney, "Tournament of Scholars over the sources of the Civil Code of 1808," 46 Tul.L.Rev. 585, 1972. See a new scholarly controversy between Davis V. Snyder [Possession: A Brief for Louisiana's Rights of Succession to the legacy of Roman Law, 66 TUL.L.Rev. 1853 (1992)] and Rodolfo Batiza [Roman Law in the French and Louisiana Civil Codes: A Comparative Textual Survey, 69 TUL.L.Rev. 1601 (1995))] and David V. Snyder, again [Ancient Law and Modern Eyes, 69 TUL.L.Rev. 1631 (1995)].

[271] "The Louisiana Civil Code of 1808: Its Actual Sources and Present Relevance" 46 Tul.L.Rev. 4, 1971.

[272] 46 Tul.L.Rev. 2, 1971.

intended to, and does for the most part, reflect the substance of the Spanish law in force in Louisiana in 1808."[273]

Let us take a close look at these conflicting theories and evaluate them in the context of the law, the veil of which they claim to have pierced.

SECTION I

PROFESSOR BATIZA'S THEORY OF THE FRENCH ORIGIN OF THE DIGEST OF 1808

The discovery in 1958 of a copy of the Digest of 1808, presently known as the "de la Vergne volume", after the family who possessed it, led to the formulation of a theory according to which the substantive law of the Digest of 1808 is apparently of Spanish origin. The basis of this theory is to be found in the handwritten "avant-propos" of that same volume. Translating from the original French language of that avant-propos, one is told "that one will find...next to the French text, and article by article, the citation of the principal laws of various codes from which the provisions of our local *statut* are drawn."[274]

---

[273] "Sources of the Digest of 1808: a reply to Professor Batiza", 46 Tul.L.Rev. 604, 1971; Pascal, "A Recent Discovery - A Copy of the "Digest of the Civil Laws" of 1808 With Marginal Source References in Moreau Lislet's Hand", 26 La.L.Rev.25, 1965.

[274] *See* the "Avant-propos" in A Reprint of Moreau Lislet's Copy of *A Digest of the Civil Laws Now in Force in the Territory of Orleans (1808)*, (The de la Vergne Volume), The Louisiana State University School of Law, The Tulane University School of Law, 1968. The word *"statute"* has been kept in its original French version because of its ambiguity. It

Three examples will explain and illustrate the technique used to support this theory:

1) next to article VII, First section, Chapter II, Title VII, Book I, one finds the following citation: L 7, t 2, Part 4. In other words: Ley 7, Titulo 2, Partida 4, the Siete Partidas therefore.

2) next to article VIII of the same Section, Chapter, Title and Book, one can read the following citations: L 4, T 23, P 4; L 5, V 1, Liv 2, T 1, S 1. Dom p.300. In other words: Ley 4, Titulo 23, Partida 4, the Siete Partidas again; Loi 5, Volume 1, Livre 2, Titre 1, Section 1, page 300 is a reference to the French version of Domat's Civil Laws in their Natural Order.

3) across from article 22, Section 1, Chapter III, Title II, Book 3 one finds a citation to: Part 6, tit. 1, loi 17 ...Fuero Real Liv. 3, tit. 5, loi 9 et tit. 12, loi 7...Rec. Cast. liv. 5, tit.6, loi 12 et tit. 8, loi 1... Dom. V 1, part 2, liv 3, tit. 3, S 1 et 2... Feb Cont V 1 .§ 5 No 72... ibid. § 7 Nos 105, 118, et 125. Feb. Jui, vol 2, liv 2, c. 1.§ 1 Nos 2,3... ["Rec. Cast." means Recopilation de Castille;" Feb. Cont." means Febrero Contratos; "Feb. Jui." means Febrero dealing with trials (Juicios).]

If we relate the above cited sentence from the Foreword of the de la Vergne volume to the three examples selected, we would probably be tempted to conclude, and logically so, that

---

could be used in a legal sense to mean "status", such as one's legal status (capacity, marriage...), or in a de facto sense to mean "condition" such as in the condition, status, of a married woman. It refers to a series of texts or provisions that regulate the situation of a particular group of people. It should not be translated by "statute" in the English sense of a text of law passed by some assembly.

the three articles of the Digest are mostly of Spanish origin[275] and, accessorily, of Roman law origin. However, Professor Batiza challenges this simple literal, textual and "superficial" conclusion: "Despite this categorical assertion and the acceptance it has received, the truth of the matter is that the de la Vergne volume is not primarily a compilation of sources, but one of concordances. The numerous citations appearing on the 245 interleaves include relatively few references to actual sources and generally fail to disclose the real origins of the Digest of 1808."[276]

The distinguished professor and legal scholar comes to this position after having conducted an extremely methodical, not to say meticulous, comparative study of the 2160 articles

---

[275] It will be noted that in two of the three examples selected, reference is made to Domat. It is explained by the author of the Avant-Propos, in the 4th §, that: "...as it would have been too long to refer to the laws of every code of Roman Law and Spanish Law, we decided, as to the Civil Laws, to cite *Domat* because each disposition of this work gives reference to texts of Roman Law where it has its origin...".

In other words, *Domat* is only a middleman between the Digest of 1808 and Roman Law then called " Civil Laws", and cannot be considered the actual source of certain dispositions of the Digest. If the words are borrowed from Domat, the substance is nevertheless Roman as required by the instructions given to Moreau Lislet and James Brown. It should be noted that Professor Batiza does not seem to have pointed to this relationship between the Digest, Domat and Roman law as established in the Avant-Propos to the Digest.

[276] Rodolfo Batiza, The Louisiana Civil Code of 1808: Its Actual Sources and Present Relevance, 46 Tul.L.Rev. 4, at 9 (1971).

which make up the Digest of 1808.[277] All in all, we are told that Professor Batiza was "led to the identification of the individual origins of 2,081 provisions...".[278] The results of Professor Batiza's painstaking research are as follows:"the French "Projet" of the Year VIII is the source of 807 provisions; the French Civil Code of 1804 is the source of 709 provisions. Thus the French "Projet" and Code, combined, account for 1,516 provisions, or about 70 percent of the Louisiana Code of 1808. Of the 709 provisions from the French Civil Code, however, 372, or more than 50 per cent, were actually borrowed from the Projet. Domat contributed 175 provisions, or 8 percent, Pothier 113, or 5 percent, and eighteen can be traced either to Domat or Pothier or both." In the end, Professor Batiza concluded,[279] 85 percent of the provisions of the Louisiana Civil Code of 1808 find their source in French texts, and the remaining 15 percent come from various sources such as Las Siete Partidas -67 provisions were borrowed-, Febrero Adicionado -52 provisions-, the Institutes of Justinian -27 provisions-, Blackstone -25 provisions-, Justinian's Digest -16 provisions-, etc.[280]

---

[277] I wish to express here my admiration and respect for my friend and colleague Rodolfo Batiza. His knowledge, scholarship and professional commitment will always be an example to be followed. May he forgive the awkwardness shown in defending a position contrary to his opinion.

[278] See supra note 13.

[279] *Id.* at pages 11 and 12.

[280] *Id.* at p. 12.

In a book with a limited publication of twelve copies only,[281] Professor Batiza describes the method he believes Moreau Lislet used in the drafting of the Digest of 1808:

"In the preparation of the 1808 code the first step would have necessarily been the undertaking of a general survey of the area of private law to be covered on the basis of the various Spanish compilations i.e. the Fuero Real, Siete Partidas, Laws of Toro, Compilation of Castile, and Compilation of the Laws of the Indies. It would have been very difficult for Moreau Lislet, who was of French ancestry and trained as a lawyer in France, not to have taken advantage of the best model for codification then available, <u>even at the risk of not adhering to the instructions received</u>.... Moreau Lislet adopted the structure, or organization, of the French code and projet as the framework for the Louisiana code. There were, however, some areas not covered, by either, e.g. slavery, master and servant... which the drafter included as an integral part of the Louisiana code.... Nearly 1700 provisions taken literally and almost literally by Moreau Lislet from French codal and doctrinal texts pervade the Louisiana code, adopted no doubt on the theory that the Roman law tradition shared by the French and the Spanish legal systems made them essentially similar.

On the other hand, there were a number of Castilian institutions, some derived from Roman law, and some from indigenous customary law, which were at variance with those of French origin, particularly in matters of illegitimacy, curatorship, succession law and community of gains. To have ignored the Spanish law in those areas would have been in open disregard of the instructions received, but even here French texts are found throughout the code. Had the drafter,

---

[281] Rodolfo Batiza, The Verbatim and Almost Verbatim Sources of the Louisiana Civil Codes of 1808, 1825 and 1870. The Original Texts, 3 v. 1973, Tulane Law Library.

however, resorted solely to the Spanish compilations in order to accomplish his task, the final product would have been at best a 17th century compilation, rather than a 19th century code."[282]

If one is to bear a judgment purely on mathematical grounds, it is logical to formulate the following conclusion on behalf of Professor Batiza: the sources of the Louisiana Code of 1808 are fundamentally French.

SECTION II

PROFESSOR PASCAL'S THEORY OF THE SPANISH ORIGIN OF THE DIGEST OF 1808

It was only in 1965 that Professor Robert Pascal put in writing, and officially so therefore, the theory he had defended over many years in conferences and classroom lectures. His thesis was, and still is, that the Digest of 1808, although written in terms literally copied, taken or adapted from provisions and texts drafted in the French language, was actually meant to reproduce, as it does to a large extent, the essence of the Spanish law in force in Louisiana in 1808.[283] Indeed, one must not forget that Spanish and Roman laws were the law of the land in Louisiana in 1806 when Moreau Lislet and James Brown were commissioned to draft a civil code on the basis of the then applicable law.[284] That law

---

[282] Rodolfo Batiza, "Sources Which Had a Substantial or Partial Influence on Provisions of the Louisiana Civil Code of 1808: The Original Texts", Volume 3, 1974. Emphasis ours.

[283] Robert Pascal, A Recent Discovery: A Copy of the "Digest of the Civil Laws" of 1808 With Marginal References in Moreau Lislet's Hand, 26 La. L. Rev. 25 (1965).

[284] See supra Part I.

existed neither in a codified form, nor in a format that would have made its codification an easy task. Besides, the requirement that the drafters write the first Louisiana civil code in the French language made their task even more difficult.

It happened that French law, which was then very close to Spanish law on account of the fact that both legal systems shared many of the same original sources, had just been presented to the French people, and the world, in a form rather unique at the time: the 1804 Civil Code of the French people. That Civil Code offered an incomparable resource of organised and structured civil law texts to the Louisiana drafters, in addition to the fact that these texts were in the French language. Furthermore, the Projet of the year VIII was closer to Roman law and the Roman-Visigothic legal institutions than the code of 1804 itself and resembled even more the Roman-Spanish legal system in force in Louisiana. This explains why the Projet of the year VIII was used by James Brown and Moreau Lislet in drafting the Louisiana "Code" of 1808. These two drafters, very practical and resourceful men as they were, quite naturally either used these available French texts whenever necessary or else they would find inspiration and guidance in them whenever they were required to transpose in the French language the institutions and rules of Spanish or Roman substantive law.

Where, on the contrary, Spanish and Roman substantive laws could not be matched with a "tailor made" French text, the two Louisiana codifiers had to resort to other texts or to drafting the articles themselves.[285] Professor Pascal offers several arguments in support of his theory.

One will note, at the outset, that the de la Vergne volume contains no express reference to either the French Civil Code

---

[285] Robert Pascal, Sources of the Digest of 1808; A Reply to Professor Batiza, 46 Tul.L.Rev. at 603 *et seq.* 1971-72.

of 1804 or the French Projet of the year VIII as potential sources for the provisions of the Digest. On the contrary, as is stated clearly by the author of the Foreword, who was none other than Moreau Lislet, the notes found in the volume refer to the "texts of the civil[286] and Spanish laws that have *some relationship*" with the provisions of the Digest. The justification for this *relationship,* and not "*actual source*" in the litteral sense, is simply that the law of Louisiana was Roman and Spanish[287] in its origin.

Much more serious is Professor Pascal's charge that Professor Batiza "failed to demonstrate that Moreau and Brown had succeeded magnificently in borrowing phraseology from French legal writings to prepare, in the French language and in civil form, all as directed by the Territorial Assembly, a statement of law so closely based on the Spanish-Roman civil laws in force that it could be entitled a "Digest" of those laws, and he failed to verify the validity of the Moreau notes in *The de la Vergne Volume* as references to the sources of the *substance* of the rules of the Digest."[288] This charge is at the center of the controversy between the two legal scholars.

Professor Pascal gave the following examples[289] to illustrate the basis of his position:

---

[286] As stated before, the expression "civil laws" must be understood as meaning "Roman Law".

[287] See supra Part I.

[288] Robert A. Pascal, Sources of the Digest of 1808: A Reply to Professor Batiza, 46 Tul.L.Rev. 603, 608-609 (1972).

[289] It will be necessary to give these examples in their French language since the controversy bears precisely on the use, or misuse, of texts in their French version.

a — First example:

Digest of 1808: Book 1, Title 7, Article 20[290]

"Lorsqu'une veuve est suspecte de se dire enceinte pour se perpétuer dans la possession des biens de son mari, par la supposition d'un prétendu héritier, l'héritier ou les héritiers présomptifs du mari pourront obtenir un ordre du juge, pour faire examiner par des matrones nommées à cet effet, si elle est enceinte ou non, et si elle l'est, pour la faire tenir dans état de contrainte jusqu'à ce qu'elle soit délivrée.

Si la veuve, sur cet examen, n'est pas jugée enceinte, l'héritier ou les héritiers présomptifs de son mari, seront envoyés en possession provisoire de sa succession, en par eux donnant caution de la restituer, si la femme vient à accoucher d'un enfant viable, dans le temps compétent fixé par la loi, depuis la mort de son mari."

Professor Batiza could not find, in either the Projet of the year VIII or in the French Code of 1804, or in Domat, or in

---

[290] "When a widow is suspected to feign herself with a child, in order to maintain herself in the possession of the estate of her husband, by the supposition of a pretended heir, the presumptive heir or heirs of the husband may obtain from the judge, an order that she may be examined by matrons appointed for that purpose, in order to discover whether she is with a child or not, and if she is, to keep her under proper restraint till delivered.

And if the widow be, upon examination, found not pregnant, the presumptive heir or heirs of the husband shall be put into a provisional possession of the inheritance, upon their giving security to return the same, if the widow should be delivered of a child able to live, within the time prescribed by law, after the death of her husband." Art. 20.

Pothier, any French text or provision that could be "matched" with this article 20 of the Digest. However, Las Siete Partidas contain such a provision which can be traced back, in fact, to the Digest of Justinian.[291] Shouldn't Professor Batiza have stopped at this point, since Moreau Lislet, himself, had indicated in the Louisiana Digest of 1808 that the source of that article 20 was, indeed, in Las Siete Partidas and in Febrero Juicios? Ignoring this reference given by Moreau Lislet, Professor Batiza was to add that it was by "chance" that he discovered the "source" of that article in the commentaries of the English jurist Blackstone, since the English version of article 20 of the Digest borrows from Blackstone's English text. Professor Batiza even asked the questions: "...was article 20 a contribution of James Brown in his capacity as a common-law lawyer? Was Moreau Lislet sufficiently familiar with both the common law and Blackstone so as to make contributions from Brown unnecessary? Would a civilian like Moreau Lislet, however knowledgeable of the common law, be likely to prefer a common law commentator over civilian sources?"

Actually, there is evidence to the effect that the first two questions were answered by Moreau Lislet himself, the former in the negative, and the latter in the affirmative.[292] Why create difficulties or an enigma where there are none, asks Professor Pascal?[293] This scholar suggested, then, that the drafters of the Digest of 1808 simply used Blackstone's English text to reproduce a rule that is Spanish in substance. One can add some support to Professor Pascal's evaluation of Professor Batiza's statement. Indeed, if one looks at

---

[291] Sexta Partida, Tit. VI, Ley XVII; Justinian's Digest, 25, 4, 10.

[292] 46 Tul.L.Rev. at 27-28, (1971-72).

[293] 46 Tul.L.Rev. at 611.

Blackstone's Commentaries, Book I, Chapter 16, Of Parent and Child, # 456, one can read the following: "and, if she be (with child), to keep her under proper restraint till delivered; which is entirely conformable to the practice of the civil law: (note o); but, if the widow be, upon due examination, found not pregnant, the presumptive heir shall be admitted to the inheritance, though liable to lose it again, on the birth of a child within forty weeks from the death of a husband." A look at "note o", as stated by Blackstone, advises us to consult a source none other than: Ff, 25, tit 4, per tot., which stands for Justinian's Corpus Juris Civilis, Book 25, Title 4 "Concerning the Examination of Pregnant Women, and the Precautions to be Taken With Reference to Their Delivery". There, under a reference to Ulpianus, we can read the following Roman law rules: "(2) In accordance with this rescript, a woman may be summoned before the Praetor and, having been interrogated as to whether she believes that she is pregnant, can be compelled to answer.

"(4)...If, however, she should deny that she is pregnant, then, in accordance with this rescript, the Praetor must summon midwives.

(6) The Praetor also must select the house of the respectable matron to which the woman must go, in order that she may be examined."

A French translation, by none other than Pothier himself, of Justinian's Digest or Pandects gives the following title to Article II of Title IV of Book XXV: Du cas où la femme se dit enceinte après la mort de son mari. (Of the instance where a woman declares that she is pregnant after her husband's death).[294]

Thus, as Professor Pascal has argued, the text of this Article 20, Book 1, Title 7 of the Louisiana Digest of 1808 is

---

[294] Pandectes de Justinien, Mises dans un Nouvel Ordre, par R.J. Pothier, Paris 1821.

very much Roman (and Spanish even more so)[295] in substance, as Blackstone himself, the so-called source of that article, had recognised in his Commentaries. Furthermore, Blackstone added a reference to "the Gothic constitutions".

b - Second example:

Digest of 1808: 3,1,6, art. 96 p. 165[296]

"L'héritier soit testamentaire, ou légitime, ou irrégulier, qui craint d'accepter une succession, ou d'y renoncer avant d'avoir eu le tems d'en connaitre les forces et les charges, peut n'accepter la succession que sous bénéfice d'inventaire."

Domat: 1, Part II, Book I, Title II, Section II, n.i.[297]

---

[295] 2 Las Siete Partidas 1024 (L. Moreau Lislet and H. Carleton, translation 1820).

[296] "The testamentary, or legal, or irregular heir, who is afraid to accept or renounce a succession, before having had the necessary time to be informed of its property and charges, may accept the succession with the benefit of an inventory." Art.96.

[297] "Every heir or executor, who doubts whether the succession be advantageous or not, and who is afraid to engage himself in it, may beforehand demand that an inventory be made of the effects, and of the deeds and writings belonging to the inheritance; and without taking time to deliberate, he may declare that he accepts the succession with the benefit of an inventory. And by this means he will be liable for the debts and charges of the inheritance only in so far as the goods belonging to the deceased shall be sufficient to acquit, and his own estate will not be chargeable therewith."

"Tout héritier, soit testamentaire ou ab intestat, qui doute que l'hérédité soit avantageuse, et qui craint de s'y engager, peut auparavant demander qu'il soit fait un inventaire des biens et des titres et papiers de l'hérédité: et sans prendre le temps pour délibérer faire sa déclaration qu'il se rend héritier par bénéfice d'inventaire."

Professor Batiza concludes from a comparison of the text written by Domat and article 96 of the Digest that the latter was substantially influenced by the former and, consequently, that article 96 has a French source. Professor Pascal replied that the rule of law found in the Digest of 1808 is also very similar to a provision of Las Siete Partidas to which Moreau Lislet made an explicit[298] reference. Besides, the reference to Domat should be interpreted as a reference to Roman law and not to French law.[299] Then, concludes Professor Pascal, Mr. Batiza "often ignores the fact that the rule may be Spanish-Roman as well as French as long as he can match the phraseology of the Digest's French text with that of a French

---

The Civil Law in Its Natural Order, by Jean Domat, translated from the French by William Strahan, in two volumes, (1853), p. 139 Section II. Art. I. § 2690.

[298] Sexta Partida, Tit. VI Ley 1.

[299] Either Professor Batiza overlooked the Avant-Propos to the Digest written by Moreau Lislet or he decided to ignore the good faith statements made therein by Moreau Lislet. One such statement is as follows (translated from the French): "But considering that it would have been too long to refer to the Laws of all the Codes of Roman Law and Spanish Law, we restricted ourselves, as far as the Civil Laws are concerned, to cite Domat, because we can find in that work (Domat's Civil Laws) on every provision it contains, the texts of the Roman Law from which they come."

language text."[300] "Had professor Batiza pretended to no more than a philological exercise — and made it clear he intended no more — there could have been no objection to his work, no cause for misunderstanding, and no reason for this reply."[301]

These are the two opposing theories in this controversy. The gap between them is deep. To a large extent, it involves a proponent of the theory that *form overrides substance*, the Batiza theory, whereas the other, the Pascal theory, would argue that there is more to a text than its form and language and that *form may disguise the substance*.

SECTION III

FORM VERSUS SUBSTANCE

Our purpose here is to attempt to reach a judgment as objective as possible - a somewhat ambitious and daring task — on the theories presented in the preceding sections. To formulate this judgment, and in support of it, we shall introduce a few yet unknown historical documents which ought to help in reaching a conclusion on the foundations and the strength of these same theories. The historical documents we have uncovered have not yet been brought into this tournament of scholars despite the fact that they have been in existence since the early 1800s. We believe that their existence should, at least, have been suspected and that a search for their discovery ought to have been undertaken to attempt to clear the cloud still hanging over the true sources of the Louisiana

---

[300] Robert Pascal, Sources of the Digest of 1808: A Reply to Professor Batiza, 46 Tul. L. Rev. p. 624, (1971-72).

[301] *Id.* at p. 607.

Digest of 1808 and, more particularly, over Moreau Lislet's intellectual integrity which was much admired in his days.

A comment on the text of the 1814 Foreword to the notes in the "de la Vergne" copy of the Digest of 1808 must be made at the outset.

One will notice that the grammatical structure of the first paragraph of the Foreword makes it an introductory paragraph meant to state the purpose of the book and to lay out the methodology used in its presentation. The purpose is described as being "to make known those texts of the civil laws and the Spanish laws which have some *rapport* (with the Laws of this State)".[302] As to the presentation or format of the book, it consists in inserting blank pages between the pages of the Digest and in writing notes on these blank pages. However, the Digest having been written and printed in two languages with the French text as the authoritative version and the English text as a mere translation,[303] it was therefore essential

---

[302] The French text of the first paragraph of the Avant-Propos reads, in part, as follows: " Le but de cet ouvrage est de faire connaitre...quels sont les textes des loix civiles et Espagnoles, qui y ont quelque rapport." *See* The de la Vergne Volume, A Digest of the Civil Laws now in force in the Territory of Orleans (1808).

[303] "Sir, The Secretary of the Territory, will transmit you a Copy of the "Civil Code", adopted at the last Session of the Legislature. You will find the English Text extremely incorrect;-This is attributable to the circumstance of the Work having been written in French, and the translation prepared by persons who were not well acquainted with the English Language; —So erroneous does the translation appear to be, that it will probably be necessary to declare by Law, that the French shall (solely) be considered the legal text...." IX Territorial Papers of the United States, p.802-803, Governor

to be very explicit and clear with regard to the controlling French version of the text of the Digest. This is what the second paragraph of the Foreword tells the reader: "To this effect, one will find next to the English text, a *general list* of all the *titles* of the Roman Laws and Spanish Laws, which are *related to the subject matters*[304] dealt with in every chapter of the Digest, and *next to the French text, and article by article, the citation of the principal laws* of diverse codes, from which *the dispositions of our local status have been extracted.*"[305] Hence, a system of general references to *titles* of laws *only* opposite the English text of the provisions of the Digest and, opposite the French text of the same provisions of the Digest, an inventory of citations to *the principal laws* selected from the *titles* appearing next to the English text. This distribution of the references between the French text, on the one hand, and the English text, on the other hand, appeared quite logical at the time since:

"The French, like the Spanish, are the languages of our law and of our doctrine. The English is nearly useless to us as *lingua juris*, since we are regulated by no code exclusively written in English, and we need not consult nor cite authors who have writen in that language, except it be for mere parade or through pedantry...".[306]

Claiborne to the Secretary of State, October 7th 1808.

[304] Emphasis ours.

[305] *Id.*

[306] Editorial, Louisiana Courier, New-Orleans, Friday, June 1, 1821.

As to the references that will be made to Domat, the author of the Foreword adds a clear explanation; he tells us that Domat is cited *"because one finds in every disposition of that book (the Civil Laws) the texts of the Roman law from which they have been taken.*"[307] Thus, Domat was cited not because he wrote *in French on French law* but, rather, because his work entitled "The Civil Laws in Their Natural Order" contains the essence of the Roman law which the drafters of the Digest of 1808 *had to use* as the basis and source of their assignment.

If we accept this formal and rational presentation of the Digest, is it still possible to conclude that the use of the French language was actually more than the mere use of a formal language of the law, its vehicle in a sense, and that it was, in reality and truly, the language of the *substance of the law,* making French substantive law the law of Louisiana in 1808?[308] According to Professor Batiza it is quite possible. In his response to Professor Pascal's reply, he wrote:

"...it is clear that Moreau Lislet took considerable liberties with the instructions since the civil law of the Territory that

---

[307] This text has been underlined to stress the technique used by Brown and Moreau Lislet in drafting the Digest. The true and primary but remote source of some provisions of the Digest of 1808 is Roman law, whereas the mediate or formal source of that same law is Domat's written work on Roman law, his treatise on les *Loix Civiles dans leur Ordre Naturel* or *the Civil Laws* as used by Moreau Lislet.

[308] *See* in particular," Le langage du droit et le langage juridique. Les critères de leur discernement". by Zygmunt Ziembinski, Archives de Philosophie du Droit, v.19, p.25 (1974).

was to be codified was almost entirely Spanish, and the Code of 1808 shows an overwhelming French influence."[309]

Professor Batiza went on to add:

"To make 'substance' the sole criterion for the identification of sources when the actual sources can be established beyond doubt on the basis of both language and substance is nonsensical. On the basis of substance alone, either Portuguese or Italian rules, or those from any other 'Roman-oriented' system could be advanced as sources of the Code of 1808 as readily as the Spanish rules."[310]

Is it really so "nonsensical"? One may wonder why Professor Batiza did not add an adjective before the word "sources" as it is first used in the above second quote, whereas the adjective "actual" appears in front of "sources" when that word is used the second time. Would that missing adjective have been "fictitious" or "artificial" to be contrasted with "actual"? Where would the proper adjectives, at least in this context, of "immediate" as opposed to "mediate" sources have been used? "Immediate", in the sense of "direct, without intervention, actual" would have been applied to those sources of Roman law and Spanish law which have a direct "rapport, relation" with Louisiana law, as the Avant-Propos to the Digest of 1808 states. On the other hand, the adjective "mediate" would have been used with the word "sources" to describe those sources which stand "in between, in the middle", the French sources of law as Professor Batiza would probably argue. But, then, why not use a "mediate" source of

---

[309] Rodolfo Batiza, Sources of the Civil Code of 1808: Facts and Speculations: A Rejoinder, 46 Tul.L.Rev. 628, at 649 (1972).

[310] Id. at 645.

law, such as the French legal language, to convey the substance of the "immediate" source of law, Roman or Spanish, if there is compatibility, as there must be, between these two kinds of sources? Is it not possible, then, to consider that French was used by Moreau Lislet as the vehicular *legal language* of the *law* as he was required to do? Let us call here on the testimony of the "legal spirit or frame of mind" of Moreau Lislet's time and cite one of his contemporaries:

"We would have chosen official representatives who would have set as a sine qua non condition that in order to be a judge, one must know French, as the Territory's language, and Spanish as the language of our governing laws. For it is in the order of things that the parts be conform to the whole rather than the whole to the parts."[311]

The language of the governing law, then, was undeniably Spanish and Moreau Lislet himself stated it in terms that leave no doubt whatsoever, even to a reasonable reader of our era. In an annoucement seeking individual subscriptions for the purchase of his translation in French of the Siete Partidas, Moreau Lislet wrote the following:" *Personne n'ignore combien l'étude des <u>lois espagnoles</u> est précieuse pour la décision des causes qui sont portées devant les tribunaux de cet état puisque l'autorité de ces lois y subsiste en matière civile, dans tout ce qui n'est pas incompatible avec notre Constitution. On sait que le Code Civil qui a été rédigé pour cet Etat ne contient en quelque sorte que les principes primitifs abstraits de <u>ce droit</u> dont on voit les développements, les exemples, les conséquences et les limitations <u>dans les lois du pays qui lui ont servi de source</u>. C'est dans <u>cette source</u> qu'il*

---

[311] Editorial, Courrier de la Louisiane, mercredi 25 juillet 1821 (author's translation).

faut aller puiser pour avoir une véritable connaissance de notre jurisprudence actuelle." [312]

---

[312] Emphasis ours. This French text was published in Le Courrier de la Louisiane, vendredi 15 octobre 1813.

The following English text appeared in the same newspaper on the 23rd and 28th of April 1813:

"No man is ignorant of the absolute necessity of a study of the Spanish laws, for the decision of causes which are brought before the tribunals of this state where the authority of these laws subsists in civil cases, in all that is not incompatible, with our constitutions or has not been altered or abrogated by our several legislatures. It is well known that the Civil Code which has been digested for this state contains in some measure, only the primitive and abstract principles of that law, the developments, examples, consequences and limitations of which are to be perceived in the ancient laws of the country, which formed its basis. It is then to that source we must recur to obtain a true knowledge of our actual jurisprudence."

Moreau Lislet added the following:

"The work intended to be offered to the public, will be preceded by a preliminary introduction, which will give an idea of the law system observed in Spain and her colonies, of the several codes published at different times, and which are still in force there, and finally of the authority enjoyed by the Roman and church laws, wherever the Royal laws are silent or deficient. At the head of each title, the translation of which will be given, will be placed a list of the several titles of the institutes of the pandects, of the code & the novels of Justinian, of the different Spanish codes, & of the canonical law, as well as the several works treating of the same matter such as Domat's civil laws, Pothier's writings, Febrero's

Examples will show that in those legal matters which had to be specifically governed by Spanish law, or Roman law, because of their differences with French law, Moreau Lislet used French as the required legal language in order to transcribe these Spanish or Roman rules of law. It is, therefore, in the Spanish or Roman laws that the *immediate* or *primary* or *actual* sources of the articles of the Digest drafted in French are to be found.[313]

---

library, and the Curia philipica. In fine at the end of each law will be placed a note showing all such laws of the civil code of this state, and of the recopilation de castilla, which contain provisions on the same subject, in such manner that it will be easy to verify what alterations the ancient law contained in the seven Partidas, may have experienced in modern or actual legislation....The said translation has been made by Mr. Moreau Lislet, counsellor at law of this city, who had made it only for his private use, but has been encouraged by his friends and colleagues to render it public....Mr. Moreau Lislet hopes to be seconded in his undertaking by Mr. Mazureau, another jurisconsult of this city, well versed in the Spanish language, and known by his talents in jurisprudence...." Louisiana Courrier, April 23, 1813.

Can't we gather from these excerpts that Mazureau could easily have denounced Moreau Lislet if the latter had betrayed the specific instructions he had received to draft a Code or Digest in 1808 according to Roman and Spanish sources? One will notice also that in this same advertisement Moreau Lislet uses the same language he used in the Avant-Propos to the Digest as regards *the Roman and Spanish laws which deal with the same subject matter.*

[313] One wonders how Professor Batiza could write the following first and third sentences of this quote: "*The fact that*

a: first example: matrimonial regimes.

The **first example** is taken from the law of matrimonial regimes or marriage contracts and, in particular, the contract of "partnership or community of acquests or gains (de la société, ou Communauté d'Acquêts ou de Gains)."[314]

Digest, article 64, p.337:

"This partnership or community consists of the profits of all the effects of which the husband has the administration and enjoyment; of the produce of the reciprocal labor and industry of both husband and wife; and of the estates which they may acquire during the marriage either by donations made jointly to them both, or by purchase, or in any other similar way, even although the purchase be only in the name of one of the two and not of both, because in that case the period of time when the purchase was made is alone attended to and not the person who made the purchase."

---

the substance of the rule expressed may conform to the Spanish-Roman law in force in 1808 is entirely irrelevant, merely proving what the writer had already pointed out himself: 'There are considerable similarities between some French and Spanish legal principles owing to the common heritage of Roman law and even some Germanic customs.' *Every "literal" ("verbatim") source is necessarily 'substantive'".* Sources of the Civil Code of 1808, Facts and Speculation: A Rejoinder, by Rodolfo Batiza, 46 Tul.L.Rev. 628 at 639.

[314] Digest of 1808, Book 3, title 5, chapter 2, section 4, articles 63 to 85.

All the references given across from this text are to Spanish texts because the substance of the law of this article 64 is undeniably Spanish. On the other hand, Planiol, writing about French law, stated that in the organization of the community from the 16th to the 18th centuries in France, "the most general practice was to include in the community: 1) all movables of the spouses; 2) the immovables acquired, that is to say the immovables acquired by onerous title during the marriage. (Coutume de Paris, art.220)."[315] By contrast, article 64 of the Digest of 1808 does not include in the community the movables of the spouses, which is perfectly consistent with Spanish law.[316]

Digest, article 65, p.337:

"In the same manner the debts contracted during the marriage enter into the said partnership or community of gains; and must be acquitted out of the common funds, whilst the debts of both husband and wife anterior to the marriage, must be acquitted out of their own personal and individual effects."

The references given by Moreau Lislet across from this article are all to Spanish texts because Spanish law provided that debts incurred by the spouses before the marriage had to be paid out of the separate property of each one of them, whereas under the Custom of Paris these debts would become the debts of the community.[317]

---

[315] Planiol, Traité Elémentaire de Droit Civil, 3e ed. 1948 "Histoire de la communauté", p. 83.

[316] See Nina Nicholls Pugh, 30 La. L. Rev. 1, 1969.

[317] Fuero Real, Ley 14, Libro III, Tit.20; Coutume de Paris art. 211; Pothier, Traité de la Communauté, Part.I,

Digest, art. 66-1, p. 337:

"The husband is the head and master of the partnerhip or community of gains; he administers said effects; disposes of the revenues which they produce, and may sell and even give away the same without the consent and permission of his wife, because she has no sort of right in them until her husband be dead."

This provision reproduces exactly the substance of its immediate and actual source which can be identified as the following:

"Quando el marido enagena constante matrimonio algunos de los gananciales, o todos, lo que puede hacer sin consentimiento ni licencia de su muger no siendo castrenses ni casi castrenses, valdra la enagenación, porque la muger no

---

Chap.II, Sect.1, n. 26. See, as an illustration, the "Marriage contract between Jean Henry Lastrapes and Geneviève Boisdore, Opelousas: 1799, June 1." Written in French (the vehicular language at the time), it refers to the "laws and Custom of Spain (the substantive law) in these words: "Les dits deux conjoints ont déclaré qu'ils ne se sont point obligés à payer les dettes l'un de l'autre créées avant leur mariage, qu'au contraire, leur volonté fut et est qu'elles le fussent par celui ou celle qui les avaient faites et de son propre bien sans que celui de l'autre ni sa personne y fut tenue en aucune manière.

Les sus dits conjoints ont entendu et entendent et veulent que la communauté de biens soit régie selon les loix, us et coutumes d'Espagne, quand bien même cette colonie viendrait à changer de domination..."

tienne uso ni dominio en los gananciales hasta que el marido muere...[318]

If Moreau Lislet had looked in Pothier's works for the source of this article, as suggested by Professor Batiza,[319] it can only be, in our opinion, for the purpose of selecting a few French words considering that the substance of this provision of the Digest is much more a transposition of its Spanish source than it is of the French text by Pothier.[320]

b: second example: law of persons.

The second example is taken from the law of persons and in particular title VII, Book I of the Digest: Of Fathers and Children.

Chapter I is entitled "Of Children in general" and is made up of six articles. Professor Batiza undertook to establish that, to draft these articles, Moreau Lislet was largely or partially influenced by at least four French sources: the Code of 1804, the Projet of the Year VIII, Domat and Pothier. Another source cited are the Commentaries of the English scholar, Blackstone. If the French sources did have an influence on

---

[318] 1 Feb. Adic. Part I, Cap. II (234), 1806 ed. Madrid.

[319] The Louisiana Civil Code of 1808: Its Actual Sources and Present Relevance, by Rodolfo Batiza, in 46 Tul.L.Rev. 4 at p.106, Appendix C.

[320] Pothier, Communauté, Part II, n.467.

"The husband, as head of the community, is deemed sole master over the community property, as long as it lasts, and he can dispose freely of the same, without the consent of his wife." (translated from the French).

Moreau Lislet, one will easily realize that they played only a role in providing a selection of French words (and here again the range of French words to chose from is necessarily limited considering the technicality of the subject matter), because the essence or substance of these articles is undeniably found in Ley 1, tit. 13 and Ley 1, tit. 15 of the Fourth Part of Las Siete Partidas.[321]

---

[321] Digest of the Civil Laws, 1808. Book I, Title VII, Chap I "Of Children in General":
Art.1: Children are either legitimate or illegitimate.
Art.2: Legitimate children are those who are born during the marriage.
Art.3: Illegitimate children are those who are born out of marriage.
Art.4: There are two sorts of illegitimate children:
Those who are born from two persons, who at the moment when said children were conceived, might have been duly married together; and those who are born from persons to whose marriage there existed at the time, some legal impediment.
Adulterous and incestuous bastards belong to this last class.
Art.5: Adulterous bastards are those who are born from an unlawful connection between two persons who at the time when the child was conceived, were either of them or both connected by marriage with some other person.
Art.6: Incestuous bastards are those who are born from the illegal connection of two persons who are relations within the degree prohibited by law.

Quarta Partida. Titulo XIII Ley I:
Legitimo fijo tanto quiere decir como el que es fecho segunt ley, et aquellos deben seer llamados legitimos que nascen de padre et de madre que son casados (1) verdaderamiente, segunt manda santa eglesia. Et aun si acaesciese que entre algunos de los que se casasen manifiestamiente en faz de la

eglesia hobiese atal embargo por quel casamiento se debiese partir, los fijos que fecienseń ante que sopiesen que habie entre ellos atal embargo, serien legitimos (2). Et esto serie tambien si amos non sopiesen que hi habie tal embargo, como si non lo sopiese mas del uno dellos (3); ca el non saber deste solo, face los fijos legitimos: mas si despues que sopiesen ciertamente (4) que habie entro ellos atal embargo, feciensen fijos, todos quantos fijos despues hobiesen (5), non serien legitimos. Pero si algunos entre quien hobiese atal embargo non lo sabiendo amos o el uno dellos, si fuesen acusados ante alguno de los jueces de santa eglesia, et ante que el embargo fuese probado (6) nin la sentencia dada, quantos fijos fecieren entre tanto que estodieren en esta duda, todos seran legitimos. Ostrosi son legitimos (7) los fijos que home ha de la muger que tiene por barragana (8), si despues deso se casa con ella (9); ca muger estos fijos atales non son legitimos quando nascen, tan grant fuerza ha el matrimonio que luego que el padre et la madre son casados, se facen por ende los fijos legitimos. Eso mesmo serie si alguno hobiese fijo de su sierva et depues deso se casase con elle; ca tan grant fuerza ha el matrimonio que luego es fecho, es la madre por ende libre et los fijos legitimos(10).

Quarta Partida Titulo XV, Ley I:
Naturales et non legitimos llamaron los sabios antiguo a los fijos que non nascen de casamiento segunt ley, asi como los que facen en las barranganas (1), et los fornecinos que nascen adulterio (2), o son fecho en parienta (3) o en mugeres de orden (4), et estos non son llamados naturales porque son fechos contra ley et contra razon natural. Otros fijos hi ha que son llamados en latin manzeres (5), et tomaron este nombre de dos partes de latin mania et scelus, que quire tanto decir como pecado infernal; ca los que con llamados manzeres nascen de las mugeres estan en la puteria et danse a todos quantos a ellas vienen: et por ende non puecen saber cuyos fijos son los que

In chapter 3 of the same title VII of the Digest are found the following three provisions which, in our opinion, reveal again the influence of the Spanish law:

Article XXIV: Illegitimate children who have been acknowledged by their father are called natural children, and those whose father is unknown are contra-distinguished by the appellation of bastards.

Article XXV: The acknowledgment of an illegitimate child, shall be made by a declaration executed by a notary public in presence of two witnesses, whenever it shall not have been made in the registering of the birth or baptism of such child.

Article XXVIII: Illegitimate children though duly acknowledged, cannot claim the rights of legitimate children.

---

nascen dellas. Et homes hi ha que dicen que manzer tanto quiere decir como mancelliento, porque fue engendrado malamiente et nasce de vil logar. Otro manera hi ha de fijos que son llamados en latin spurri (6), que quiere tanto decir como los que nascen de las mugeres que tienen algunos por varraganas de fuera de sus casas, et son ellas atales (7) que se dan a otros homes sin aquellos que las tienen por amigas, et por ende non saben quien es su padre del que nasce de tal muger. Otra manera hi ha de fijos que son llamados notos (8), et estos son los que nascen de adulterio: et son llamados notos, porque semeja que son fijos conoscidos del marido que la tiene en casa, et non lo son. (...)."

Mr. Batiza cites article 331 of the French Civil Code as the source of the above-referenced article 4 of the Digest and does not even mention Law 1, Title XV of La Quatra Partida, to which in our opinion article 4 of the Digest is closer, not only as to its form, but also as to its substance.

The rights of natural children are regulated under the title of successions.[322]

Particular attention must be paid to the definition and concept of a natural child in article XXIV. This definition is none other than the one found in Las Siete Partidas: "Are natural and illegitimate as they were called by our forefathers, the children born out of wedlock, such as the concubine's children. Are called bastards those born from adultery, incest or from a mother belonging to a religious order."[323] This definition is much more restrictive than the definition found in French law which included, under the notion of natural filiation, not only the simple natural filiation (equivalent to the

---

[322] Professor Batiza cites, as the sources of these articles, the following provisions of the French Civil Code of 1804: articles 334 of the French Civil Code as the source of Digest art. 25 and article 338 for Digest art. 28. 46 Tul.L.Rev. at 53.

[323] Law I, Title 15, Quatra Partida.

The source of article XXIV would be, according to Mr. Batiza, the Compilation of Castilla Lib. V, Tit. VIII, Ley IX. Mr. Batiza was unable to cite a French source for this article (although the French Civil Code is cited as the source of the preceding or following articles) because, in our opinion, the substance of this article corresponds to Spanish law and not to French law. Besides, in a volume of the Digest of 1808 containing Moreau Lislet's handwritten notes and references, there is a footnote (a) facing the title of Chapter III which reads "Of Illegitimate Children". This footnote in Moreau Lislet's handwriting, at the bottom of the page, gives several references to either Latin or Spanish texts.

concept of Las Siete Partidas) but also the incestuous and adulterous natural children.[324]

c: third and fourth examples: Blondeau on the Digest.

The **third and fourth examples** we have selected are taken word for word from a commentary on the Louisiana Civil Code of 1825 written that very same year by a French Professor, Blondeau.

In its articles 357 to 366, on the curatorship of minors, the Code of 1825 reinstated exactly articles LXXVIII to LXXXVI of Chapter II, Title VIII, Book I of the Digest of 1808. It is possible, therefore, to transpose the comments made by Blondeau on the articles of the Code of 1825 into the framework of the Digest of 1808 from which these same articles were copied.[325]

In his general introduction to "The New Civil Code of the State of Louisiana" of 1825, Blondeau expresses his disappointment with the form of that Code, its structure, much of its style and the length of many of the articles.[326] When addressing some of the substantive issues dealt with in the

---

[324] Planiol, Traité Elémentaire de Droit Civil, Vol. I p.454 4ème édition, 1948.

[325] Blondeau, "Sur le nouveau Code Civil de l'Etat de la Louisiane." Thémis ou Bibliothèque de Jurisconsulte, 1826 p. 62 *et seq.* Author's translation from the French.

[326] Strange and surprising comment made by a French law Professor on a Code "supposedly" French in style, wording and substance according to Professor Batiza! Did Blondeau fail to "recognize" the French Code of 1804 or the French Projet of the Year VIII?

Louisiana Code, this is what he had to say about the curatorship of minors:

"By adopting the distinction so wisely established by Roman Law between persons under the age of puberty and adults (*i.e.* minors above the age of puberty), which distinction consists in submitting the former to the authority of a tutor who can altogether devise and carry out all the juridical acts required to protect the interest of his ward, whereas only one curator is given to the adult to approve, if necessary, the acts for which the adult has the initiative, the new Code has not however fully determined, as the Roman legislator had done, the condition of either those persons who are under the age of puberty or of those who are adults. Instead of one curator, as we have already said, adults will now be given two: one in charge of the assets or estate (ad bona), to assist the minor in the ordinary acts of his life, and a curator ad litem who has no other function than to assist the minor in the courts of justice and to substitute himself to the curator ad bona when the acts or interests of the latter can be in conflict with those of the minor. As in Roman Law, the curators (except for what will be said concerning the curator ad litem) are appointed only at the minor's request; but the Louisiana Code orders the judge to appoint the person designated by the minor, if that person is not prohibited from exercising the functions of tutor or curator. The curator ad litem is general or special; it is only a special curator that a judge can appoint against the will of the minor, which occurs in the event the latter goes to court before having requested a curator or having lost the one appointed, and he does not want to propose one."

Hence, according to this prominent scholar and a contemporary of Moreau Lislet, the law of curatorship in the Louisiana Civil Code of 1825 and, therefore, in the Digest of 1808, would have its origin, or immediate source, in Roman

Law.³²⁷ On his part, Moreau Lislet gives references to different laws from "Partida 6", laws or leyes which express the substance of the articles of the Digest. Professor Batiza acknowledges the influence of both Roman and Spanish law, but classifies these "sources" under the category of "other sources" after citing as the primary source either Domat or Pothier.³²⁸ This example may help to point out that there is something artificial in Professor Batiza's methodology and his classification of the "actual" sources of the Digest of 1808.

---

³²⁷ In light of the time and the circumstances in which Blondeau was writing, it would be very difficult to suspect him of any bias in this controversy on the "actual sources" of the Digest of 1808. His impartial analysis of some provisions of the Code of 1825 gives all the more value to the theory of the Roman and Spanish sources of the Louisiana Digest of 1808.

³²⁸ It is interesting to note here that in his article on the sources of the Digest of 1808, 46 Tul.L.Rev. p.58 and 59, Mr. Batiza lists Pothier and Domat, and only in the third place La Sexta Partida, as sources of the articles of the Digest on curatorship. In our opinion, the reference to Pothier is not justified, especially as regards "mandate". In addition, between 1971 and 1974 Mr. Batiza, as he admits himself, corrected mistakes he had made in a number of his classifications and findings. For instance, in 1971, Mr. Batiza had listed Pothier as having had a substantial influence on article LXXXIV of the Digest. In 1974, this influence is no longer cited and no reference is made to Pothier. On the contrary, we find a reference to Febrero Adicionado as having had a partial influence. In other words, between 1971 and 1974, the sources have changed!!

This criticism is even more relevant and justified in the second example borrowed from Blondeau. This example deals with the law of emancipation:[329]

Emancipation in the new Code can be compared to what Roman Law calls *venia aetatis*, rather than to our French notion of emancipation. Indeed, the emancipated minor does not have a defender anymore, except to receive an accounting from his tutor or curator, or to go to court, although this last restriction does not exist when emancipation results from marriage; he (the emancipated minor) is able to receive, without authorization, not only his wages but also all other amounts due to him; finally he can lawfully bind himself for an amount equal to one year of his revenues. This emancipated minor is not bound to return anything, on account of the juridical acts he entered into as stated above, either on the ground of lesion or on the ground of lack of use."

The articles of the Code of 1825 which were the objects of Blondeau's comments were articles 367 to 381, Chapter 3, Title VIII, Book I. They corresponded to articles LXXXVII to XCVII, Chapter 3, Title VIII, Book I of the Digest of 1808. Whereas Blondeau traced the origin of these articles on emancipation to their Roman law sources, Professor Batiza would consider these sources to be French. Out of the eleven articles of the Digest, five, according to Professor Batiza, had their source (verbatim or almost verbatim) in the Projet of the

---

[329] Blondeau, "Sur le nouveau Code Civil de l'Etat de la Louisiane". Thémis ou Bibliothèque de Jurisconsulte, 1826 p. 195 et seq. See also, Robert Pascal, Contracts of the Minor or His Representative Under the Louisiana Civil Code. 8 La.L.Rev.383-396, at p. 388-389, (1948).

Year VIII and the Code of 1804; two had their source in the Code of 1804 and one had its source in Pothier.[330]

Mr. Batiza does not cite any Roman Law source, not even any Spanish law source for that matter, in reference to Blondeau's statement to the effect that "emancipation in the new (Louisiana) Code can be compared to what Roman law calls *venia aetatis*, rather than to the French notion of emancipation." In the volume of the Digest of 1808 which contains Moreau Lislet's handwritten notes and references, one can find, following the title "Of Emancipation", a note (a); this note at the bottom of page 75 reads:" For authorities on emancipation see at the bottom of page 51". At the bottom of page 51 one can read:[331]

"Adoptions and Emancipations teatro vol 2, p.354 Dig. Li.1, t.7. De Adoptionibus et emancipationibus et aliis modis quibus potestas solvitur.....

46 laws
    -inst. Liv. 11 t. 11 idem   12 laws
    -cod. Liv.8 t.48 idem   11 laws
    -Partida 4 t 18 de hos hijos profijados   10...

These handwritten notes confirm Blondeau's analysis of the concept of emancipation in the Louisiana Code of 1825,

---

[330] Batiza, The Louisiana Civil Code of 1808, Its Actual Sources and Present Relevance, 46 Tul.L.Rev. p.59. Mr. Batiza could not tie the 11th article to a particular source.

[331] These references do not appear as such in the De La Vergne Volume. Almost all of them, however, can be found in the introduction to the Title XVIII of the Fourth Part of the translation of Las Siete Partidas by Moreau Lislet and Carleton.

even if the text of the code articles was written in the French language. Blondeau, a contemporary of Moreau Lislet, after having undertaken a research of sources of the substantive law of the Code of 1825 laid down in a French text, would not suspect any wrongdoing by Moreau Lislet even though he could, very easily, have been tempted to say so since, as a French jurist, he would have been naturally inclined to relate as much of the Louisiana civil Code as possible to the Code Napoléon!

These examples — as well as others that could be given — are enough to illustrate what we believe was the technique used by Moreau Lislet. Since Spanish law had been declared applicable in the Territory, this law had to be regarded as the actual and immediate source of the dispositions of the Digest whereas the French texts that had to be used by necessity should be considered only as the vehicle, as the "formal" and "litteral" source of these dispositions.

When one tries to put oneself in Moreau Lislet's place and role as he was carrying out his mission, one can only conclude that he had no alternative but to obey the instructions he had received. Not only James Brown, who knew Spanish, was working with him, but Brown, as far as we know, and even though he may not have worked as hard on the Digest of 1808 as Moreau Lislet did, has never been accused of surreptitiously importing French law into the Digest of 1808 or even allowing Moreau Lislet to do so. In addition, when in 1806 Moreau Lislet was appointed to the committee of two to draft the Digest, he undoubtedly must have been conscious of the fact that one day, as a lawyer at least, he would have to handle legal issues and cases based on that very same Digest and that the solutions to be brought to these issues and cases would necessarily have to be found in the provisions he was working on. Could he, then, have decided, all alone, that he could pull a veil over the eyes of an "uneducated" legal community of the time by seizing the opportunity to draft a code based on French law and not on the "Laws in force in the territory"? It is hard to believe that Moreau Lislet, a man of integrity, dedication and high moral values as he demonstrated in his personal life and legal profession, would not have been aware that neither the courts, nor his fellow members of the Bar, Mazureau and Livingston in particular, would have been inclined to listen to his arguments or attach any credit to his word if he had failed them, if he had cheated on them. Had Moreau Lislet violated the trust placed in him in 1806, he would quite obviously have banned himself. And why would he have undertaken, on his own, the translation of Las Siete Partidas in French first and in English subsequently, if there was to be no connection, no "rapport", between the Digest of 1808 and the Spanish law?

It is hard to accept even the slightest suggestion that a man of such an excellent reputation and exemplary life could have committed "fraud". His contemporaries, whether trained in the law or not, did not think so and legal scholars who, in the 19th and 20th centuries, were to evaluate his contribution to the science of codified law, would not think so either.

CHAPTER II

19TH AND 20TH CENTURIES VARIATIONS ON THE SAME THEME.

We have attempted to gather here as many as possible of the opinions and evaluations expressed either by contemporaries of Moreau Lislet or by scholars who, at a later time, became interested in his work and who, in their writings, addressed, either directly or indirectly, the crucial issue of the actual or presumed sources of the Digest of 1808.

These opinions will be presented as they were expressed originally by their authors. We will abstain from bearing any judgment or making any commentary that would inevitably lead to a search and an evaluation of the subjective reasons which may have inspired an author in expressing a "partisan", because personal, opinion. Such is not the scope of this study at this time. Therefore, we will transcribe these opinions as faithfully and honestly as can be done in order to illustrate the fact that the current controversy on the actual sources of the Digest of 1808 is as old as the Digest itself. The reader will be the only ultimate judge, convinced one way or the other by the evidence brought forth.

SECTION I

MOREAU LISLET AND THE SPANISH SOURCES OF THE DIGEST OF 1808: 19TH CENTURY SPANISH VARIATIONS.[332]

The supplement to issue 2077 of the Louisiana Courier of Wednesday, January 3rd, 1821, includes a very instructive report of a session of the House of Representatives. The following excerpt has been selected for its relevance:

"The report of the committee to whom had been referred the letter of the translators of the Partidas, was then taken up and read in the following words:

Your committee to whom had been referred the joint letters of Messrs Moreau Lislet and H. Carlton, translators of such part of the Partidas as are considered to have the force of law in this state, by virtue of an article passed for that purpose, approved on the 3rd of March 1819, beg leave to report that in the opinion of your committee the said translators have discharged the duties imposed by said act with zeal and ability,....

Your committee are of opinion that the labors of the translators in this invaluable work have been greater than they first imagined; that the original Partidas is composed in about 3,000 folio pages and written in an antiquated dialect, alike unconnected with the living and dead languages,...; that they have bestowed more labour than necessary to comply with the provisions of the act, inasmuch as each title of the work is

---

[332] These opinions are presented in chronological order.

preceded by a list of the titles of the Roman and Spanish laws, and the civil code of this state, relative to the subject of which it treats, thereby adding to the utility of the work, and rendering it more complete and satisfactory, and which must have required uncommon research in traversing the immense codes of Roman jurisprudence and pausing the less expanded but more complete abstract provisions of our civil code...."

In the Louisiana Courier of Wednesday, May 16, 1821, the author of an editorial, signed "A LOUISIANIAN", had this to say about a recent decision of the Louisiana Supreme Court:

"The Supreme Court of this State, has recently pronounced a decision, by which all those who are incapable of passing an examination in the English language, are excluded from the profession of the law. The style of this Anglo-Gallican Legislative regulation, and the violation of the rules of grammar and sound reasoning which characterise it, sufficiently designate the author. None but a man desirous of effacing all trace of his own origin, could have entertained the idea of a regulation so outrageous to the ancient population of Louisiana....

But what excuse can they pretend to allege, when entertaining the most exaggerated idea of their own powers, they arrogate to themselves an authority purely legislative? In this regulation they declare that the English language is the *legal language* of the state of Louisiana. Have they duly reflected on the consequences of so palpable an error? When the law says *white*, the Supreme Court may decide that it says *black*, but their power extends no further; and it is vain that they undertake to change the immutable nature of things. The *political language* of Louisiana is unquestionably the English language, but its *legal language*, that is, the language in which the legislative will is expressed, is in the first place the

Spanish, and second the French, in which the intelligible part of the civil code is written, and it is the knowledge of these two languages which the legislature, and not the supreme court (who are not authorised) might reasonably require in a lawyer...."[333]

The controversy went on for several months in 1821 as illustrated by the following excerpts:

"Who can predict where the torrent may stop? Who can vouch that the usages and habits of the ancient population shall· not be forever eradicated?...It is only from the Representatives of the people, that we ought to expect a remedy to so great an evil. Let us therefore hope, that the next legislature will put an end to those odious machinations, and will allow both populations peaceably to enjoy advantages which a paternal government grants to all its children....What? Shall we not be allowed to raise our voice against the most tyrannical and arbitrary acts, without finding in the way, men. so unreasonable as to charge us with throwing the brands of discord into society? What? to say that the Supreme Court have transgressed their powers, and to call the attention of the

---

[333] Louisiana Courier, New-Orleans, Wednesday, MAY 16, 1821. We cannot but call the attention of the reader to that section of this editorial where the LOUISIANIAN states that the *Spanish language is the language "in which the legislative will is expressed"* whereas *the French language is the language "in which the intelligible part of the civil code is written".* A definite distinction was made, then, between the language of the intent of the legislator, the Spanish language as the language of the substantive law, and the language of the formal or outward expression of that intent, the French language. This distinction made in 1821 is, we believe, reminiscent of the theory espoused by Professor Pascal!

Legislature upon a measure, which, if it is not modified, must overthrow the existing order of things, and disturb the peace and good harmony which ought to exist among the two populations, it is to conspire against the state? it is to wring the alarm bell, it is to call a civil war, it is to give the signal of hostilities between the Americans and the French? What a curious reasoning indeed! and what an excess of good faith...."[334]

"The writer in the Advertiser, to whom we answered in our last, about the remarks to which the *celebrated regulation* of the Supreme Court has given rise, is truly tenacious in *his* opinion. He wants, at all events to show that we were wrong...; he is endeavoring to make it appear that we have committed an outrage against the *whole of America* by reproaching (as he pretends) to the judges of the Supreme Court, some time their *low origin* and some time *the land that gave them birth*...."[335]

"Vexatus toties, nunquamne reponam?"

"Let us start from a principle which is the basis of the eternal justice of a democratic republic. Our mandataries are nothing but the organs of the law. Whenever they speak by themselves they cease to be anything; for, although we must respect the autorities, we owe obedience to law alone;...

In the first instance, I think that the supreme court in making that regulation have usurped the powers of the

---

[334] Louisiana Courier, New-Orleans, Monday, May 21, 1821.

[335] Louisiana Courier, New-Orleans, Wednesday, May 23, 1821.

legislature....[I]f an attorney who is unacquainted with the English language (which in this state is nothing but the instrument of conversation) cannot give advice to his fellow citizens, how can a judge who is unacquainted with the French, the Spanish and the Latin languages which are the languages of our jurisprudence, be able to decide in the controversies arising among his fellow citizens? How will he be able to understand the argument, the law, and the doctrine, which must be cited in those languages? It is true, a few of the laws of the *Partidas* have been translated into English — but is ever a translation as good as the original? And does that small number of translations of our laws, suffice to give a thorough knowledge of our jurisprudence? Neither the French laws, which come next to the Spanish, nor the works of the Spanish and French law writers are translated. There is no translation of the Roman civil laws nor of its commentators. I now ask, how could a judge who is ignorant of those languages, understand the spirit of our fundamental laws?...The French, like the Spanish, are the languages of our law and of our doctrine. The English is nearly useless to us as *lingua juris*, since we are regulated by no code exclusively written in English, and we need not consult nor cite the authors who have written in that language, except it be for mere parade or through pedantry, since we find in abundance all the laws we stand in need of, in the three codes which are in force among us, as well as in the learned authors who have written in those three languages, whereby we are dispensed to have recourse to the monster called the common law, and to its able commentators...."[336]

On July 25, 1821, the Louisiana Courier published a very elaborate and somewhat scholarly piece entitled "PROMISSA ADIMPLETO". It read, in part, as follows:

---

[336] Louisiana Courier, Friday, June 1, 1821.

"...To judge one suit by another would be the height of absurdity and ignorance. *Illud in primis observare debet Judex, ne aliter judicat quam legibus, constitutionibus aut Moribus. (de. offic. jud. inst.).* By so doing we should become a kind of casuists in law, even more contemptible than the casuists in morals. I know that such is the manner of judging according to the common law, and that the common law is followed in other states of the Union; let it be followed elsewhere as much as they please, but it shall never be our law here, and we shall always repeat to our judges what was said to Pilate nineteen centuries ago: *"Nos legem habemus & secundum legem nostram judicare debes."*

There is a fact unfortunately too true, it is that the trash known by the name of *Martin's Reports*, has infected our bar to such a point, that all our young lawyers and even some of our old practitioners, have their heads full of nothing else but those little tales of suits, equally insipid and out of place, and that their only occupation is to find some similitude or analogy between the cases reported and those confided to their care. They cite nothing but decisions of the courts of this State or of the courts of Virginia, Pennsylvania, etc.. which they endeavor to adapt to our practice, and which by the bye serves only to form an Harlequin's coat...

I have shown that the legislator alone could, and ought to explain the doubts of the law. Now the question is to know, whether there is actually any doubt. I think that the Supreme Court alone find some or fancy they discover it. The Constitution (General Provisions) says positively that the judicial proceedings shall be in the language in which the constitution of the United States is written, that is to say in english....If we could have suspected so much weakness in [our representatives], we would have chosen individuals, who identifying themselves with our true interest, would have supported it with energy, instead of betraying us, and who, instead of suffering themselves to be deprived of the use of our language, of that language in which we uttered our first accents,...would have declared that no man should be called to public office, unless he could speak French. They would have stipulated as a *sine qua non*, that in order to be a judge, one would be obliged to know the French language, which is the language of the country, and the Spanish which is the language of the laws by which we are governed, for it is more in order, that the parts should yield to the whole, than the whole to its parts....The Spanish government did, at least, religiously respect our habits and our language; it never thought of enacting a law, nor of issuing a decree to deprive us of them...."

The controversy continued into the year 1824 at a time when Moreau Lislet, Edward Livingston and Pierre Derbigny were in the process of drafting the Louisiana Civil Code of 1825. Again in January 1824 the issue of the sources of laws that were in force in Louisiana came up in an editorial in support of Edward Livingston:

"About twenty years ago, Mr. Livingston came to fix his residence among us. He brought with him as a stateman and a jurisconsult, profound knowledge, a mind as vast as liberal, which naturally placed him on the first rank, as he had been in his native place. Too great to be accessible to those national prejudices unworthy of a civilized man, he soon identified himself with the population of Louisiana. Too enlightened, too equitable, to favor any innovation dangerous to that population, altho he might have found in it the means of establishing and increasing his fortune, he seemed to make an abnegation to himself, to sacrifice the fruits of long studies as a lawyer at the school of Blackstone, to become the disciple and the apostle of the civil law which constituted the basis of the laws of *Alfonso the wise*, then exclusively in force in this extensive territory....Mr. Livingston had been hardly fifteen months in New Orleans, when Congress were pleased to form Louisiana into separate territories, and to give us, as a constitution, the ordinance of 1787, which had been framed for a country almost desert to the northwest of Ohio. By that ordinance....Congress gave us a Superior Court, consisting of one single judge,....As if to crown the work, that famous ordinance did contain a clause providing that that Superior Court should exercise a *jurisdiction of Common Laws*....If that clause was put in force, every thing was at an end in our jurisprudence; our ancient laws would have disappeared, and upon their venerable ruins would have been erected a system which none of us was acquainted with, which no where exists in a body of law, and which its warmest advocates themselves do hardly know; and the codes under which the ancient inhabitants of the country had inherited the estates of their fathers and passed all their contracts, would have been annihilated....Livingston, consulting nothing but the interest of his adopted country, setting aside all views of private interest, pleaded during three days the cause of Louisiana....The Superior Court declared itself in his favor, and in so doing, freed us from that inextricable labyrinth of incoherent decisions, scattered in thousands of volumes, and which people have been please to decorate with the pompous name of *Common law*...."[337]

In 1837, Etienne Mazureau, Attorney General and Dean of the New Orleans Bar, extolled the virtues and merits of Georges Mathews who had presided over the Supreme Court of Louisiana. On that occasion Mazureau made some remarks about the primary sources of the Digest of 1808 and the Code of 1825:

---

[337] The Courier, New Orleans, Thursday, January 15, 1824.

"...As early as 1805 the Spanish and Roman laws, written it is true, in languages unfamiliar to several public functionaries, as well as to the greater part of the old and new inhabitants, gave umbrage to persons whose reason, being obscured by national prejudices, repulsed the idea however simple that laws, collected and put together since numerous centuries, might in the nineteenth century be suitable to the administration of civil justice amidst a free people....

The attack was brisk, they made the most heroic efforts to insure victory! But Livingston spoke, at his voice the menacing and thundering work of the new Titans crumbled to its base, and the oracle which then emanated from the mouth of Hon. John B. Prevost swept away the light rubbish and dispersed it.

...persons prone to doubt would probably be much surprised when told that several of the great principles consecrated by our constitutions, had likewise been consecrated by Roman and Spanish law a few hundred years before the immortal Columbus discovered our hemisphere. Open the Roman code of Alfonso the Wise, you will find,...that rule,...'that no law may have retroactive effects.'...

Let us not dissimulate it, we must have master minds, jurists of vast erudition and of rare sagacity, highly enlightened, foreseeing and very wise legislators to make better digests than that of Justinian and better laws than those of Alfonso the Wise....

Our code of 1808, whose co-existence with the ancient laws that were not incompatible was wisely maintained, remained in vigor during almost eighteen years. If, as it must be acknowledged, imperfections were noticeable in it, jurisprudence aided by the enlightenment found in the Roman and Spanish laws had ended by embodying itself into a corps of legal doctrines which, if not perfect, (what work of the human mind can be so), was at least sufficiently complete, suffciently comprehensible to all slightly studious minds, to satisfy in great part the exigencies of reason and justice.

But,...,clamors arose against this same digest, against its insufficiency, and above all, against the necessity under which we still labored of going to sources from which were taken the principles which rule our civil tribunals. They wanted a code comprehensible to all;...They wanted a code covering everything, foreseeing everything, providing for everything, as if a code could ever emanate from man! A new code was made. Less incomplete and in this respect less imperfect than the first. However, it was so far from fulfilling the exigencies of justice that our tribunals were continually obliged to dig into the old compilations of Castilian and Latin laws to find rules that might be applied to cases to which the general rules in that voluminous collection could with difficulty be applied..."[338]

In 1838, the Revue des Deux Mondes published, under the signature of Mignet, a very interesting biography of Edward Livingston who is said "to be known for having participated in the work of the French jurisconsults Moreau Lislet and Derbigny, who gathered in one book the old Louisiana civil laws."[339]

---

[338] Panegyric delivered January 1837 by Etienne Mazureau, Attorney General and Dean of the Bar, Georges Mathews - President of the Supreme Court of Louisiana. 4 Louisiana Historical Quarterly 154-188, 1921.

[339] Livingston, Sa Vie et Ses Travaux, par Mignet, in Revue des Deux Mondes, p.31-53, at 41 (1838). (translated from the French).

Tracing back the first years of the Territorial Government of Louisiana, Mignet wrote the following:

"With the territorial form of government, [Louisiana] adopted the writ of habeas corpus and the jury system, two institutions which accompany the American in any country where he settles, in order to ensure his enjoyment of liberty and justice. But this preliminary law which brought before a jury all civil and criminal facts affecting his property as well as his person, was not sufficient. It remained to decide which body of law would control those facts as well as the procedure that would be followed in a case all the way to the judgment. Was the law of Louisiana to be maintained, a mixture of Roman law, French customary law and Spanish texts? Or was English law to be introduced in Louisiana, with all the uncertainties attached to its precedents, the subtelties of its fictions and the prolixity of its expressions? This was the subject of debates before the Supreme Court. American lawyers pushed for the exclusive adoption of English law in civil and criminal matters. But, following the arguments presented by Mr. Livingston who reminded to the new possessors of the land the dispositions of the treaty according to which Louisiana was to participate fully in all the benefits flowing from belonging to the American Union without losing its own privileges, it was decided that Louisiana would keep its civil laws...."[340]

Charles E. Fenner, who was a Justice of the Louisiana Supreme Court and a passionate defender of the Civil Law, wrote the following in 1887:

"In 1808, the Commission presented its report to the Territory Legislative Assembly, report that was adopted and

---

[340] *Id.* at p.40.

is known as the Code of 1808. This Code preserved former laws in force, except to the extent they were contrary to or incompatible with the Code itself.

Although the Napoleonic Code was promulgated in 1804, at that time when transportation was slow and imperfect, no copy of this code had then reached New Orleans. The drafters of the Code of 1808, however, used the Projet of this work they had in their possession and imported in their report important parts from this projet....

The period from 1803 to 1825, illustrated by the reports of Judge Martin, was the formative era of our jurisprudence. In the beginning of that period, there was a juridical chaos; all things were without form and void. This condition of uncertainty is amusingly described by Mr. Ellery, one of the lawyers in Beauregard vs. Piernas (1 M.293): "The navigation among the Codes and Recopilacion is certainly difficult and dangerous, thick set with points, and abounding in sands and shoals; the path dazzled by the deceitful lights of expositors, and pursued with unskilful pilotage; we might have weathered the Partidas and Recopilacion, we have steered clear of the laws of Madrid and Toro, but is there no risk of striking upon the Fuero Real, or the Fuero Inezga, or being lost on the shoals of the Ordonamiento. Even a Senatus Consultum Velleianum or an unheeded law of Justinian might prove fatal to our voyage...

Although the origin of the laws was Spanish, French was the mother tongue of the people, and Pothier, with his precise and logical method, exercised, in all probability, more ascendancy here than in France....In fact, it has been held (15 L. 112, 1A.456, 2 A.201), that the articles of the Civil Code, derived from the Code of 1808, are to be interpreted by reference to the Spanish laws not repealed by the Code of 1808."[341]

In a series of articles on Louisiana published in 1892, we read:

"It must be remembered, however, that while the Code Napoleon has served as the model of our municipal law, it has not been servilely copied, and that free scope has been given to American inventiveness in adapting it to the requirements of modern times and the genius of free institutions. So, many principles of Spanish law which had proved salutary in their practical operation were retained, and many modifications were introduced suitable to the habits and wants of a progressive people in a new country....

In 1808, very shortly after the organization of the territorial courts, a code was prepared and published, but this consisted merely of an abstract of the Spanish laws then prevailing, with such modifications from the Code Napoleon lately introduced into the territory as seemed compatible with the existing law....We see,...,this singular anomaly in the first series of reports, that while the organic structures and statutory provisions of the law were mainly of Spanish origin, there was a rapid transition to the French modes of criticism and interpretation so that when the new code of 1825 gave legal authority for this transition to the French system by positive statutory enactment, the new jurisprudence founded on the Code Napoleon was so congenial to the spirit of the old,

---

[341] The Genesis and Descent of the System of Civil Law Prevailing in Louisiana, A Lecture by Hon. Charles E. Fenner, 1886.

that it seemed rather its natural and logical evolution than the introduction of a foreign outgrowth.[342]

Parts of the last two opinions reproduced above are somewhat in conflict with respect to the issue of the influence that the Code Napoleon may have had on the Digest of 1808. Yet, they concur on that same single and most important conclusion that Spanish Law was actually the fundamental source of the Digest.

It is proper now to present the opinions of those who have chosen to adopt the opposite theory according to which the sources of the Digest of 1808 are French, not only in form but likewise in substance, rather than Spanish.

SECTION II

MOREAU LISLET AND THE FRENCH SOURCES OF THE DIGEST OF 1808:[343]
19TH CENTURY FRENCH VARIATIONS.

Mr. Batiza, following in the footsteps of a few prominent scholars who preceded him, wrote that "Moreau Lislet adopted the structure, or organization, of the French Code and *projet* as the framework for the Louisiana Code."[344] Professor Pascal

---

[342] Biographical and Historical Memoirs of Louisiana, 3 v., The Goodspeed Publishing Company, 1892, Chapter VIII "Bench and Bar", p.77-101.

[343] The opinions of the different authors will be presented in chronological order.

[344] Preface of volume 3 on the "Sources which had a substantial or partial influence on provisions of the Louisiana

is not at all critical of this broad statement as the evidence is too overwhelming to be challenged. However, these two contemporary scholars are at odds on the importance to be given to the "form" of the law over its "substance" and they reach opposite conclusions as concerns the respective sources of the former and the latter.

Following are a series of positions taken by a number of authors who have supported the theory of the French origin of the Digest of 1808. Some of these opinions, as we shall see, take the position that one can witness an influence of French sources more on the *form* of the Digest of 1808 than on the *substance* of the law therein contained; other authors accept *in toto*, without any qualification or distinction between form and substance, the French origin of the Digest of 1808.

Edward Livingston, one of the co-drafters of the Louisiana Civil Code of 1825, had an extensive correspondence with the Presidents of the United States and in one of his numerous letters to President Jefferson, he wrote:

"You are aware, Sir, that in the year 1808 a civil Code was adopted in that State (Louisiana), founded chiefly on that of Napoleon but very hastily and therefore imperfectly executed..."[345]

Civil Code of 1808: The original texts." Copyright 1974 by Rodolfo Batiza.

[345] "Letters of Livinsgton to Presidents", Padgett, p.20. Letter of March 9, 1825 from Livingston to Jefferson. The same opinion was expressed in a report that Judge Workman addressed to the Louisiana House of Representatives: "Our civil code, erroneous as it confessedly was, has nevertheless been of great utility....Those portions of it which were copied from the Napoleon code, were excellent, as far as they went...." in Sampson's Discourse and correspondence with

Another contemporary of Moreau Lislet, François Xavier Martin,[346] Justice of the Supreme Court of the Territory and author of a History of Louisiana, wrote this about the Digest of 1808:

"The professional gentlemen, who had been appointed in 1805 to prepare a civil and criminal code, Moreau Lislet and Brown, reported "a digest of the civil laws now in force in the territory of Orleans with alterations and amendments adapted to the present form of government." Although the Napoleon code was promulgated in 1804, no copy of it had as yet reached New Orleans; and the gentlemen availed themselves of the projet of that work, the arrangement of which they adopted, and *mutatis mutandis*, literally transcribed a considerable portion of it. Their conduct was certainly praiseworthy; for, although the projet is necessarily much

---

various learned jurists upon the History of the Law, 1826, p.165-166.

[346] "Judge François Xavier Martin was born at Marseilles, in France, March 17, 1762, and died December 11, 1846. He was appointed judge of the highest court of the territory March, 1810, and judge of the supreme court February 1, 1815, where he labored industriously until the organisation of the court under the constitution of 1845, having served as chief justice for many years."(see supra note 11, Bench and Bar, in Biographical and Historical Memoirs of Louisiana, p.83.) See also, A Discourse on the Life, Character, and Writings of the Hon. François Xavier Martin, LL.D., p.17-40, by Henry A. Bullard in Historical Collections of Louisiana embracing translations of many rare and valuable documents relating to the Natural, Civil and Political History of that State compiled with Historical and Biographical notes and an Introduction by B.F. French, Part II, 1850.

more imperfect than the code, it was far superior to anything, that any two individuals could have produced, early enough to answer the expectation of those who employed them....Anterior laws were repealed, so far only, as they were contrary to or irreconcilable with any of the provisions of the new....In practice, the work was used as an incomplete digest of existing statutes, which still retained their empire....The Fuero Viejo, Fuero Juezgo, Partidas, Recopilationes, Leyes de las Indias, Autos Accordados and Royal schedules remained parts of the written law of the territory, when not repealed expressly or by a necessary implication....To explain them, Spanish commentators were consulted and the *corpus juris civilis* and its own commentators were resorted to; and to eke out any deficiency, the lawyers who came from France or Hispaniola read Pothier, d'Aguesseau, Dumoulin, etc.[347]

---

[347] The History of Louisiana, by F.X. Martin with a memoir of the Author by Judge W.W. Howe, 1882. One will notice the ambiguity of the statements by Judge Martin: on the one hand he states that the gentlemen who drafted the digest used the projet of the French code," the arrangement of which they adopted, and *mutatis mutandis*, literally transcribed a considerable portion of it", but, on the other hand, he states also that "certain laws were repealed so far only as they were contrary to or irreconcilable with any of the provisions of the new...". This last statement is followed by a listing of Spanish sources of law in addition to references to Spanish commentators. On the basis of these two statements, Judge Martin could as well be placed in the category of those scholars who supported the Spanish origin of the Digest of 1808.

In 1829, Barbé de Marbois[348] published his "Histoire de la Louisiane et de la cession de cette colonie par la France aux Etats-Unis de l'Amérique Septentrionale" in which he made a brief comment about the influence of the French Civil Code on the Louisiana Code of 1825:

"The laws of Spain, France and the United States have ceased in 1825 to conflict on this land where these three powers have succeeded one another; learned men have undertaken a great work to reconcile them. A Civil Code was adopted and the Code now applicable in France was used to a large extent in its drafting."[349]

The most forceful and unwavering opinion on this matter may have been expressed in 1842 by Gustavus Schmidt:[350]

"The jurisprudence of Louisiana is a mixture of the Roman, French and Spanish law, tinctured with no inconsiderable portion of the common law of England, as

---

[348] Barbé de Marbois (1745-1837), French politician, French consul to the United States, Minister of Finances under Bonaparte and Minister of Justice. [Grand Larousse Encyclopédique, 1960].

[349] Histoire de la Louisiane et de la cession de cette colonie par la France aux Etats-Unis de l'Amérique Septentrionale, par Barbé-Marbois, Paris, 1829, at p.364.

[350] Gustavus Schmidt was a counsellor at law and the editor of the Law Journal which was "devoted exclusively to subjects connected with the science of jurisprudence, including every thing, which has a tendency to illustrate its progress; and to exhibit its present condition." from "To The Public",p.III, The Louisiana Law Journal, volume 1, 1841-1842.

understood and expounded in the sister States of the Union,...[T]he first territorial legislature appointed, in the year 1806, Messrs. James Brown and Moreau Lislet,....These gentlemen, thus appointed to prepare a digest of the laws in force in Louisiana, instead of looking to the Spanish colonial law, and consulting exclusively the *Partidas* and the *Recopilacion de las Indias,* etc, as they surely would have done, had the Spanish law alone been in force, transcribed literally, and incorporated into their Digest large portions of the *projet of the Code Napoleon.*"[351]

However, in a letter dated October 12, 1841, under the title "Were the Laws of France, which governed Louisiana, prior to the cession of the country to Spain, abolished by the Ordinances of O'Reilly?", another legal scholar apparently endorsed by Gustavus Schmidt had this to say:

"...the laws of a country cannot be rooted out so entirely as to leave no vestiges of their existence, and the learned jurists who, in 1806, compiled our old Civil Code, were well apprized of it, and took care to blend, with the Spanish laws, such parts of the French laws, as were consonant with the feelings of the people, and the ancient customs of the territory."[352]

A former Justice of the Supreme Court, Henry A. Bullard, in " A Discourse on The Life and Character of the Hon. François Xavier Martin", referred to the sources of the Digest of 1808 in these terms:

---

[351] The Supreme Court and its Decisions, p.135, in The Louisiana Law Journal Edited by Gustavus Schmidt, v. 1 No. 4 April 1842.

[352] *See* supra note 87, at p.24-25.

"Seven years before the period of which I am speaking, Louisiana was a Spanish Province; governed by a system of laws written in a language understood by only a small part of the population, and which had been forced upon the people at the point of the bayonet by O'Reilly, and which superceded the ancient French laws by which the Province had been previously governed.... In 1808 was promulgated the Digest of the Civil Laws then in force in Louisiana, commonly called the Old Code. This compilation was little more than a mutilated copy of the Code Napoleon. But instead of abrogating all previous laws and creating an entire system, as had been done in France by the Code Napoleon, our code was considered as a declaratory law, repealing such only as were repugnant to it, and leaving partially in force the voluminous codes of Spain."[353]

Henry J. Leovy, a jurist and owner as well as publisher of the New Orleans Delta, wrote the following in 1851:

"The first territorial legislature met in 1806, and one of its acts was the appointing of Messrs. Brown and Lislet, two members of the bar, a committee to prepare a *Digest* of the laws then in existence in the territory. Instead of complying with their orders and digesting the laws in existence, these gentlemen made a code based principally on the *Code Napoleon*. This was adopted by the Legislature, and is now known as the "old Civil Code of 1808." This code did not repeal former laws; "the old Civil Code repealed such parts of the Civil law as were contrary to or incompatible with it." It

---

[353] A Discourse On The Life And Character of the Hon. François Xavier Martin, Late Senior Judge of the Supreme Court of the State of Lousiana, Pronounced at the Request of the Bar of New-Orleans, by Henry Bullard, New-Orleans, 1847 at p 11.

did not contain many and important provisions of the Spanish law nor any rules of judicial proceedings. It was therefore decided that the Spanish laws were to be considered as untouched when the Digest or Civil Code did not reach them. The legislature, therefore, in 1819 ordered the publication of such parts of the *Partidas* as were still in force."[354]

In 1856, Antoine de Saint-Joseph published his second edition of "Concordance Between Foreign Civil Codes And The Code Napoleon". In his introduction to the Louisiana Civil Code of 1825, he wrote the following:

"Louisiana is the only State in North America to have undertaken to coordinate its customs and its laws so as to make a regular Civil code. Before 1824, it was governed by Spanish laws, the custom of Paris and by a large number of statutes of the United States.

In 1824, the Sixth Louisiana Legislature put an end to this confusion of such voluminous and contradictory laws by voting the adoption of a Civil Code comprised of 3522 articles for which ours has largely been the model...."[355]

---

[354] Louisiana and her Laws, by Henry J. Leovy, in The Louisiana Book Selections from the Literature of the State, Thomas M'Caleb, 1894, at p. 8-9.

[355] Antoine de Saint-Joseph, Concordance entre les Codes Civils étrangers et le Code Napoléon, 2e ed. 1856, T.2 p.459. Could that statement be interpreted to mean that the author acknowledges the fact that before 1824, therefore under the era of the Digest of 1808, the law was based on the Spanish laws, the Custom of Paris,...?

SECTION III

20TH CENTURY VARIATIONS ON THE SAME THEME

Among the many of our contemporary scholars and legal writers[356] who have written in this century on the enigma

---

[356] *See*, John H. Tucker, Bench and Bar, Source Books of Louisiana Law, 6 Tul. L. Rev. 280 et seq.(1931). This author quotes from Saunder's 2d ed. of the Louisiana civil code of 1870:"(Moreau Lislet and Brown) either did not understand that their mission was to compile the Spanish laws, or else they assumed that the French laws were substantially the same as the Spanish laws, or they may have believed that, in fact, no one system of laws was definitely the law of the colony, and, as they found already prepared a Code of French laws which did not seem to differ much form the laws in common use, they proceeded to make such alterations and modifications in this Code as would, in their opinion, adapt it for use in Louisiana."-- See, Ben Robertson Miller, The Louisiana Judiciary, 1932.— In the New Orleans Morning Tribune, The Item Tribune, New Orleans Sunday May 1, 1932, one can read on p.20: "Seated in his law library at 1124 Royal Street, HENRY L. GARLAND, veteran attorney, is shown reading from an original copy of the Code Napoleon of France, which belonged to Moreau Lislet 127 years ago and which he believes was used by Lislet and James Brown in their compilation of the first Louisiana Code which was enacted into law by the legislature of 1808. Legend says that the original Code Napoleon was not used in the compilation of the Louisiana law." —In the Times Picayune Sunday May 1, 1932, p.25, under the heading: "Moreau Lislet had code at hand as model, old tome indicates" one can read: "It has been supposed generally that when the Louisiana civil code of 1808

of the actual sources of the Old Civil Code of 1808, we will quote from only two of them: they were Judge Hood and Professor Dainow. They will be considered, then, as the advocates and representatives of the school of thought which has argued and still supports the view that the Digest of 1808 was French in its sources.[357]

---

was compiled by Moreau Lislet with the assistance of James Brown, they had as their model not the original Code Napoleon, but only a project of that code....Mr Garland's book is the first real evidence that has been produced to show that Moreau Lislet did have a copy of the code." This statement is far from being very convincing; indeed, nothing in the article can be taken as establishing beyond any doubt that Moreau Lislet had the French code in his possession before 1808 although it is a fact that he had this code in his library at the time of his death in 1832. We have not been able to find any evidence that Moreau Lislet had the French code in front of him when he drafted the Digest of 1808.— See also Mitchell Franklin, Eighteenth Brumaire in Louisiana, XVI Tul. L. Rev. 514-561, (1942); — Joseph T. Hatfield, William Clairborne: Jeffersonian Centurion In The American Southwest, The USL History Series, 1976.

[357] Beside Judge Hood and Professor Dainow, two legal scholars will be identified here as supporting strongly the influence of French law on the Digest of 1808. In "Tradition and Technique of Codification in the Modern World: The Louisiana Experience", 25 La. L. Rev. 698-719, at p.706 (1965), John H. Tucker, Jr. wrote: " The Code of 1808 was not based on Spanish law, but it was adopted with the title "A Digest of the Civil Laws....". The jurisconsults appointed to prepare this Digest chose as their model the *Code Napoleon* of France, although Spanish law prevailed. Later, the Supreme Court of Louisiana held that Spanish law still prevailed unless

This doctrine, it will be noticed, qualifies very narrowly the influence and authority of the French texts that are claimed to have been used as models by the drafters of the Louisiana Code of 1808. The fluid, almost vacillating, position of this doctrine could, in the end, easily lead one to the temptation of actually including these authors among those of the opposite school, those who have argued, and continue to argue today with Professor Pascal, that the fundamental sources of the Old

---

it had been repealed expressly or by necessary implication by the Digest (Code of 1808). This led to the redaction of the Code of 1825, and upon its adoption all former Spanish law was repealed."-- Writing on the specific topic of the law of marriage contracts, Professor Hans W. Baade made these assertions:"This brings us to the crucial question of the intent in 1808 of the redactors and the Legislative Council of Orleans Territory. The historical context shows the chief aim was to consolidate the civil law of the territory into code form to forestall the infiltration of the common law. This objective had to be achieved speedily, in an increasingly unfavorable environment....The French *Code Civil* of 1804 had to serve as the basic text and was generally acceptable to the extent it reflected or harmoniously advanced the "living law" of the Territory, the Custom of Paris. Yet this borrowing could not be publicly acknowledged. On the contrary, every effort had to be made to find support for the various provisions of the Code of 1808 in *enacted* Castilian law formally applicable in Spanish *Luisiana* after 1769, and as yet not formally repealed. It now appears that the furnishing of such a "positive law alibi" was the primary purpose of the source notes to the 1808 codification, which Moreau Lislet prepared for publication in 1814, and which were recently discovered by Professor Pascal." 53 Tul. L. Rev. 3-92, at p. 83-84, (1978). These assertions by Professor Hans Baade are just that: assertions without support.

Code of 1808 are to be found in the Roman law and, more particularly, in the Spanish law.

Judge Hood was very much interested in the history of Louisiana Law and, in one of his numerous articles, he expressed his views as follows:

"The Civil Code prepared by Brown and Moreau Lislet, however, was not based on the Spanish law, as the Legislature had directed, but was based instead on the then newly adopted French Code, the Code Napoleon. No satisfactory explanation has been offered to this date as to why this was done. *It is probable, however, that these two attorneys and the Legislature had a high regard for the codification experience in France, not only as to form but also as to content, since both the French and the Spanish systems had many common sources in Roman law; for that reason they may have used the Code Napoleon as a model without any intent to displace the Spanish law. This theory is supported by the fact that there are many differences between the Code Napoleon and the Louisiana Code of 1808, due largely to the fact that there were incorporated into the Louisiana Code a substantial number of Spanish laws, which had not been included in the French Code.*"[358]

Judge Hood gives a very plausible explanation of the methodology used by James Brown and Louis Moreau Lislet, even though we cannot find any convincing "legal" evidence of the argument he wishes to make. All in all, for Judge Hood, the adoption of the French code, not only as to its form but also as to its "content", is perfectly justified. Indeed, the Code Napoleon, or French Code, was the expression of the

---

[358] John T. Hood, Jr., The History and Development of the Louisiana Civil Code, 33 Tul. L. Rev. 7 at p.14 (1958). Emphasis ours.

most recent technique of codification and its mediate sources found in Roman Law were the same, to a large extent, as the sources of Spanish law. The French Code was then a perfectly appropriate go-between, given the circumstances prevailing in Louisiana. Still, the existence of typically Spanish dispositions in the code of 1808, is evidence that the drafters of the Digest had obviously no intention at all to repudiate Spanish law in its entirety and to ignore intentionally the specific instructions they had been given.

It appears to us that we would not betray Judge Hood's viewpoint if we venture to argue that Judge Hood would be more a supporter of the theory "form may conceal the substance", than an advocate of the theory "form reveals the substance".

Such was also, we believe, the conclusion reached by our colleague, Joseph Dainow. In an historical introduction to his second edition of the Louisiana civil code, Joseph Dainow wrote the following:

"One of the questions to which there has not been a conclusive answer is "Why did the 1808 code follow so closely and borrow so much from the French law, since the existing civil laws were Spanish?" There has also been the secondary question: "Which French materials were the ones actually used?" In view of the fact that there is not available, neither from the commissioners nor from anyone else, a written record of the reasons for the use of French basic materials, the answer later attributed to these questions must necessarily include a degree of conjecture....The use of the French code as a model and as a source could not have been intended as the displacement of Spanish law by French law. Considering their close relationship as the two most prominent and well developed systems of civil law, as well as the extensive area of common sources in Roman law, and the actual similarity of the textual provisions, it was only to be expected that the Louisiana jurists would take advantage and make use of the French unification experience instead of attempting the impossible task of making one order of their own out of the multiplicity and chaos which existed....Not to be overlooked at this point is the fact that the Louisiana Civil Code of 1808 contained a substantial amount of laws incorporated directly from Spanish sources....Given that neither the drafting commissioners, nor any other person have left archives or written notes explaining the reasons for the use of French documents, the answers given at a later time must necessarily present an element of speculation. The use of the French Code, as a model and as a source, could not have expressed the intent to substitute French law to Spanish law. Being that these two very close legal systems were the most advanced and remarkable of the Civil Law, considering the vast scope of their common sources in Roman Law and the true similarity of their dispositions, one could not have expected anything else but that the two Louisiana jurists took advantage of and used the French experience of the unification, instead of undertaking the impossible task of creating a unique system that would be their own, based on the multiple systems and the chaos then existing."[359]

---

[359] Civil Code of Louisiana, Revision of 1870 with Amendments to 1960, Second Edition, by Joseph Dainow, West Publishing Co. 1961. See, A System of Penal Law for the State of Louisiana, Edward Livingston, the Legal Classics Library 1991. In an Introduction, Professor Thomas G. Barnes writes: "While the drafters of both the 1808 *Digest* and 1825 *Civil Code* preferred the French version of Civil Law rules... the *Projet* of 1800 that led to the 1804 French *Code Civil,* and the *Code Civil* (Napoleon) itself, so many of the specific rules in effect before the purchase were common to both French and Spanish Civil Law that precise attribution becomes Trivial Pursuit. Clearly the Louisiana Civil Code was (and is) not an English translation of the "Code Napoleon," contrary to a very widely held misconception." at p. 18 - 19.

This opinion seems to us the wisest and the closest to the historical facts, under the condition, however, that the word "source" as used by Joseph Dainow be given the qualification retained by this author, and in our opinion, by Moreau Lislet himself. This qualification is that if the Digest of 1808 has its apparent sources in the French Codes and other French texts, these sources are only *indirect* because it was not the intention of the drafters, Louis Moreau Lislet and James Brown, to substitute French law for Spanish law, the *mediate* source of the dispositions of the Digest of 1808.

CHAPTER III

THE DIGEST OF 1808 AND THE COURTS

A short presentation and some brief comments will be made here of a few cases heard by the Superior Court of the Territory of Orleans between the years 1809 and 1812. The purpose of this survey is two-fold: first, to ascertain whether the legal issues raised before the Court were considered and decided according to the provisions of the Digest which had just been promulgated and, second, whether, beyond these provisions which had just become positive sources of law, the court had embarked upon an examination of the original sources of law which predated the Digest and had served as the actual sources of the applicable provisions of the Digest.

"In 1812 the Territory of Orleans adopted a constitution... [and] on April 8, 1812, Congress admitted it to the Union as the State of Louisiana."[360] As a consequence of these two landmark events it will be necessary to study some additional court decisions handed down between 1812 and the early eighteen twenties to find out if statehood had altered, to some extent or not at all, the legal scholarship of the Louisiana judges and the practicing attorneys. Were they concerned with the necessity to establish a relationship between the provisions of the Digest and their actual sources? We shall see that the historical and legal analysis applied by the Louisiana courts was remarkably consistent during the years 1808 to 1823 and that the courts themselves held that the Digest of 1808 had its actual sources in Spanish and Roman law.

---

[360] Richard H. Kilbourne, Jr. "A History of the Louisiana Civil Code, The Formative Years, 1803-1839", 1987 at p.61.

SECTION 1

THE DIGEST OF 1808 AND THE SUPERIOR COURT OF THE TERRITORY OF ORLEANS: 1808-1812.

As Richard H. Kilbourne very wisely stated, "[T]he extent to which the Territorial Superior Court followed the rules stated in the Digest cannot be determined with certainty because of the brevity of the period between the enactment of the Digest and the admission of the territory to statehood,..".[361] Nevertheless, five cases decided during this brief period of time may be singled out and used to illustrate the purpose of this study. For each case, a succinct diagram under the form of columns listing the sources of law referred to by the parties and the court will be made in an attempt to compare them with those sources which Professor Batiza has stated and "identified" as being the "actual" sources of the Digest. Lastly, all these sources will be compared to the sources which Moreau-Lislet himself, in his own handwriting, listed in a copy of the Digest of 1808 which came to be known as "The de la Vergne volume".

A.

Dewees v. Morgan, Fall Term 1809, 1 Mart.(O.S.) 1.

The issue in this case was one of redhibition following the sale of a slave who was carrying a disease.

Sources of law cited:

---

[361] *Id.* at p.61.

Plaintiff	*Defendant*
BROWN, ATTORNEY	HENNEN, ATTORNEY
Digest p. 358 art. 80	Domat,(Justinian):1,T.2,S.7
Partida L.64,65,T.5,P.5	Partida 5, T.5,L.23
Pand. L.21,T.1,L.4,§6	
LEWIS, Judge	*BATIZA*
Digest, 358, art. 71,72,73.	French Projet, art. LXVI,LXVII,LXVIII
	Code Napoleon, art. 1645,1646,1647.

MOREAU LISLET's Notes to the DIGEST of 1808
Domat, Pothier, Partida 5

COMMENT: One will notice, on the one hand, the similarity of the sources of law cited by the attorneys for the parties, one such attorney being James Brown, himself a co-drafter of the Digest, and the sources or references cited by Moreau Lislet in his handwritten annotations to the Digest. There is, on the other hand, a definite discrepancy with the sources cited by Professor Batiza who is the only one to refer to the French Projet and the Code Napoléon. It is most relevant, and instructive at the same time, to point out here that **three contemporaries** of the Digest, all members of the legal profession at that time, agreed on finding the law applicable to the case in the same **Spanish** sources, in addition to Roman law referred to either directly or through Domat's Treatise on the Civil Laws in their Natural Order. None of these attorneys cited an exclusively French source of law. Is it not revealing that two attorneys, one of them a co-drafter of the Code of 1808, although pitted one against the other, agreed nevertheless on finding the actual sources of the law of their case in the same sources which happen to have been cited by Moreau Lislet as having a relationship with the articles of the Digest?

B.

Caisergues v. Dujarreau, Fll Term, 1809, 1 Mart.(O.S.) 7.

The issue in this case was one of the lawful amount of interest payable under the law.

Sources of law cited:

Plaintiff	*Defendant*
ALEXANDER, ATTORNEY.	MAZUREAU, ATTORNEY.
Recopilacion de las leyes	Febrero, Partida, Recopilacion de Castilla
LEWIS, Judge	*BATIZA*
Laws of Spain	Projet year 8, Code Napoléon.

MOREAU LISLET's Notes to the DIGEST of 1808
Recopilacion, Domat, Febrero, Pothier

COMMENT: One will have noticed, again, the similarity, not to say the identity, between the **Spanish sources** cited by the two attorneys, Mazureau most specifically since he was a very prominent citizen, a **French speaking attorney** and a leader of the Bar, and the same Spanish sources of law referred to by the Court in an opinion written by an **English speaking judge**. On the other hand, Professor Batiza gives only two French sources of law as the law of the case. Lastly, it is worth pointing out, again, that the sources **listed** by Moreau Lislet match those cited by the attorneys and the court. As far as the contemporaries of the Digest of 1808 are concerned, they all agree!

C.

Debon v. Bache, Fall Term 1810, 1 Mart.(O.S.) 100.
Spring Term 1811, 1 Mart.(O.S.) 240.

In this particular case the issue was one of an insolvent debtor who had given a preference to one of his creditors over his other creditors.

Sources of law cited:

Plaintiff	*Defendant*
ELLERY, ATTORNEY	ALEXANDER, ATTORNEY.
Ordinance of Bilboa	Ordinance of Bilboa
	Recopilacion de las leyes de Castille, tit.5, ley 19.
	Curia Phil. lib.2, chap.9.
The Court	*BATIZA*
Spanish authorities cited in support of plaintiff's	Projet art.LXI Code Napoleon, opinion. art.1166,1167

MOREAU LISLET
Pothier.

COMMENT: To the extent that the Digest of 1808 did not include an express provision which could have been relied upon by the Court, Spanish law controlled as the law in force in the Territory in 1803. The court, being unable to cite a specific article of the Digest, relied on Spanish law as did the two attorneys for the parties. In his annotated version of the Digest of 1808, Moreau Lislet referred to Pothier "on Obligations" to the extent that Pothier offerred some comments on this very topic.

D.

Daublin v. Mayor &c. of New Orleans, Fall Term, 1810, 1 Mart.(O.S.) 185.

In this case the issue was one of the authority of the city's rights to tear down a building.

Sources of law cited:

Plaintiff
MAZUREAU & PAILLETTE, ATTORNEYS
Laws of Spain
Leyes del Ordonamiente Real
Recopilacion de Castille

Defendant
DUNCAN & MOREAU, ATTORNEYS
Partida 3, lib.23.

MARTIN, JUDGE.
-Pothier
-Partida 3
-Roman law, Dig.43, 10.

COMMENT: The Digest of 1808 was not at issue in this case and, therefore, no comparison can be made between the selection of the relevant sources of law by Professor Batiza on the one hand, and Moreau Lislet on the other hand. We must point out, however, that three most prominent jurists (Moreau Lislet, Mazureau and Judge François Xavier Martin) were involved in the above-cited case and that all three of them were, undoubtedly, very familiar with the history of Louisiana and Louisiana law in particular. In the above cited case these same jurists did not hesitate to rely on Spanish law as the actual source of law applicable to the issue. According to them, Spanish law and Roman law were the legal systems controlling in Lousiana before the Digest of 1808 as well as beyond that date whenever there did not exist any specific legislation to the contrary.

E.

Hayes v. Berwick, Spring Term 1812, 2 Mart.(O.S.) 138.

The issue was raised by the plaintiff seeking the opening of her husband's succession on account of his absence for some twenty years.

Sources of law cited:

Plaintiff	*Defendant*
BALDWIN, ATTORNEY	PORTER, ATTORNEY.
No retroactivity of Code	Civil Code 16, art.9; 17, art.19.
THE COURT	BATIZA
Civil Code or Digest	French Civil Code, art.115, 120-129
French authors	French Projet p.31 art.9
Roman law	

MOREAU LISLET's Notes to the DIGEST of 1808
-Pothier, successions
-Partida 3 t.14 l.14.
-Feb. 2, Liv.3

COMMENT: Professor Batiza is the only one to cite the French Projet and the French civil Code as sources of the relevant articles of the Louisiana Digest of 1808. Actually, an analysis of the **actual** sources of the French Projet and the French civil Code articles cited by Professor Batiza, would reveal that the **actual** source of the articles of the Projet and the civil Code was the French jurist Pothier in his treatise "on successions, ch.3, S.1." This treatise is one of the three sources cited by Moreau Lislet as being a source of the corresponding articles of the Digest, the other two sources listed being Spanish. One could then make the legitimate comment that the articles of both the French Projet and the French civil Code should only be considered as **indirect and**

242

formal sources whereas the actual substantive source of law existing behind these articles was, in fact, Pothier as cited by Moreau Lislet. Strangely enough, Professor Batiza fails to identify Pothier as being the source of the articles of the French Projet as well as of the French civil code articles in this particular instance!

SECTION 2

THE SOURCES OF THE DIGEST OF 1808 AND THE SUPREME COURT OF THE STATE OF LOUISIANA: 1812-1823.

"In 1812 the Territory of Orleans adopted a constitution that embodied the essential institutions of Jeffersonian democracy....The indigenous laws of the area had survived the territorial period more or less untouched, and the Digest of 1808 had no doubt helped to substantiate and preserve the influence of the civil law in Louisiana's legal system....Once Louisiana became a state it was free to develop its legal system in any way it saw fit; so statehood opened up vast possibilities for enrichment of the legal system.[...]; the post-1812 decisions of the new Louisiana Supreme Court demonstrate that the authoritativeness of the Digest tended to diminish in the decade after statehood."[362]

Although the years between 1812 and 1825 do, indeed, reveal that the Digest of 1808 lost some of its authority as a result of a concurrence of events which led to its subsequent

---

[362] A History of the Louisiana Civil Code, the Formative Years, 1803-1839, by Richard Holcombe Kilbourne, Jr. The Publications Institute, Paul M. Hebert Law Center, LSU, May 1987, at p.61 et seq.

replacement by the Louisiana Civil Code of 1825[363], the Digest remained nevertheless the primary legislative source of law to be relied upon by the Supreme Court in solving legal issues raised within the purview of the articles of the Digest. Therefore, the questions concerning the actual sources of this Digest should have remained the same after the Territory of Orleans became a state of the Union and until the Digest gave way to the Civil Code of 1825[364]. From 1812 onward, it will appear that the Court manifested a tendency to make an even greater use of the Spanish sources of law as the Digest's role and purpose of providing an inventory of formal and positive written rules of law become more and more restricted. The Court also showed a propensity to look more and more beyond the French text of the provisions of the Digest.

A survey of a few important and illustrative cases handed down by the Supreme Court after 1812 will demonstrate this trend and, at the same time, buttress the theory that the Spanish and Roman laws were the substantive law of the land in 1806-1808 during these crucial years in the formation of Louisiana law. The Supreme Court will exhibit a definite inclination to place the same Digest of 1808 in the wider and wider realm of Spanish law by resorting to additional Spanish, and not French, sources of law considered not in conflict with the provisions of the Digest.

---

[363] Id. at p.62 and 63.

[364] Act of April 12, 1824 promulgating the Civil Code of 1825.

A.

Le Breton v. Nouchet, June Term, 1813, 3 Mart. (O.S.) 60.

The point of law raised in this case concerned the validity of a contract of marriage: was the law applicable that of the domicile, lex fori, or was it the law of the place, lex loci, of the celebration of the marriage?. Although not referred to by the Court, at issue was the application of article 10 of the Preliminary Title of the Digest. One most interesting aspect of this case is that it brought one against the other the two most prominent lawyers of the time, Edward Livingston and Louis Moreau-Lislet, who were to joint forces later on to draft the Civil Code of 1825.

Sources of law cited:

Plaintiff, mother of deceased wife.	Defendant, husband.
MOREAU LISLET, ATTORNEY Partida 4, tit.11, 1.24. Gregorio Lopez	LIVINGSTON, ATTORNEY 4 Part. tit.11, 1.24. Commentary by Gregorio Lopez Las Leyes de Toro, 626, n.75.
The Court. Law of nations L.24, T.11, P.4. L.15, T.14, P.3.	*BATIZA* French Projet, art. VI.

MOREAU LISLET's Notes to the DIGEST OF 1808
L.15, t.14, part.3
L.24, t.11, part.4. No 289.
Ch.1.V.1. p.243. Feb.Cont.

Comment: Professor Batiza, in citing the French Projet as the source of article 10 of the Preliminary Title of the Digest, stands alone against the two legal giants who "lived" the law of their days and who, both, rely on the Siete Partidas to further explain the legal meaning and scope of application of that article 10. Most important also is the fact that Moreau-Lislet is "vindicated" by the Supreme Court decision since the Court sided with him in turning to Spanish law, and not to the French Projet, in finding in the Spanish law the source of article 10 of the Preliminary Title of the Digest. It is worth to quote here from the Supreme Court opinion:" It is necessary to enquire...whether the special provision of the Spanish statute, which directs, that the customs of the place where a marriage has been contracted, shall govern the effects of such marriage, is applicable to the present case....There is, indeed, such a provision in the 24th law of the 11th title of the 4th partida; but the Court is of opinion, that it is not applicable to this case. That provision is evidently intended to have effect only within the dominions of Spain... Were it not so, it would be at war with the 15th law of the 14th title of the 3d partida, which expressly forbids the Spanish tribunals to recognise any authority in the foreign laws cited before them, except as to controversies arising between foreigners upon contracts by them made abroad...."[365] Moreau-Lislet was to win this case against Livingston!.

B.

Pizerot et al. v. Meuillon's Heirs, 3 Mart.(O.S.) 97, 1813.

Several issues bearing on Spanish law were raised in this case. Two were particularly interesting. One concerned "the

---

[365] Le Breton v. Nouchet, 3 Mart.(O.S.) 60, at 71 and 72, 1813.

necessity of compliance with the solemnities required for a renunciation of a testamentary bequest, and the other concerning whether upon the death of a spouse the community of acquets and gains formerly existing between the spouses might continue between the surviving spouse and the heirs of the deceased."[366]

Plaintiffs,

LIVINGSTON, ATTORNEY
Numerous Spanish sources
of law
cited: ex: Febrero, Matienzo,
Velasco, Azevedo, Partidas,
Nueva Recopilacion,...
Also: Pothier, Custom
of Orleans.

Defendants,

MAZUREAU, ATTORNEY
Numerous Spanish sources
of law
cited: ex: Rodriguez,
Partidas, Febrero de
Juicios, Rodriguez...
Also: Domat

The Court
Laws of the Partidas, Fuero real,
Azevedo, Febrero, Laws de Toro...

Comment: On the above two issues the Court gave no reference to articles of the Digest. It dealt exclusively with "other" sources of law, Spanish in particular. It stated, for example, that "this doctrine of the continuation of the community is founded in the fuero real of the kingdom of Spain. We think it would be easy to show, from the authority of Febrero, Azevedo and others, that it is necessary to prove the fuero real to be in use and force in the place where the continuation of the community is contended for....We can never believe that it was the intention of the monarchs of

---

[366] See Richard Kilbourne, p.66-67.

Spain to require all that strictness in the execution of acts in their distant colonies,.."[367]

Since the Supreme Court "overlooked" the provisions of the Digest on these issues and went "behind" the Digest to focus on its Spanish sources, we cannot evaluate Professor Batiza's listing of the sources of the Digest. Suffice it to say that, with respect to the two most important issues raised concerning, on the one hand, the solemnities required for a renunciation of a testamentary bequest and, on the other hand, the continuation or not of the community of acquets and gains upon the death of a spouse, the Court considered that the controlling law was Spanish law. The Court did so rule even though the Digest included many specific provisions, in French, directly applicable to partnerhsips (p.389-401), marriage contracts (p.323-345), successions (p.145-209), etc...

C.

Sennet v. Sennet's Legatees, 3 Martin's Reports (O.S.) 411, 1814.

In this case, the Court was asked to rule whether a deceased could bequeath all his property to his natural children although he had three legitimate brothers and a niece living at the time of his death.

Plaintiff,	*Defendant,*
PORTER, ATTORNEY	BRENT, ATTORNEY
Digest or Civil Code, p.212, art.21; p.208, art.4; p.210, art.14.	Same references as plaintiff, plus: Code, p.154, art.43; Spanish law.

---

[367] 3 Martin's Reports (O.S.) 97 at 115 and 120.

THE COURT.	BATIZA
Civil Code, p.210, book 3. tit.2, chap. 2, art. 14.	Digest, art.21 = French Projet, p.286,art. chap.2, art.14; XVI, and Code Nap. art.916; Digest, art.14 = French Projet, p.138, art. LV; Code Nap. art. 757; Partida 6, T.XIII, L.IX; Digest, art.4 = French Projet, p.285, art.XV; Code Nap. art.902.

MOREAU LISLET's Notes to the DIGEST of 1808
Digest (of Justinian), art.14, p.210 = Part.6, tit.13,1.8; Rec. Cast. Liv.5, tit.8, L.8; Feb. Cont. vol.1 ch.1 §7; Feb. Jui. v.2 liv.2 ch.1 §3... Digest (of Justinian), art.21, p.212 = Part.6, tit.7, L.1 & 2; tit.8, L.2; Fuero Real Liv.3, tit.6, L.1; Feb.Cont. v.1, C.1 §7, §14.

Comment: It is tempting to state here that the two attorneys in the case, being very likely of the English language and having been trained in the common law, restricted themselves to the language of the Digest and reasoned exclusively on the basis of its French text. One may also venture to say that these attorneys probably had little or no knowldege of the Spanish language. Except to a very limited extent on the part of the lawyer for the defendant, the two attorneys, following the traditional common law reasoning of focusing on the text of a statute, did not go beyond the Digest to look at the sources of the law they were dealing with. These sources, once again, were very much Spanish as explained by Moreau Lislet in his handwritten notes in The de la Vergne Volume.

D.

Cottin v. Cottin, 5 Martin's Reports (O.S.) 93, 1817.

The issue presented to the Court in this most important case was whether a child who lived a few hours and died could nevertheless inherit? "According to the Roman law, and the laws of many modern nations, this child would be deemed capable of inheriting. In Spain, however, the laws which were, and have continued to be ours, where not repealed, there exists a particular disposition, by which it is further required, that the child, in order to be considered as naturally born, and not abortive, should live twenty-four hours."[368]

The Court, Derbigny, J.
Civ.Code 8, art.6.
Sect.I.
Law 2, tit.8, book 5
of Recopilacion de Castilla;

BATIZA
Domat, 1, Liv. Prél. Tit.II,

MOREAU LISLET's Notes to the DIGEST of 1808
L.2, t.8, Liv.5 Rec. Cast.
L.5, S.1, T.2, Liv. Prel. V.1 p.10 Domat
No 112 ch.1 v.1 p.112.103 Feb. Cont.

Comment. The importance of this case lies in the fact that the Court brushed aside a litteral reading of the provisions of the Digest or Civil Code of 1808 to find the roots of Louisiana law in the legal system which was then in existence. Consider the following statements by the Court:" It must not be lost sight of, that our civil code is a digest of the civil laws, which were in force in this country, when it was adopted; that those laws must be considered as untouched, wherever the

---

[368] Cottin v. Cottin, 5 Mart.(O.S.) 93 at 93 and 94, Derbigny, J.

alterations and amendments, introduced in the digest, do not reach them; and that such parts of those laws only are repealed, as are either contrary to, or incompatible with the provisions of the code. Is the definition given of abortive children in the code, incompatible with the disposition of the law 2, tit.8, book 5, of the Recopilacion de Castilla, which declares that those will be deemed abortive who shall not live twenty-four hours? We think not. The definition given in the code, must hold as good in Spain as any where else, for it is dictated by nature itself;...So our civil code provides that, in order to inherit the child must be born capable of living (viable); and the Recopilacion de Castilla, requires a legal presumption that he was capable of living- that he shall have lived twenty-four hours."

"Significantly, Edward Livingston, in an unsuccessful motion for rehearing of the Cottin case, argued that the Digest established a rule sufficiently different from the Spanish rule there at issue as to make it "mathematically demonstratable" that the court could not give effect to the Spanish rule if the Digest were followed. Thus Livingston argued for a more liberal construction of the Digest's articles under which they, and not the prior Spanish rules, would be given the benefit of the doubt when the crucial question of conflict *vel non* was raised. Had Livingston's view prevailed, the history of the Digest in the interim between the two codifications would have been very different, and probably the magnum opus of 1825 would have been unncessary...Justice Derbigny's description of the Digest of 1808 as merely a compilation of the laws previously in force thus seems unfortunate in retrospect, even though that pronouncement was justified by the terms of the Digest enactment itself."[369]

---

[369] A History of the Louisiana Civil Code, The Formative Years, 1803-1839, by Richard H. Kilbourne, Jr. at p.65, The Publications Institute, Paul M. Hebert Law Center, 1987.

E.

Bruneau v. Bruneau's Heirs, 9 Martin's Reports (O.S.) 217, 1821.

In this opinion by François Xavier Martin, J., the Court was asked whether a plaintiff-widow could claim half the property acquired during her marriage to the deceased and an additional sum of money which she had brought into the marriage.

The Court.	*BATIZA.*
Civ. Code, 337, art.64 and 67.	Art.64 influenced by Pothier, Fuero Real and Recop. de Cast.
Recop. de Cast.5,9,2.	
1 Febrero, Contratos, 1,2,n.9.	
	Art. 67 influenced by Recop. de Cast.

MOREAU LISLET's Notes to the DIGEST of 1808
Art. 64 = Fuero Real; Rec.Cast.;
Feb.Cont.; Feb. Jui....
Art. 67 = Rec. Cast.; Feb.Cont.;
Feb. Jui.

Comment. One will have noticed that, this time, Professor Batiza recognised that the two relevant articles of the civil code, although written in French, had been influenced by Spanish law; it could not be otherwise in this particular case since the law of marriage contracts in the Digest was definitely Spanish. Judge Martin was to add the following illuminating statement: " As the marriage took place while this country was under the dominion of Spain, the laws of that kingdom afford us the only legitimate rule of decision; unless it should appear what are the goods, and their value, which each party brings in marriage, or which had been given to him separately, or which he has inherited during the marriage, all are presumed common. 1 Febrero, Contratos, 1,2, n.9. This part of the

Spanish law has been transcribed in one of our statutes. Civ. Code, 337, art.64 and 67."[370]

F.

Dufour v. Camfranc, 11 Mart. (O.S.) 675, June Term, 1822.

The main issue in this case was whether an immovable property sold at a sheriff's sale could pass to the buyer by mere adjudication, or whether an act was also essential to the transfer.

Moreau, attorney.
Civ. Code, 344, art.2
Id. 346, art.4
Id. 490, art. 1, 2 and 3.
Partida 5, 5, 52.
Partida 3, tit.30, 1. 4 & 5.
Domat, liv.3, tit.7, sec.4, n.13
Part. 3, tit.28, 1.39; id. 1.40

The Court, Porter, J.
Civil Code (Digest) several articles;
Prior Louisiana cases citing Spanish;
Law; Domat, liv. 3, tit.7, sec.3,
art.5; Pothier, Traité de prescription;
Digest, lib.41, ti.4, 1.11; Digest,
lib. 50, tit. 16, 1. 109

Livingston, attorney.
D. 41, 4, 6, in notis, n.42
D. 41, 4, 2, sec.15.
Carlivallio, tit. 3,
Des.2,4,7,

Batiza.
Tercera Partida, Tit,XVIII
Ley XVI.
French Projet of the year VIII
Pothier, Domat and French Code Civil

---

[370] Bruneau v. Bruneau's Heirs 9 Mart. (O.S.) 217 at 219, 1821.

Comment: Two of the most prominent attorneys and legal scholars of the time were, again, facing each other in this case, Moreau (Moreau Lislet) and Livingston. Shortly thereafter they were to work side by side to draft the Louisiana Civil Code of 1825. Both, as well as the Court, referred to the traditional sources of law in use at the time, to wit: Spanish sources and Roman sources. One would think that if French sources of law had been "copied" and transplanted into the Digest of 1808, as Professor Batiza argues, these attorneys would most likely have mentioned them and used them. If, indeed, Moreau Lislet had extensively "borrowed" from French sources in 1806-1808 and not disclosed that evil and unethical fact at all, it is very likely that Edward Livingston would have brought it up, even long before this particular case. It is worth pointing out here this very revealing statement made by Moreau Lislet in his argument: "In translating this law (of the Siete Partidas, 3, 28,40), an error has been committed, *and though part of the blame may attach to me*, still it is true that there is a mistake, and it is *my duty to show it.*"[371] One can only speculate, then, that had Moreau Lislet copied the French Projet and the French Civil Code, he would have admitted that fact long ago in order not to run the obvious risk of being humiliated by such a revelation. It would have been very easy for any other attorney or legal scholar, such as Edward Livingston, Etienne Mazureau or François Xavier Martin, to break through that secret and covert activity, had Moreau Lislet had anything to hide when he embarked, with James Brown, on the drafting of the Digest. If an error in *translation*, a minor "sin" in relation to "plagiarism", could so easily have been discovered, wouldn't it have been even much easier to establish that Moreau Lislet had "betrayed and miscarried" the instructions he had been given to make use of Spanish law and Roman law

---

[371] Emphasis ours.

in drafting the Digest of 1808?. One will have noticed in the above case that Professor Batiza is the only one to claim that French sources of law, particularly the French Projet and the French Civil Code, were the actual sources of the articles of the Digest applicable here.

CONCLUSION.

We believe that the above few cases of both the Territorial Court and the Supreme Court establish, for their part, that the Digest of 1808 had its sources in the Spanish law and the Roman law as these were the "laws inforce in the Territory of Orleans" in May 1806 and as incorporated, thereafter, in the Digest. In his conclusion to a comprehensive and scholarly evaluation of the Louisiana courts' decisions of these years, Richard H. Kilbourne firmly believed that "the redactors' approach, moreover, merely reflected the predominant view among the members of the bench and bar of the period....The early decisions of the Louisiana Supreme Court demonstrate that, at least after Louisiana became a state, the court found it congenial to approach the Digest as a kind of "Restatement of the Civil Law" that still drew its substance from the uncodified law of the region...For the Anglo-American lawyers and judges who came to predominate in Louisiana after 1812, law, whether civil or common, was revealed in courtrooms, not in the halls of the legislature. The use that those men made of Spanish legal sources, moreover, coincided with contemporary views about the effects of the 1803 cession, and the survival of Spanish institutions after that cession. Their reliance on Spanish law to substantiate the Digest's provisions, even where those provisions had been taken verbatim from the Code Napoleon or were contrary to the old law, was credible insofar as the civil law at that moment in history was not identified with any single state but was instead deemed the *jus commune* of all of the civilian world....[That] trade (with Cuba, Mexico, and the rest of the Spanish Caribbean) frequently brought Spanish law into the courtroom, so that the bench and bar of early Louisiana remained familiar with many of its institutions long after the cession had severed Louisiana from Spain itself."[372]

We can but join Richard Kilbourne in another of his conclusions: "that, whatever sources the redactors of the 1808 Digest employed in their labors, the legislature's enactment of the Digest made those laws Louisiana's laws. Thus they tended to be construed within the context most familiar or available to the Louisiana attorneys and judges who applied them, which, during the period in question, were the Anglo-American and Spanish "common laws." It is thus not surprising that the supreme court largely ignored French sources in interpreting the Digest, despite the fact that much of its language was taken from the Code Napoleon and its Projet. Moreover, the change in sovereignties had already given local practitioners one new legal system to work with, and they must therefore have been the more unwilling to embrace a second. In any event, there is no indication that either the redactors of the Digest of the Territorial Legislature ever intended to adopt the French legal system. In sum, the supreme court's continuing reliance upon Spanish commentators and compilations during the Digest period did not undermine the integrity of the traditional legal principles epitomized in that enactment."[373]

---

[372] Richard H. Kilbourne, History of the Louisiana Civil Code, The Formative Years, 1803-1839, at p.75-77.

[373] Id at p.94.

CONCLUSION

MOREAU LISLET on MOREAU LISLET

It is time, we believe, to bring to an end the constructive, but divisive, tournament of scholars triggered thirty years ago with the publication of The de la Vergne Volume. We have provide here, in this conclusion, an acceptable re the sometimes acrimonious debate that has lasted fo years over the single issue of the identification o sources of the Louisiana Digest of 1808. Where parts of the work completed here were written on materials and sources provided by "third parties historians, legal scholars, politicians, public official journalists and many others, this conclusion w appropriately, give to the most directly concern Moreau Lislet himself, an opportunity, at last, to p own personal views and contribution to the fun question raised in the introduction to this work: did Lislet betray the trust placed in him by the people of L in not following the specific instructions of the L legislature of 1806?

It is fitting to give to the party "charged", *Moreau* in this unusual trial, the last word before the jury of H Ideally, those who have debated and argued over the t the research undertaken in this work should have resist dangerous temptation of elaborating ursuban "speculations" fueled by their personal feelings or b intellectual bents. Although, as we found out, the ostaci the research in the field were many and the hurdl vexi times, nevertheless one should have attempted, and r every effort possible, to ascertain what Louis Cas Elisabeth Moreau Lislet himself had actually done be taking these speculations for the stated reality. All of Mo Lislet contemporaries, associates, peers and friends alw referred to him as a modest, honest, virtuous, ethical, true-hearted, just and trustworthy man. These impressive human qualities remained constantly for us like a haunting theme or, better, a refrain, so much at odds with the charge leveled against Moreau Lislet that the personality of Moreau Lislet himself became, originally, the main focus of our research. Once we determined to our satisfaction that Moreau Lislet was truly who "they" said "he" was, it did not come as a surprise to us to find the "man" behind his work and, most specifically, the "honest hand" behind the Digest of 1808.

So let us allow Moreau Lislet himself to come forward to the bar to present to us, in his own handwriting, for lack of other means of communication in his days, the arguments he can bring forth to counter the charge made against him.

Such is the purpose of the two consultations and the one opinion presented here as a formal conclusion to this research as well as the "last word of the defense". These documents are presented, first, in their original French version and, second, in an English translation. Our personal contribution, besides the work of translation, will consist only in adding a few footnotes to the texts handwritten by Moreau Lislet so as to re-emphasize our own conclusions supported by the research reported in the three parts of this book: Moreau Lislet was truly an *honest* man!

No 3008
29 avril 1825
Déclaration et Opinion
par
Messieurs L. Moreau
Lislet et Pierre
Derbigny, avocats
à la requête
de
Mr Jn.Bte. LaBranche
en sa qualité.

En la ville de la Nouvelle Orléans, dans l'Etat de la Louisiane, le vingt neuf avril mil huit cent vingt cinq, et dans la quarante neuvième année de l'Indépendance des Etats-Unis d'Amérique.

Pardevant Hugues Lavergne, notaire public dûment commissionné dans et pour la ville et paroisse de la Nouvelle Orléans, y résidant, et en présence des témoins ci-après nommés et soussignés.

Est personnellement comparu Mr Jean-Baptiste LaBranche habitant sucrier demeurant dans la paroisse St Charles, de présent en cette ville, et agissant au nom et comme fondé de pouvoir ad hoc de Mr. A.G.M.Suriray De la Rue, Gardemagasin des Tabacs en feuilles à Bordeaux, dans le Royaume de France, ainsi qu'il résulte d'une lettre en date de Bordeaux, le premier Août mil huit cent vingt quatre, adressée par le dit sieur de la Rue au dit sieur LaBranche qui l'a représentée au notaire soussigné qui la lui a rendue après en avoir pris lecture, ce qu'il certifie;

Lequel dit sieur comparant, en sa qualité, a déclaré que le dit Sieur son constituant ayant un procès en France, relativement au partage d'une succession dont la base principale repose sur un contrat de mariage passé à la Louisiane, en dix-sept cent soixante et quatorze, qui ne stipule point de société d'acquets entre les époux, il a été chargé par le dit Sieur son constituant de prendre l'attestation en bonne forme, de deux avocats éclairés, de la Nouvelle Orléans, sur la question de savoir, "si dans les partages de successions qui s'effectuent maintenant à la Louisiane, la société d'acquets ou la communauté entre mari et femme, est reconnue ou non exister de plein droit quoiqu'il n'y en ait point de stipulation expresse de la part des époux, dans les contrats de mariage, qui ont été passés à l'époque où la Louisiane était une colonie espagnole, et qu'en conséquence il a requis le notaire soussigné de prendre la déclaration de Messrs Louis Moreau Lislet et Pierre Derbigny, anciens avocats en exercice près des Tribunaux de l'Etat de la Louisiane et demeurant à la Nouvelle-Orléans; -à quoi obtempérant:

Sont personnellement comparus Messrs Louis Moreau Lislet et Pierre Derbigny, avocats, chargés par la Législature de l'Etat de la Louisiane, de la rédaction du code civil dudit Etat;

Lesquels, répondant à la question mentionnée dans le préambule de cet acte, ont dit et déclaré qu'ils ont parfaite connaissance et ont fait une étude particulière des lois qui ont régné à la Louisiane, depuis l'époque de son établissement comme Colonie Française et sous les divers changemens de gouvernemens qu'elle a éprouvés jusqu'à ce jour; - Qu'avant la cession de la Louisiane par la France à l'Espagne, elle était gouvernée comme toutes les autres colonies françaises par la coutume de Paris;- Qu'en l'année dix sept cent soixante neuf, lors de la prise de possession de la Louisiane, par le Comte O'reilly revêtu des pleins pouvoirs de sa Majesté Catholique, les lois françaises furent abolies et qu'on y substitua les lois espagnoles telles qu'elles s'observent en Espagne et dans les colonies du nouveau monde;- Que d'après ces lois qui sont encore en force aujourd'hui à la Louisiane, il existe de plein droit, par le seul fait de la célébration du mariage, une communauté ou société d'acquets ou de gains entre mari et femme, dans laquelle entrent tous les conquets meubles et immeubles faits durant le mariage et les fruits des biens propres des deux époux. Recopilacion de Castille, livre cinq, titre neuf, lois une, deux et quatre - Febrero adicionado, édition de Madrid de mil huit cent dix-huit, première partie, chapitre deux, paragraphe unique numéro un, pages deux cent trente-cinq et deux cent trente-six- et seconde partie livre un, chapitre quatre, paragraphe un, numéro un à six, pages deux cent douze à deux cent quatorze; - Digeste des lois de l'Etat de la Louisiane, articles soixante-trois, soixante-quatre, soixante-cinq, page trois cent trente-six; - Que d'après les dispositions de ces lois, la coutume constante qui a été suivie sous leur empire, et les décisions des tribunaux de la Louisiane, les avocats ci-dessus nommés déclarent qu'ils n'ont point de doute, que dans tout partage de succession qui s'effectuerait aujourd'hui à la Louisiane, et dont la base serait un contrat de mariage passé à l'époque où la Louisiane était une colonie Espagnole et dans lequel il n'y aurait point de stipulation expresse établissant une communauté ou société d'acquets ou de gains, cette communauté ou société d'acquets ou de gains serait censée exister de plein droit et par le seul effet de la loi, et que la même chose aurait lieu quand même il n'y aurait pas eu de contrat, si le mariage avait été célébré sous l'empire des lois Espagnoles.

Et les dits sieurs comparans ont ajouté de plus que pendant tout le tems que la Louisiane est restée sous la domination Espagnole, il était assez rare que les époux fissent un contrat de mariage, ce qui n'empêchait pas que la communauté n'eut lieu de plein droit.

Fait et passé en l'Etude, les jours, mois et an que dessus, en présence des sieurs Jean-Baptiste Desdunes fils et Charles Janin, témoins requis domiciliés qui ont signé avec tous les comparans et le notaire, après lecture faite.

Signatures de Moreau Lislet, P.Derbigny, Labranche, Janin, Desdunes et Lavergne.

N° 3008[374]
April 29, 1825
Declaration and Opinion
By
The Sirs L. Moreau Lislet and Pierre
Derbigny, Counsellors at Law,
At the request of
Mr. J-B LaBranche,
in his capacity.

In the city of New Orleans, State of Louisiana, the twenty ninth of April one thousand eight hundred and twenty five, and the forty ninth year of the Independence of the United-States of America.

Before Hugues Lavergne, notary public duly commissioned in and for the city and parish of New Orleans, there residing, and in the presence of the named and undersigned witnesses.

Has appeared in person Mr. Jean-Baptiste LaBranche, resident and sugar manufacturer residing in St Charles parish, presently in this city, and acting in the name and as agent ad hoc for Mr. A.G.M. Suriray de la Rue, Wharehouse of Tobacco Leaves in Bordeaux, Kingdom of France, as is established by a letter dated in Bordeaux on the first of August one thousand eight hundred and twenty four, addressed by the said Mr. de la Rue to the said Mr. LaBranche who presented that letter to the undersigned notary who, after he took cognizance of it returned the same to him [LaBranche], which he certifies;

The said appearing Gentleman, in his capacity, has declared that the said Gentleman his principal was involved in a trial in France, in a matter of partition of a succession raising a main issue based upon a marriage contract entered into in Louisiana, in seventeen hundred and seventy four,

---

[374] Notarial Archives, New Orleans, Lavergne, notary. Original text in the French language as reported above.

which stipulates no community of acquets between the spouses; he was instructed by his said principal to obtain the proper affidavits from two learned New Orleans counsellors at law on the question, "whether in the partitions of successions being opened now in Louisiana, the partnership of acquets or the community between husband and wife is considered to exist or not as of right, although there has been no express stipulation to that effect made by the spouses in the marriage contracts which were entered into at the time when Louisiana was a Spanish colony"; in consequence of which, he did request that the undersigned notary record the statement of Mrs. Louis Moreau Lislet and Pierre Derbigny, two former counsellors at law who practiced before the Courts of the State of Louisiana and who are residents of New Orleans;- in compliance with the above:

Have personally appeared MM. Louis Moreau Lislet and Pierre Derbigny, counsellors at law, mandated by the Louisiana Legislature to draft the civil code of the said State;

Who, in answer to the question set forth in the preamble of this act, have stated and declared that they have a perfect knowledge of and have made a specific study of the laws that have been in force in Louisiana, since the time of its settlement as a French colony and all through the various changes in government that have taken place until this day; - That before Louisiana was transferred by France to Spain, it [Louisiana] was governed, as were all other French colonies, by the Custom of Paris; That in the year seventeen hundred and sixty nine, when Count O'Reilly, vested with full powers by His Catholic Majesty, took possession of Louisiana, *the French laws were repealed and were replaced by the Spanish laws* as they are in force in Spain and in the colonies of the New World; - That *according to these laws which are still in force in Louisiana today*,[375] there exists as a matter of right, by the sole fact of the celebration of a marriage, a community or partnership of acquets or gains between husband and wife, in which are included all movable and immovable property acquired during the marriage and the fruits of the personal property of the spouses. Recopilacion de Castilla, Book V, Title IX, Laws 1, 2 and 4.- Febrero Adicionado, Madrid Edition of one thousand eight hundred and eighteen, Part I, Chapter II, Paragraph 1, pages two hundred and thirty five and two hundred and thirty six,- and Part II, Book 1, Chapter IV, Paragraph 1, n°1 to 6, pages two hundred and twelve to two hundred and fourteen. Digest of the laws of the State of Louisiana, articles sixty three, sixty four, sixty-five, page

---

[375] The emphasis is ours. It is meant to call the reader's attention to Part I of this work as it concerns the history of the Louisiana legal system. In this consultation we have two French speaking attorneys, trained in the French legal tradition in France and living witnesses, since 1804, of that period in time when the Louisiana legal system was being shaped, molded and couched in a Digest and subsequently in a Code, informing us in no uncertain terms that Spanish law was still the law of Louisiana in 1825 when this consultation was given. This historical state of things could only lead Moreau Lislet and Derbigny to write, in the next sentences to come, that the legal issue they were addressing here had to be considered in light of the Recopilacion de Castilla and Febrero Adicionado as these sources of law were transcribed in the Digest of the laws of the State of Louisiana. We believe that we can read in these statements the specific indication of the methodology and writing technique used by Moreau Lislet and James Brown in their making of the Digest. See supra Part III of this work.

three hundred and thirty six;[376] - That, according to the dispositions of these laws, the constant custom followed under the control of these laws, the decisions handed down by the courts of Louisiana, the above named two counsellors at law have declared that they have no doubt, that in every partition of a succession that would take place today in Louisiana, and the basis of which would be a marriage contract entered into

---

[376] *In his article on "The Louisiana Civil Code of 1808: Its Actual Sources and Present Relevance", 46 Tul. L. Rev. 1-165 (1971-72), Professor Batiza "finds"* the sources of articles 63, 64 and 65 cited by Moreau Lislet in this consultation, in no other than "Pothier, Communauté; Coutume de Paris"; the Professor also adds, and by necessity, the "Fuero Real, Partida 1, Compilation of Castille, Febrero Adic." Professor Batiza states, then, that these articles of the Digest were *substantially influenced* by these sources.(at p.105-106). Which sources, one could ask, and was the influence of these sources on the substance of the articles or on their terminology or wording? Is it not possible to find here an illustration of the technique resorted to by Moreau Lislet, to wit: use French words and, thus, French texts where Spanish law or Roman law and French law reflected the same substantive law, or where *French texts could be used to reflect Spanish law and substantially influence the wording of the provisions of the Digest*? Professor Batiza himself stated that "because the Code of 1808 was originally drafted in French and then translated into English and because identity or substantial identity of wording is necessary to classify a source as "verbatim" or "almost as verbatim", only the French and Louisiana sources can be either "verbatim" or "almost verbatim"...All other sources, whether in Spanish or Latin, had to come under either of the two remaining categories, "substantially" or "partially" influenced, since only *their concepts and not their language were adopted.*" Id. at p. 13-14.[Emphasis ours].

when Louisiana was a Spanish colony, and in which contract of marriage there would be no express stipulation creating a community or partnership of acquets or gains, the said community or partnership of acquets or gains would be deemed to exist as of right and by the mere effect of the said law, and that the same would occur in the event there would have been no marriage contract, if the marriage had been performed under the control of Spanish laws.

And the said appearing two Gentlemen have added that as long as Louisiana was under Spanish domination, it was rather exceptional for spouses to enter into a contract of marriage, which would not prevent the community from existing as of right.

Done and signed in this office, on the day, month and year stated above, in the presence of MM. Jean-Baptiste Desdunes, Jr. and Charles Janin, witnesses summoned to that effect, who have signed with all the parties appearing and the notary, after the act had been read.

Signatures of:
- Moreau Lislet,
- Pierre Derbigny,
- LaBranche,
- Janin,
- Desdunes,
- Lavergne.

Consultation, 18 décembre 1818.[377]

Consultation.-

Pierre s'est marié en premières noces et a eu sept enfans de ce premier mariage. La première femme lui avait apporté environ 74000 piastres avec lesquelles Pierre avait acheté une habitation et une centaine de nègres. Après la mort de sa première femme, Pierre est passé à de secondes noces ayant sept enfans du premier lit existans. Depuis son second mariage deux de ces mêmes enfans sont morts sans postérité et Pierre s'étant vu dans la nécessité de faire cession de biens à ses créanciers a fait liquider les droits qui revenaient à ses enfans du premier lit et il s'est trouvé qu'en comprenant les parts des deux enfans décédés, ces droits s'élevaient à une somme de 52500 piastres aux environs, c'est-à-dire 7500 pour chaque enfant. Les syndics des créanciers de Pierre ayant mis ses biens en vente, trois des enfans de Pierre ont acheté son habitation et quelques uns des esclaves y attachés et le surplus a été vendu à des étrangers, les syndics n'ont pas encore fait de répartition et ont demandé s'ils peuvent répartir les 15000 piastres qui revenaient aux deux enfants décédés de Pierre comme un bien qui était acquis à Pierre, en toute propriété, comme héritier naturel de ces deux mêmes enfans.

L'avocat soussigné pense que si Pierre ne fut point passé à de secondes noces il n'y aurait pas de doute qu'ayant hérité de ses deux enfans du premier lit qui étaient décédés, ses droits sur leur succession ne fussent passés à ses créanciers, en vertu de la cession de biens qu'il leur avait faite de manière que les sindics pourraient pleinement en disposer.

---

[377] *The Favrot Papers, 686-770, Document # 725; Manuscripts Department, Special Collections Division, Tulane University Library.*

En effet la loi porte en général, que les pères et mères succèdent à leurs enfans décédés sans postérité à l'exclusion des autres ascendans ainsi que des collatéraux:
Code Civil Art - 30 page 150-
Loi 1,- 1-5, - tit 8 de la récopilation de Castille.

Mais Pierre est passé à de secondes noces et c'est depuis ces secondes noces, que deux de ses enfans du premier lit sont décédés, il en résulte qu'il ne leur a succédé qu'en usufruit seulement et qu'il n'a pu céder et transporter à ses créanciers par sa cession de biens, plus de droits qu'il n'en avait lui-même, comme héritier de ses enfans,-

En effet c'est une disposition formelle de la loi Espagnole, que le père ou la mère qui se remarie, est tenu de réserver à ses enfans du premier lit les biens qu'il tient de la libéralité de l'époux prédécédé, ou de la succession de quelques uns du précédant mariage.-

C'est ce qu'on lit dans Febrero addicional vol.1 part.1 Chap 3 § unique page 242 et suivantes.

"La femme qui contracte un second mariage, dit Febrero, est obligée de réserver aux enfans du premier lit, la propriété de tous les biens qu'elle a reçus de son premier mari par donation pour cause de noces, (arras), fidéicommis, legs, donation entre vifs ou pour cause de mort ou à quelque autre titre lucratif. Febrero, vol.1 - part 1 - chap.3 - § unique, No 1---"

"La femme, ajoute ensuite Febrero, est non seulement obligée de préserver les biens mentionnés dans le numéro précédent, mais encore ceux dont elle hérite ab intestat de quelques uns de ses enfans du premier lit, mais dans ce cas elle leur réservera seulement les biens dont les dits enfans ont hérité de leur père. Febrero, ibid. No 2-"

Enfin Febrero termine pour dire que dans tous les cas ou la femme est obligée à faire cette réserve envers ses enfans, le mari y est également obligé sans exception s'il vient à se remarier, ce qui est conforme aux dispositions de la Loi 4. tit-1.-liv.5 de la récopilation de Castille. Febrero ibid. No 3.

Or cette réserve que la loi Espagnole prescrit de faire en faveur des enfans du premier lit dont les pères ou mères se remarieraient, bien loin d'avoir été abrogé par le Code s'y trouve au contraire pleinement quoiqu'indirectement confiné lorsque le code, après [.?.] dit, en parlant de la donation que l'époux qui se remarie pourra faire à son nouvel époux "que cette donation ne peut porter en aucun cas que sur les biens propres de l'époux qui passe à de secondes noces et ne peut rien comprendre de ceux qui lui sont venus du prédécédé, soit par donation faite avant ou depuis le mariage, ou autrement, ou de la succession de quelqu'un des enfans du précédant mariage" ajoute "ces biens devant, d'après la loi, être réservés aux enfans dudit mariage, dans le cas ou leur père ou mère passerait à de secondes noces-" Code civil, Art. 227 - page 259 -

Le code civil maintient donc les lois précédentes qui prescrivaient cette réserve puisqu'il les cite à l'appui de la disposition qu'il établit pour restreindre les donations que les maris ou les femmes qui passent à de secondes noces, ayant des enfans du premier lit, peuvent faire à leur nouvel époux.-

On ne doit pas croire que cette réserve soit uniquement relative au nouvel époux; le mari et la femme qui se remarient, ayant des enfans du premier lit, ne peuvent pas plus disposer des biens compris dans la réserve, en faveur d'autres personnes, qu'il ne le peuvent à l'égard de leur nouvel époux. - C'est ce qu'enseigne Febrero après avoir parlé de la réserve à laquelle est obligé le mari ou la femme qui a passé à de secondes noces, lorsqu'il dit:

"En conséquence, elle (la femme qui se remarie ayant des enfans du premier lit) ne peut aliéner ni hypothéquer, ni engager ces biens (ceux compris dans la réserve) ni en disposer en faveur de ses enfans du second lit, ou de ses autres parens ou d'autres personnes, attendu que ces biens ne sont pas sa propriété, quoique les biens seraient tacitement affectés...et elle doit même donner caution et sureté qu'elle les restituera et en usera en bon père de famille, parce que par le seul fait de s'être remariée, elle perd le droit qu'elle avait sur

eux et ne lui reste plus que l'usufruit pour en jouir sa vie durant." Febrero ...part.1. ch-3- § unique, No-1 vers le milieu.

Il semble, d'après ces autorités, que si le mari ou la femme a hérité de quelques uns de ces enfans du premier lit, avant même d'avoir passé à de secondes noces, leurs droits de propriété sur les biens de cette succession, se [condensent?] en un simple usufruit. Il en doit donc résulter que lorsque le mari et la femme ne succèdent à leurs enfans du premier lit, qu'après avoir passé à de secondes noces, leurs droits de succession se réduit à un simple usufruit et que la propriété des biens qui la composent appartiennent aux enfans du premier lit. On conclut de la loi, que Pierre n'ayant hérité des biens de ses deux enfans du premier lit qui ne sont décédés que depuis son second mariage, n'a pu transmettre à ses créanciers, que l'usufruit des 15000 piastres qui revenaient à ses deux mêmes enfans et qu'ainsi, lors de la distribution à faire par les sindics de ses créanciers du produit de la vente de ses biens, les autres enfans du premier lit comme héritiers de leurs frères décédés quant à la propriété, peuvent valablement s'opposer à ce que 15000 piastres sur ce prix, ne soient distribuées aux derniers créanciers en ordre, qu'à la charge pour eux de donner bonne et valable caution de bien restituer cette somme à la mort de Pierre.

Délibéré à la Nlle Orléans le 18 Décembre 1818.

*(Signé) L. Moreau Lislet
avocat*

La loi ne prévoyant pas le cas ou le père ou la mère convole à de secondes noces, après avoir hérité par le décès d'enfans du premier lit de ce qui était échu à ces enfans par la mort de leur père ou de la mère, il semblerait, au premier coup d'oeil, que la réserve n'est pas d'obligation, lorsque l'enfant décède après le second mariage. Mais si l'on veut réfléchir que l'esprit et le but de la loi sont de ne favoriser les secondes noces qu'autant que les enfans d'un premier lit n'en souffrent pas, et d'empêcher, à cet effet que les biens du père ou de la mère de ces enfans n'enrichissent ceux d'un second mariage, on doit sans peine souscrire à l'opinion ci-dessus émise. En méditant cette loi on découvrira que les voeufs restent simples usufruitiers des biens maternels et paternels de leurs enfans décédés depuis la mort de leurs conjoints. Ainsi, que le second mariage ait lieu avant ou après la mort de l'enfant du premier lit, cela ne peut rien changer à la qualité. Il serait ridicule que dans le cas ou la mort de l'enfant précède le convol en secondes noces, le père fut seulement usufruitier et que lorsqu'elle n'a lieu qu'après il fut propriétaire. Ajoutons que cela blesserait les droits des enfans frères du défunt aux intérêts desquels la loi a voulu prévoir. Pour ces raisons, je partage l'opinion de Mr Moreau.

(Signé)   Mazureau

[Translation]
Consultation given on December 18, 1818.[378]

Consultation[379]

Pierre was married a first time and had seven children from this first marriage. His first wife had brought to him about 74000 piastres with which he had bought a dwelling and about one hundred negroes. After the death of his first wife, Pierre remarried still the father of seven children from his previous marriage. Since his second marriage, two children have died without leaving any descendant and Pierre being under the necessity to surrender his assets to his creditors proceeded to sell the rights of his children of his first marriage, including the shares of the two previously deceased children; the total amount of the sale was about 52500 piastres, or 7500 for each child. The trustees for Pierre's creditors having sold his assets, three of Pierre's children bought back his house and some of the slaves whereas the remaining assets were sold to third parties; the trustees have not yet distributed the monetary amount received and have asked whether they can divide the 15000 piastres which were due to the two deceased children of Pierre as if it were an asset acquired by Pierre, in full ownership, as the natural heir of these same two children.

The undersigned counsellor at law believes that had Pierre not married a second time there would have been no doubt that having inherited from his two deceased children from his first marriage, his right to their succession would have been

---

[378] The Favrot Papers, 686-770, document # 725, Manuscripts Department, Special Collections Division, Tulane University Library.

[379] Liberal translation into English from the French text of this consultation as reported above.

transferred to his creditors, by virtue of the surrender of assets he had made to them, in such a manner that the trustees could have proceeded with the full disposition of such assets.

Indeed the law provides in general, that fathers and mothers inherit from their children who have died without leaving any descendant, to the exclusion of any other ascendant as well as collateral:

Civil Code art: 30 page 150 - Law 1, b.5, tit.8 of the Recopilacion de Castille.[380]

But Pierre married a second time and it is since his second marriage that two of his children from the first marriage have died; it follows that he inherited from them the *usufruct only*[381] and that he could not transfer and deliver to his creditors by the surrender of his assets, more rights than he, himself, had received as heir of his children.

Indeed it is an absolute disposition of the Spanish law, that the father or the mother who remarries, is bound to reserve to his/her children of the first marriage the assets which he/she

---

[380] If one looks at the sources of this same article as they are cited in the Digest annotated by Moreau Lislet, page 150 of the De La Vergne volume under the title "of the succession of descendants", this same reference to the Recopilacion is mentioned in exactly the same format. Many additional references to Spanish laws, in particular, and to Domat are also given. Professor Batiza could only give the Compilation of Castille as the source of this same article of the Digest: see The Louisiana Civil Code of 1808: Its Actual Sources and Present Relevance, by Rodolfo Batiza, 46 Tul.L.Rev.1-165, at p.73, (1971-72).

[381] Underlined in the original French text.

received by gratuitous act from the predeceased spouse, or from the succession of whomever from the first marriage.
This is what one can read in Febrero addicional, vol.1, part.1, chap.3, § 1, page 242 and following:

"The wife who remarries, says Febrero, is *bound to reserve*[382] to the children of the first marriage, the ownership of all assets which she has received from her first husband by way of donations on account of the marriage, (arras) fideicommis, legacies, donations inter vivos or mortis causa or by any other onerous title. Febrero, vol.1- part 1- chap.3- § 1---"

"The wife, adds Febrero, is not only bound to hold the assets mentioned in the preceding paragraph, but also those assets which she inherits *ab intestat* from any one of her children of her first marriage, but in this case she will hold back for them only those assets which the said children have inherited from their father. Febrero, id. No 2-"

Lastly Febrero ends by saying that in every case where the wife is bound to hold back in reserve some assets for the benefit of her children, the husband is bound likewise to the same obligation without any exception should he remarry, which is in total compliance with the dispositions of law 4. tit.1. book 5 of the Recopilacion of Castille. Febrero id. No 3.

Moreover, this particular reserved share that the Spanish law requires that it be kept in favor of the children of the first marriage when the father or the mother remarries, far from having been repealed by the Code is, quite to the contrary, fully incorporated in the Code, although indirectly where the Code, referring to the donation that the spouse who remarries can make to the new spouse, states "the donation...can, in no

---

[382] Id.

case, affect any property, but the estate belonging to the man or woman who contracts a second marriage, and cannot comprise any effects which came to him or her, from the deceased spouse, either by donation made before or after the marriage or otherwise *or by the succession of some of the children of the preceding marriage; these effects being, according to law, reserved to the children of said marriage, in case their father or mother marries again.*[383]" Civil Code, art.227 - page 259.

Thus the Civil Code maintains the preceding laws which had provided for this particular reserved share since it refers to them in support of the provision it lays down to restrict the donations that husbands or wives who remarry, and who have children of their first marriage, can make to their new spouse. This is not to say that this special reserved share is of concern only to the new spouse; the husband and the wife who remarry, and who have children of their first marriage, cannot any more dispose of the assets which make up this reserved share in favor of any other person, than they can in favor of their new spouse.- This is what Febrero states after he has addressed the issue of the reserved share to which is held the husband or the wife who has remarried, where he says:

"As a consequence, she (the wife who remarries and who has children of a first marriage) can neither dispose, nor give a

---

[383] Underlined in the original French text. In the De La Vergne Volume, Moreau Lislet gives many Spanish texts as the sources of this article 227, p.259 of the Digest. In his search for the sources of the Digest, Professor Batiza can only give Spanish texts also, Quinta Partida and Feb. Adic.: see supra note 3. It is obvious, therefore, that where Spanish law was different from French law and any text written in French, Spanish law was to be included in the Digest drafted by Moreau Lislet and James Brown, leaving no room for Professor Batiza to speculate.

mortgage, nor commit those assets (i.e. the assets making up that reserved share), nor transfer them to the children of the second marriage, nor in favor of her other relatives or third persons, since these assets are not her property, and she must even give a personal security and a surety to make sure that she will return these assets and will make use of them as a faithful administrator, *because by the mere fact that she remarried she lost the right that she has over them, and she is left only with the usufruct to enjoy for the rest of her life.*[384]" Febrero 1, ch.3,- single §, No 1 around the middle.

It appears, from these authorities, that if the husband or the wife has inherited from some of the children from their first marriage, even before he or she enters into a second marriage, the assets, rights of ownership over the assets of that succession, are transformed into a simple usufruct. We draw the conclusion from the law, that since Pierre did not inherit assets from his two children from his first marriage and who died after his second marriage, he could transfer to his creditors, only the usufruct of the 15000 piastres who were the shares of these two children, and that, therefore, the children of the first marriage, as heirs of their predeceased brothers with respect to the ownership of these 15000 piastres, can validly raise objections to these 15000 piastres being distributed to the creditors in their proper order, or only if these creditors agree to give adequate security to ensure the return of this amount of money upon Pierre's death.

Prepared and done in New Orleans, this 18th of December 1818.

L. Moreau Lislet
Counsellor at law

---

[384] Underlined in the original French text.

Since the law does not provide for the case where the father or the mother would remarry, after having inherited from their deceased children of their first marriage the share of inheritance which these children had themselves inherited on account of the death of their father or mother, it would appear, at first glance, that the reserved share is not a requirement of the law when the child dies after the second marriage. But if one does understand that the spirit and the goal of the law are to encourage second marriages only to the extent that the children of the first marriage do not suffer from them, and to prevent, in that respect, that the assets of the father or the mother of these children lead to the enrichment of the children of the second marriage, one must necessarily endorse the opinion given above. When meditating over this law one will find out that a widower or a widow is only a usufructuary of the assets inherited from their father or mother by those children who have died since the death of their spouse. Thus, whether the second marriage takes place before or after the death of the child of the first marriage, this cannot change anything in the legal relationships. It would be ridiculous to have a case where in the event the child would die before his father remarries, the father would be only a usufructuary, whereas should the child die after the second marriage the father would become a full owner. We can add that such a situation would prejudice the rights of the children who are the brothers of the deceased child, rights which the law did intend to protect. For these reasons, I share the opinion expressed by Mr.Moreau.

Mazureau

GAZETTE D'ETAT DE LA LOUISIANE
Mardi 20 Juin 1826

Journal de la Cour d'Accusation
(Impeachment)

Opinion de L. Moreau Lislet, sénateur, sur les chefs d'accusation portés contre le juge Chinn.

"....Pour démontrer que le juge Chinn s'est rendu coupable à cet égard d'une violation manifeste des devoirs que lui prescrivait la loi, les commissaires chargés de la poursuite, ont cité une loi de la Recopilacion de Castille en force dans cet Etat, par laquelle ils ont soutenu qu'il était formellement défendu aux juges et aux officiers de justice de se rendre adjudicataires dans les ventes publiques faites par leur ministère.

.....il s'agit ici d'examiner si le juge Chinn en achetant ainsi, a commis sciemment une infraction à la loi qui puisse lui mériter d'être destitué....Or à l'égard de la loi de la Recopilacion de Castille, sur la traduction de laquelle les commissaires de la poursuite et les défenseurs de l'accusé n'ont point été d'accord....je pense que le juge Chinn ne peut pas être puni d'avoir ignoré les dispositions d'une loi qui aurait contenu une semblable prohibition, lorsque l'on considère que cette loi se trouvait insérée dans un recueil écrit dans une langue étrangère qui n'est point entendue généralement par les habitants de cet Etat, que les lois de la Recopilacion de Castille n'existent que dans un petit nombre de bibliothèques de cet Etat et qu'elles n'ont jamais été traduites en Anglais et publiées par l'ordre de la Législature comme l'ont été les lois des Partidas.....

[Translation]
Gazette of the State of Louisiana
Tuesday, June 20, 1826.

Journal of the Cour d'Accusation
(Impeachment)

Opinion of L. Moreau Lislet, senator, on the charges brought against judge Chinn.[385]

"...To establish that judge Chinn is guilty of an obvious violation of the duties he is bound to under the law, the commissioners in charge of the prosecution, have cited a law of *the Recopilacion de Castilla* in force in this State, according to which they have argued that it was expressly prohibited for any judge and any officer of the court to become a successful bidder in public sales held under their supervision and authority.

...Our purpose here is to determine whether Judge Chinn, in so acquiring, has willfully committed a violation of the law to such an extent that he should be removed from office.

...As to the law of *the Recopilacion de Castilla*, on the translation of which the commissioners for the prosecution and the counsels for the defense have not agreed ... I believe that Judge Chinn should not be punished for having been unaware of the existence of a statute which would have included such a prohibition, when one must be aware of the fact that such a statute was a part of a compilation written in a foreign language by and large not understood by the inhabitants of this State, that the laws of the *Recopilacion de Castilla* can be found only in a few libraries in this State and that they have

---

[385] Liberal translation from the French text published in the "Gazette d'Etat de la Louisiane", Mardi 20 juin 1826.

never been translated in English, nor published by order of the Legislature, as has been the case of the laws of the *Partidas*...[386].

---

[386] Once again, we have included this published "opinion" by Moreau Lislet for the purpose of emphasizing that Spanish law was the law of the land in Louisiana: here, in this case, we may have an issue of litigious rights. Moreover, it was a controlling law even though it was written in Spanish, a language unknown to many "inhabitants", including Judge Chinn who was supposed to enforce a law or legislation he, apparently, could not understand. It is also important to point out that this opinion was given by Moreau Lislet who had just contributed to the writing of the Louisiana Civil Code of 1825, a progeny of the Digest of 1808 itself drafted mainly by Moreau Lislet. It definitely shows consistency in the sources of law of the Louisiana legal system from 1808 to 1825 and establishes, in conjunction with the previous two consultations cited in this Conclusion, that these sources were Spanish in substance.

APPENDICES

1) 1796 map of Saint-Domingue 282

2) Olographic Will: Moreau Lislet, 1832 283

3) Juridical Acts 285

4) Moreau Lislet as Council: Cases 296

5) Spanish Sources of Law of the Digest of 1808 (Feliú) 304

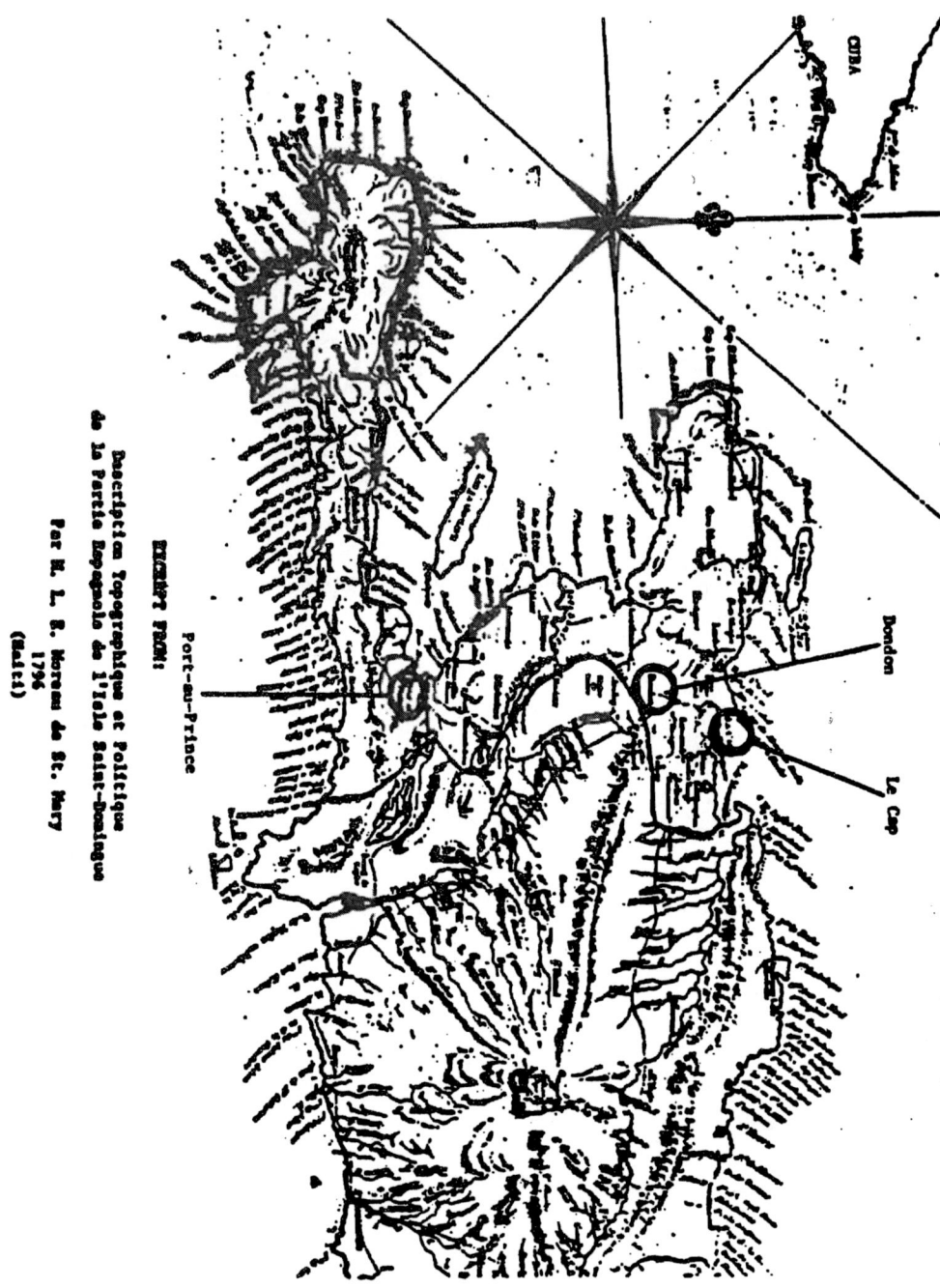

Moreau Lislet

Olographic Will
filed 6 Dec. 1832

Recorded folio 417 vol.4

Ne Varietur

Charles Maurian, Judge.

Ceci est mon testament olographe et l'acte de mes dernières volontés.

Je m'appelle Louis Casimir Elisabeth Moreau, le surnom de Lislet que je porte m'ayant été donné pour me distinguer de Benjamin Moreau mon frère ainé décédé;

Je suis né à St Domingue dans le quartier du Dondon dépendance du Cap Français. Mes père et mère sont morts depuis longtems.

Je n'ai été marié qu'une fois à feue Dlle Anne Philipine de Peters, duquel mariage est née ma fille Julie Elisabeth Athée épouse divorcée de Mr Jean Baptiste Desdunes fils.

Quoique j'aie plus de dettes que de biens, en raison des endossements considérables que j'ay eu le malheur de donner à mon frère Louis Deynaut et ensuite à mon neveu Camille Bruslé, néanmoins s'il arrivait qu'à mon décès, je laissasse quelques biens libres, je déclare en léguer les deux tiers à mes trois petites filles, Joséphine, Adèle et Louise Desdunes a parts égales, d'après le droit que la loi ... accorde, n'ayant qu'une fille; sauf cependant les legs particuliers cy après décrits.

Je déclare donner et léguer à mon gendre Jean Baptiste Desdunes fils pour le récompenser des soins qu'il prendra comme mon exécuteur testamentaire, ma bibliothèque avec tous les livres qu'elle contiendra et une commission de dix pour cent sur l'estimation de tous les biens que je délaisserai lors de mon décès.

Je prie mon gendre d'acheter pour mes petites filles, ou pour lui, s'il en a les moyens, ma négresse Louise et sa fille Elina ou de faire en sorte qu'elle ne devienne pas la propriété de ma fille, ayant des raisons pour cela.

Je déclare faire remise et donner décharge à mon frère Louis Deynaut et à mon neveu Camille Bruslé de toutes les sommes que j'ai pu ou pourrai payer pour eux, sur les endossements que je leur avais donnés ou les billets que je leur avais prêtés.

Je donne et lègue à ma soeur Madame de la Grange et à ma nièce...Bruslé à chacune une bague de la valeur de cent piastres que je les prie de garder comme un témoignage de mon attachement.

Je nomme Mr. Jean Baptiste Desdunes fils mon exécuteur testamentaire, lui donne la saisine de mes biens et l'autorise à les vendre et à en faire le partage, après liquidation de mes dettes. Je révoque tous testaments et codicilles antérieurs, s'il y en a. Fait à la Nouvelle Orléans par <u>Duplicata</u> le vingt deuxième jour du mois de juillet de l'année mil huit cent vingt neuf.

Moreau Lislet

Ne Varietur
Charles Maurian, Judge.

List of Juridical Acts to which Moreau Lislet or members of his family were parties.

Louisiana Notarial Archives
Notaire: Narcisse Broutin 1804 - 1818

Années	Acte	Contenu
1805	26 août	Moreau Lislet et Pierre Derbigny donnent pouvoir à Boucard négociant à Nantes.
	25 septembre	[Mêmes dispositions que l'acte du 26 août]
	26 septembre	Acte de dépôt de documents par Moreau Lislet.
1808	15 septembre	Notification d'une sentence arbitrale par Moreau Lislet au Sr Ducournau.
1809	7 février	Enregistrement par le Sr Moreau Lislet d'un document d'achat d'un noir cuisinier de 50 ans et d'une négresse de 18 ans.
	13 mai	Quittance. Louis Moreau Lislet au nom de Jean Blanque à Alex. Bonamy.
	15 juin	Enregistrement Louis Deynaut: achat d'une boulangerie.

Années	Acte	Contenu
1809	25 juillet	Obligation Hyp^{re} L^s Deynaut à Louis Moreau. Louis Deynaut reconnait devoir au sieur Moreau Lislet la somme de 1,000 piastres pour prêt pour payer le fond de boulangerie, ustensiles de deux nègres en dépendant.
1811	26 mars	Enregistrement à la requête de L. Moreau Lislet.
	31 mai	Enregistrement à la requête de L. Moreau Lislet.
	12 juin	Power of attorney by Moreau Lislet to Chevas.
	30 août	Enregistrement à la requête de L. Moreau Lislet.
	7 septembre	Enregistrement à la requête de L. Moreau Lislet. [acte de vente d'esclave sous signature privée consenti par L. Deynaut à L. Moreau Lislet]
	16 novmebre	Power of attorney by Moreau Lislet.
1812	27 janvier	Mainlevée d'hypothèque par L. Moreau Lislet au profit de L. Deynaut.
1813	26 février	Quittance par Louis Deynaut à Vatelle Vve Boyer.

Années	Acte	Contenu
1813	2 juillet	Vente d'esclave par L. Moreau Lislet à Antoine Foucher.
1814	27 avril	Hypothèque par L. Moreau Lislet à Pierre Colette et Jean B^{te} Desdunes.
1817	7 mars	Obligation hyp^{re} de Moreau L'Ilet en faveur de Desdunes.
	7 mars	Quittance par Mr. Jn. Bte. Desdunes fils à Mr. Moreau Lislet.
	13 juin	Vente de terrain de maison par Mr. Moreau Lislet protuteur de Uranie Thierry à Mr. Dorfeuille.
	23 juillet	Vente d'esclave par Louis Deynaut à Mezelle Baudry [Moreau Lislet se porte caution et garant de la propriété de l'objet, une négresse nommé Sophie].
1818	8 mai	Vente de maison et terrain par L. Moreau Lislet à J. Bte Desdunes fils.
	20 mai	Main levée en partie. J. Bte Desdunes père à Louis Moreau Lislet.

Louisiana Notarial Archives
Notaire: H. Lavergne 1819 - 1826

Années	Acte	Contenu
1820	4 janvier (acte 286)	Vente d'esclave par Mr. Moreau Lislet à Marie Antoinette Dupard.
	22 mars (acte 753)	Meeting of the creditors of Louis Deynaut [Louis Moreau Lislet créditeur pour 10.498 dollars et plus consent à la cession de biens et renonce à ses droits contre Louis Deynaut ...]
	20 juin (acte 537)	Vente d'esclave par le Sr Pierre Verain Desbordes au Sr L. Moreau Lislet
1821	28 avril (acte 814)	Moreau Lislet agissant comme syndic des créanciers de Louis Deynaut.
	28 avril (acte 815)	Vente d'esclave par Mr. Moreau Lislet, syndic.
	28 avril (acte 817)	Main-levées par Mr. L. Moreau Lislet syndic des créanciers de Louis Deynaut.
	28 avril (actes 818 à 823)	Ventes d'esclave aux enchères par L. Moreau Lislet, syndic.

Années	Acte	Contenu
1821	1 mai (acte 829)	Vente de terrain et maison par Mr. L. Moreau Lislet esqualités à Mr. Antoine Abat.
	9 mai (acte 841)	Vente d'esclave par J.B. Desdunes fils à L. Moreau Lislet.
	1 août (acte 944)	Quittance par Mr. Moreau fondé de pouvoirs d'Aubry Dupuy.
	29 octobre (acte 1008)	Quittance par Mr. Joseph Abat à Mr. Louis Moreau Lislet contenant subrogation d'hypothèque en faveur de Mme Marie Thérèse Vallade épouse du Sieur Louis Christophe Deynaut.
1822	11 janvier (acte 1075)	Hypothèque Spéciale par L. Moreau Lislet en faveur de J.B. Desdunes fils.
	27 septembre (acte 1535)	Obligation hypth^{re} de L. Moreau Lislet à Mr. J.B. Desdunes fils.

Années	Acte	Contenu
1822	20 septembre (acte 1536)	Vente de deux portions de terrains par Mr. Jean Baptiste Haget à Mr. L. Moreau Lislet [comparant a vendu à Mr. Louis Moreau Lislet, Président de la loge l'Etoile Polaire, numéro cinq ... agissant pour et au nom de la dite loge ...]
	13 novembre (acte 1573)	Prorogation d'hypothèque par M. Moreau Lislet en faveur de Mr. J.B. Desdunes fils.
	19 novembre (acte 1576)	Quittance et décharge partielle entre Mess. J.B. Desdunes père, Moreau Lislet et J.B. Desdunes fils.
1823	11 janvier (acte 1638)	Prorogation d'hypothèque par Mr. L. Moreau Lislet en faveur de Mr. Lucien Guillaume Hiligsberg.
	14 janvier (acte 1641)	Prorogation d'hypothèque par Mr. L. Moreau Lislet en faveur de J.B. Desdunes fils.
1824	31 mai (acte 2480)	Enregistrement et Dépôt à la requête de Mr. Louis Moreau Lislet.

Années	Acte	Contenu
1826	30 août (acte 3726)	Dépôt par J.B. Desdunes fils [Dépôt de l'inventaire avec estimation des biens meubles et immeubles dépendant de la communauté qui a existé entre J.B. Desdunes fils et Julie Elizabeth Althée Moreau Lislet époux séparés de corps et de biens et dépôt du partage en nature daté du 25 août 1826]

Louisiana Notarial Archives
Notaire: Louis T. Caire 1829 - 1835

Années	Acte	Contenu
1829	1 août (acte 634)	Hypothèque spéciale consentie par Louis Moreau Lislet à Pierre Soulé sur la plusvalue d'un terrain qu'il possède rue de Condé et sur la plusvalue de certains esclaves.
	31 octobre (acte 758)	Echange et vente d'esclaves entre Louis Moreau Lislet et sa fille Julie Elizabeth Althée, épouse divorcée de Mr. J.B. Desdunes.
	30 novembre (acte 798)	Vente d'esclaves par Louis Moreau Lislet à Pierre Soulé.
	17 décembre (acte 830)	Acte de notoriété établi au bénéfice de Julie Elisabeth Althée Moreau Lislet et à sa demande.
	18 décembre (acte 833)	Vente d'un esclave par Louis Moreau Lislet à Jean Baptiste Desdunes fils.

Années	Acte	Contenu
1830	24 août (acte 715)	Quittance et mainlevée accordées par D^{me} Julie Elizabeth Althée Moreau Lislet épouse divorcée de J.B. Desdunes fils à Louis Moreau Lislet.
	22 septembre (acte 766)	Hypothèque par D^{me} Julie Elizabeth Desdunes, née Moreau Lislet à Mr. J.B. Desdunes fils.
1831	24 janvier (acte 45)	Héritiers de Dame Marie Marthe Aimée Bancio Piemond Desdunes Leclair en faveur de James H. Shepherd.
	12 février (acte 102)	Inventaire des biens et papiers de la succession de Dame Desdunes Jr. née Moreau Lislet.
	23 février (acte 134)	Family meeting of the minors J.B. Desdunes, Jr.
	24 février (acte 139)	Mainlevée par J.B. Desdunes Jr. et Pierre Soulé à L. Moreau Lislet.
	25 février (acte 150)	Vente de terre et édifices par L. Moreau Lislet à Pierre Edouard Sorbé.

Année	Acte	Contenu
1831	18 mai (acte 527)	Vente d'esclaves par les mineurs Desdunes au sieur Pierre Marie Boixel.
1832	9 janvier (acte 14)	Inventaire des biens et papiers de la succession de Dame Vve Deynaut née Vallade.
	10 janvier (acte 24)	Quittance et mainlevée par J.B. Desdunes fils à Manuel Prados.
	6 novembre (acte 1040)	Dépôt et Enregistrement par J.B. Desdunes fils.
1833	janvier (acte 44)	Vente de propriété par Dame Perro à J.B. Desdunes fils.
	13 février (acte 277)	Contrat de mariage entre J.B. Desdunes et Dlle. Elizabeth Mathilde Hatrel.
1833	5 juillet (acte 808)	Vente d'esclaves par J.B. Desdunes père à J.B. Desdunes fils.
	22 octobre (acte 1075)	Dépôt, par J.B. Desdunes fils, de papiers trouvés en possession de feu Mr. Louis Moreau Lislet, avocat, en sa qualité d'avocat de la ville [Suit une liste de 206 papiers de toute sorte].

Année	Acte	Contenu
1835	17 mars (acte 146)	Vente du tiers d'une propriété par Dlle. Josephine Rossignol Desdunes à J.B. Desdunes, son père.
	18 mars (acte 150)	Contrat de mariage entre Jean Jules Guérin et Dlle Thérèze Josephine Rossignol Desdunes.

CASES IN WHICH MOREAU-LISLET APPEARED AS COUNSEL BEFORE THE SUPREME COURT OF LOUISIANA

1 Martin O.S. (1809)
1. Miner v. Bank of Louisiana 12
2. St.Marc v. La Chapella & Harrison 36
3. Folk et al v. Solis 64
4. Livingston v. D'Orgenoy 87
    (*District ct. case)
5. Moreau v. Duncan 99
    (Moreau is P here)
6. Hudson v. Grieve 143
    (Moreau denied permission to appear)
7. Daublin v. Mayor & Co. of N.O. 185
8. Territory v. Barran 208
9. Ramozay et al v. Mayor & Corp. of N.O. . . . 241
10. Orleans Navigation Co. v. The Mayor of N.O. 269
11. Beauregard, Exec. v. Piernas & Wife 281

2 Martin O.S. (1811)
12. Orleans Navigation Co. v. The Mayor et al of N. O. 10
13. Moreau v. Duncan (s.c. 1-99) 47
14. Riviere v. Spencer 79
15. Orleans Navigation Co. v. Boutte's Execs. 84
16. Orleans Navigation Co. v. Mayor of N.O. . . . 214
17. Ellery v. Amelung's Syndics 242

3 Martin O.S.(1813)
18. LeBreton v. Nouchet 60
19. Meunier v. Duperron 285
20. Mayor of N.O. v. Metzinger 296
21. St. Maxent's Syndic v. Sigur 371

22.	Kemper v. Smith	622
23.	Bourcier v. Lanusse	661

4 Mart. O.S. (1815)

24.	Mayor v. Magnon	2
25.	Cox v. Rabaud's Syndics	11
26.	Harang v. Dauphin	27
27.	Cresse v. Marigny	50
28.	Baron v. Phelan	88
29.	Olinde v. Gougis	96
30.	Renthorpe v. Bourg	97
31.	Poydras v. Robillard	174
32.	Syndics v. Mayhew	175
33.	Doubrere v. Papin	184
34.	St. Maxent's v. Amphoux's Syndics	192
	St. Maxent's v. Puche	193
35.	Victoire v. Dussuau	212
36.	Bernard v. Curtis	214
37.	Roussel v. Dukeylus' Syndics	218
38.	LeBlanc v. Croizet	272
39.	Enet v. His Creditors	307
40.	Prampin v. Andry	314
41.	Beard v. Poydras	348
42.	Allard v. Ganusheau	384
43.	Forsyth v. Nash	385
44.	Enet v. His Creditors	401
45.	Smith v. Kemper	409
46.	Blanque v. Peytavin	458
47.	Dukeylus' Syndics v. Dumontel	466
48.	Esteve v. Rochon	481
49.	Mayor v. Davis	533
50.	Duncan v. Cevallos' Heirs	571
51.	Enet v. His Creditors	599
52.	Robillard v. Robillard	603
53.	Amory v. Grieve's Syndics	632
54.	Jones v. Gale's Curatrix	635

55.	Gale v. Davis' Heirs	645
56.	Allard v. Ganushau	662
57.	Girod v. Mayor et al	698
58.	Ducournau v. Marigny	708
59.	Fortier v. McDonogh	718

5 Martin O.S. (1817)

60.	Murphy's Heirs v. Murphy	83
61.	Cottin v. Cottin	93
62.	Greffin's Execs. v. Lopez	145
63.	Broutin et al v. Vassant	169
64.	Poydras v. Livingston	292
65.	Decuir v. Packwood	300
66.	Mayor v. Duplessis	309
67.	D'Apremont v. Peytavin	323
68.	Rogers v. Smith	359
69.	Zanico v. Habine	372
70.	Loze v. Zanico's Estate	391
71.	Mouchon v. Delor	395
72.	La. Bank v. Dubreuil	416
73.	Peytavin v. Hopkins	438
74.	Augustin v. Cailleau	464
75.	State v. Edward	474
76.	Joublanc's Ex. v. Delacroix	477
77.	Lefevre v. Boniquet's Syndics et al	481
78.	Cuffy v. Castillon	494
79.	Doubrere v. Papin	498
80.	Metayer v. Noret	566
81.	Berthole v. Mace	576
82.	D'Apremont v. Peytavin	641

6 Martin O.S. (1819)

83.	Metayer v. Metayer	16
84.	Morgan v. Livingston et al	19
85.	Peytavin v. Hopkins	256
86.	Davis v. Preval	422

87.	Smith v. Kemper	563
88.	Trègre v. Trègre	665
89.	Andry v. Foy	689
90.	Musson v. Bank U.S.	707

7 Martin O.S. (1819)
91.	Claiborne v. Police Jury	4
92.	Police Jury v. McDonogh	8
93.	Carrell's Heirs v. Cabaret	375
94.	Durnford v. Patterson	460
95.	Viales v. Viales' Syndics	634
96.	Nagle v. Mignot	657

8 Martin O.S. 1820)
97.	Livaudais' Heirs v. Fon et al	161
98.	Catin v. D'Orgenoys' Heirs	218
99.	Dufour v. Camfrancq	235
100.	Brown v. La. Bank	393
101.	Nagel v. Mignot	488

9 Martin O.S. 1821)
102.	La. Bank v. Bank of U.S.	398

10 Martin O.S. (1821)
103.	Wiltz v. Dufau et al	20
104.	Ferrers v. Bosel	35
105.	Chauveau v. Walden	100
106.	Lecesne v. Cottin	174
107.	Frederic v. Frederic	188
108.	Conrad v. La. Bank	700

11 Martin O.S. (1822)
109.	Chretien v. Theard	11
110.	Ferrer v. Bofil	234
111.	Aubrey & Wife v. Folse & Wife	306
112.	Preval v. Moulon	530

113.	Dufour v. Camfranc	607
114.	Mayor v. Gravier	620
115.	Copelly v. Deverges	641
116.	Dufour v. Camfranc	675

12 Martin O.S. (1822)

116A.	Mayor v. Hunter	3
117.	McCarty v. Foucher	11
118.	Powers v. Foucher	70
119.	Davis' Heirs v. Provost's Heirs	445
120.	Fleckner v. Nelder	503
121.	Trepagnier's Heirs v. Butler et al	534
122.	Pepper v. Peytavin	671
123.	Lazare's Executor v. Peytavin	684
124.	Tilghman v. Dias	691
125.	Tilghman v. Dias	699

1 Martin N.S. 89 (1823)

126.	Belanger v. Gravier	89
127.	Peytavin v. Paloe	153
128.	Baudin v. Roliff & Robertson	165
129.	Lafon's Execs. v. Gravier et al	243
130.	Boismarre v. Jourdan	304
131.	Fleitas v. Mayor N.O.	430
132.	Delery v. Bunle's Under Tutor	451

2 Martin N. S. (1824)

133.	Desdunes v. Miller	53
134.	Doubrere v. Grillier's Syndic	171
135.	Le Cesne v. Cottin	475
136.	Le Changeur v. Gravier's Heirs	545
137.	Labat v. Labat's Syndics	652
138.	Mayor v. Griffon et al	653

3 Martin N.S. (1825)

| 139. | Dreux v. Dreux's Syndics | 239 |

140. Guibert v. Herpin 395
141. Guirot v. Guirot's Syndics 400
142. Barbarin v. Deschaut's Heirs 639
143. Lafon's Heirs v. His Executors 707

4 Martin N.S. (1825)
144. Lewis v. Petayvin 4
145 Moulon v. His Creditors 29
146. Corporation v. Paulding 189
147. Malchaux v. Lefebvre 489
148. Baudin v. Dubourg & Baron 496
149. Parish of Orleans v. Kennedy 511
150. Corporation v. Paulding 614
151. Lartigue v. Duhamel's Exec. 664

5 Martin N.S. (1826)
152. Griffon v. Mayor 279
153. Police Jury v. Hampton 389
154. US v. Baulos' Exec. 567
155. Beon v. Morgan 701

6 Martin N.S. (1827)
156. Parish of Orleans v. Morgan 3
157. Lanusse v. Lanna 103
158. McCarty v. Fanchon 116
159. Martel v. Tureaud's Estate 118
160. Pimpinella v. Lanusse's Syndics 124
161. Mayor v. Peyroux 155
162. Mayor v. Hennen 428
163. Dreux v. His Creditors 502

7 Martin N.S. (1828)
164. Mayor v. Morgan 1
165. Acosta v. Robin 387
166. Loiseau v. Laizer et al 580
167. Cornie v. LeBlanc 591

168.	Gravier v. Lafon	612
169.	Dreux and His Creditors	635
170.	Pilie v. Lalande et al	648
171.	Oger v. Daunoy	656
172.	LeBlanc v. Landry	665

8 Martin N.S. (1829)

173.	Baudin v. Roliff et al	98
174.	Bulloc v. Parthet	123
175.	Rochelle v. Alvarez	171
176.	Cormier v. LeBlanc	457
177.	Savenet v. LeBriton et al	501
178.	Tourne v. Lee	548
178A	Cambre v. Kohn	572

1 La. (1830)

178B	Oakey v. Mayor	1
179.	Laralde v. Derbigny	85
180.	Croizet v. Police Jury of Pte. Coupee	103
181.	Thibaud v. Thibaud's Heirs	493
182.	Savenat v. LeBreton	520

2 La.(1830)

183.	Morano v. Mayor et al	217
184.	Elliott v. Labarre	326
185.	Mayor v. Ripley	344
186.	Pontalba v. Pontalba	466
187.	Dorfeuille's Minors v. Duplessis et al	484
188.	Baudin v. Conway	512
189.	Crocker v. Bland	531

3 La.(1831)

190.	Cauchoix v. Dupuy et al	206
191.	Cornie v. LeBlanc	213
192.	Kohn & Bordier v. Packard	224
193.	Lafferranderie v. Mayor	246

194.	Dufau v. Duflechier's Syndics	304
195.	Arnaud's Heirs v. His Exec.	336

4 La.(1831)
196.	LaRosa v. The Mayor et al	24
197.	Bouligny v. Urquhart	29
198.	Goicochea v. Ricarte	44
199.	Lanfear v. Mayor	97
200.	Gravier v. Perrillat	208
201.	Rochelle v. Alvarez	218
202.	St. Amand v. Lisardi et al	243
203.	Bauduc v. His Creditors	247
204.	Fletcher v. Cavalier	267

5 La.(1832)
205.	McCarty v. Steam Cotton Press Co. et al	16
206.	DeArmas v. Mayor N. O.	132
207.	Morand's Heirs v. Mayor N.O.	226
208.	Chiapella v. Moni	380

Appendix: Spanish Sources of Law of the Digest of 1808
By Vicenç Feliú*

Examination of Spanish Sources of Law:
The selection of Spanish sources for inclusion in this appendix is based on three original documents closely contemporary to the creation of the Digest of 1808. These documents are the de la Verne Volume[1], an annotated first edition of the Digest of

---

* Vicenç Feliú is the Foreign Comparative and International Law Librarian at the Paul M. Hebert Law Center at Louisiana State University Law Library. He graduated from Franklin Pierce Law Center, Concord, NH, with a JD and a Masters in Intellectual Property and from the University of Washington, Seattle, WA, with a MLIS with an emphasis in Law Librarianship. He is the author of *Meeting the Informational Needs of Constitutionalist Patrons: A Guide for Reference Librarians*.

[1] The de la Vergne Volume is a reprint of an original copy of the Digest of 1808 "bound with interleaves containing references in manuscript to various civil laws and commentaries. According to the preface to these manuscript annotations, the references opposite the English texts of the Digest are to various laws of civilian jurisdictions on the same subjects as the texts and those opposite the French texts are to the actual sources of the texts themselves. These latter are very predominantly to Spanish laws and works, even in those many instances in which it is obvious that the words of the particular texts were taken from the French Code Civil of 1804 or one of its *projets*. The annotations, therefore, lend support to the conclusion that the Digest was indeed in substance primarily a digest of the Spanish laws in force in the Territory of Orleans in 1808, even though the formal source of many of its provisions was the French Code Civil or one of its *projets*, and tend to refute the popular notion that the Digest

1808[2] (Fig. 1 and Fig. 2), and the inventory of Moreau Lislet's possessions made shortly after his death.[3] Therefore, we will begin this exploration by examining the principal Spanish sources

---

represents an acceptance of French Law in what is now the State of Louisiana." There is strong evidence that the annotations in the volume were made by Moreau Lislet. This evidence is strongly corroborated by three other copies of the Digest of 1808 that contain annotations made in Moreau Lislet's own hand. A REPRINT OF MOREAU LISLET'S COPY OF A DIGEST OF THE LAWS NOW IN FORCE IN THE TERRITORY OF ORLEANS (1808) Preface to the Reprint (The Louisiana State University School of Law and the Tulane University School of Law 1968)

[2] This annotated first edition, mentioned in footnote 6 *supra*, is the one discovered by Professor Robert Pascal, Professor Emeritus Paul M. Hebert Law Center, Louisiana State University, in 1965 in the Louisiana Room of the Louisiana State University Library. It is presently located in the Hill Memorial Library of Louisiana State University and was made available for the original research of the conference and this article. Our thanks also go to Professor Pascal who was instrumental in the selection of members for the original panel of presenters and who provided invaluable insight into the collection of original resource materials.

[3] All the facsimiles of original documents pertaining to Moreau Lislet's life were gathered by Professor Alain Levasseur, during his research for the original edition of this book. Professor Levasseur's research in original materials from such diverse sources as the French National Archives, the New Orleans Notarial Archives, and even the parish records of Dondon, Haiti has resulted in a collection of facsimiles materials spanning and documenting the life of Moreau Lislet which is presently held in the Rare Book Collection of the Paul M. Hebert Law Center Law Library. His original research is one of the corner stones supporting the argument for Spanish law as the primary substance of the Digest of 1808.

A DIGEST

OF THE

CIVIL LAWS

NOW IN FORCE

IN THE

TERRITORY OF ORLEANS,

WITH

ALTERATIONS AND AMENDMENTS

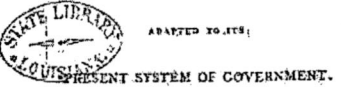

ADAPTED TO ITS PRESENT SYSTEM OF GOVERNMENT.

By Authority.

NEW-ORLEANS:

PRINTED BY BRADFORD & ANDERSON, PRINTERS TO THE TERRITORY.

1808.

New Hill Memorial Library,
Louisiana State University

Fig. 1 – Title page of annotated first edition of the Digest of 1808, in Moreau Lislet's hand and bearing his signature at the top of the page, held by the Hill Memorial Library of Louisiana State University.

included in those documents: *Las Siete Partidas, La Recopilación de Castilla, La Recopilación de las Indias, El Fuero Real de Castilla,* the *Curia Philipica,* and *Febrero Adicionado*. The three original documents also cite to Spanish Royal Ordinances and Decrees but since these are, in essence, not much different from the royal ordinances and decrees of other European countries at the time, we will not examine them here.

Las Siete Partidas:

In medieval European codification the *Partidas* comes down as a unique code of civil law.[4] Certainly there are other examples of contemporary legal collections; *e.g.* The *Constitutions of Melfi, De legibus et consuetudinibus Angliae,* the *Coutumes de Beauvaisis,* and the statutes of Edward I, the Law Giver, but none of these approach the level of depth and organization of the *Partidas*.[5] The *Partidas* are a legal encyclopedia and a codification rolled into one and it was meant to be in force as a code of law for the whole kingdom.[6] It is a true code, following the model of Justinian's *Corpus iuris civilis*;[7] it is comprehensively and systematically organized in

---

[4] JOSEHP F. O'CALLAGHAN, *Alfonso X and the Partidas* in 1 LAS SIETE PARTIDAS xxx (Robert I. Burns, S.J. ed., Samuel Parsons Scott trans., University of Pennsylvania Press, 2001)
[5] *Supra*
[6] E. N. VAN KLEFFENS, HISPANIC LAW UNTIL THE END OF THE MIDDLE AGES 155 (Edinburgh University Press 1968)
[7] CORPUS IURIS CIVILIS (Theodore Mommsen et al. eds., Weidman, 1915-1928)

books, titles and laws.[8] The *Partidas* were composed during the reign of King Alfonso X (1252-1284), the Wise, between 1256 and 1265 and it might not have been known by its present name during the life of Alfonso X.[9] The present title comes from the work's division into seven parts following the divisional format of the *Corpus iuris civilis* and keeping with the

---

[8] O'CALLAGHAN, *supra* at xxx
[9] In his last will, dated 10 January 1284, Alfonso refers to the book as the *Setenario* and in other documents it has been referred to as the *Libro de las Leyes* or Book of Laws. *Supra* at xxxvi

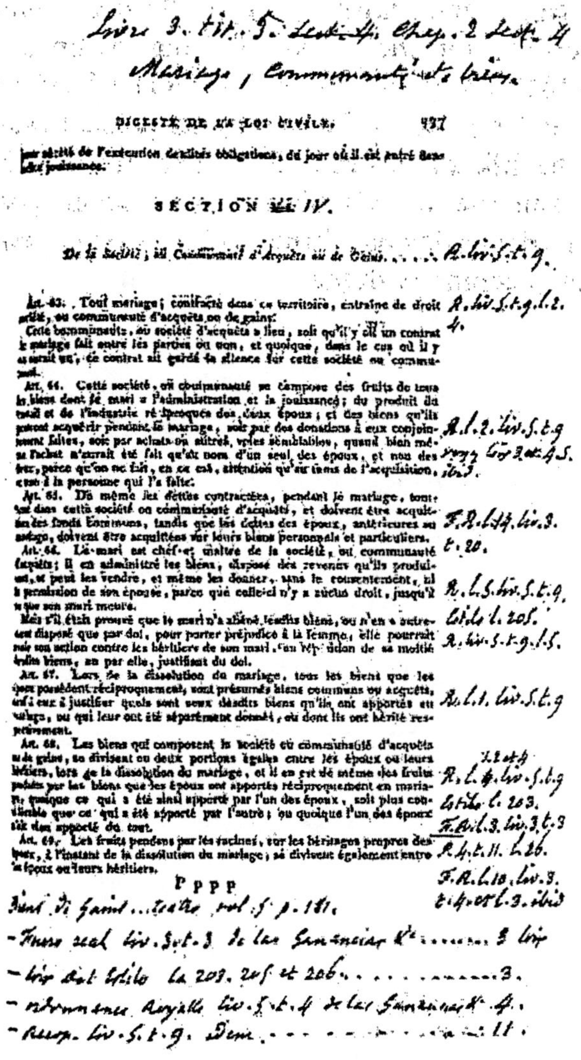

DIGESTE DE LA LOI CIVILE. 437

par sûreté de l'exécution desdites obligations, du jour où il est entré dans ladite jouissance.

SECTION IV.

De la Société, ou Communauté d'Acquêts ou de Gains.

Art. 63. Tout mariage, contracté dans ce territoire, entraîne de droit société, ou communauté d'acquêts ou de gains.

Cette communauté, ou société d'acquêts a lieu, soit qu'il y ait un contrat de mariage fait entre les parties ou non, et quoique, dans le cas où il y en aurait un, ce contrat ait gardé le silence sur cette société ou communauté.

Art. 64. Cette société, ou communauté se compose des fruits de tous les biens dont le mari a l'administration et la jouissance; du produit du travail et de l'industrie réciproques des deux époux; et des biens qu'ils peuvent acquérir pendant le mariage, soit par des donations à eux conjointement faites, soit par achats ou autres voies semblables, quand bien même l'achat n'aurait été fait qu'au nom d'un seul des époux, et non des deux, parce qu'on ne fait, en ce cas, attention qu'au tems de l'acquisition, et non à la personne qui l'a faite.

Art. 65. De même les dettes contractées, pendant le mariage, tombent dans cette société ou communauté d'acquêts, et doivent être acquittées des fonds communs, tandis que les dettes des époux, antérieures au mariage, doivent être acquittées sur leurs biens personnels et particuliers.

Art. 66. Le mari est chef et maître de la société, ou communauté d'acquêts; il en administre les biens, dispose des revenus qu'ils produisent, et peut les vendre, et même les donner, sans le consentement, ni la permission de son épouse, parce que celle-ci n'y a aucun droit, jusqu'à ce que son mari meure.

Mais s'il était prouvé que le mari n'a aliéné lesdits biens, ou n'en a autrement disposé que par dol, pour porter préjudice à la femme, elle pourrait avoir son action contre les héritiers de son mari, en répétition de sa moitié desdits biens, en par elle, justifiant du dol.

Art. 67. Lors de la dissolution du mariage, tous les biens que les époux possèdent réciproquement, sont présumés biens communs ou acquêts, sauf à eux à justifier quels sont ceux desdits biens qu'ils ont apportés en mariage, ou qui leur ont été séparément donnés, ou dont ils ont hérité respectivement.

Art. 68. Les biens qui composent la société ou communauté d'acquêts ou de gains, se divisent en deux portions égales entre les époux ou leurs héritiers, lors de la dissolution du mariage, et il en est de même des fruits produits par les biens que les époux ont apportés réciproquement en mariage, quoique ce qui a été ainsi apporté par l'un des époux, soit plus considérable que ce qui a été apporté par l'autre; ou quoique l'un des époux n'eût rien apporté du tout.

Art. 69. Les fruits pendans par les racines, sur les héritages propres des époux, à l'instant de la dissolution du mariage, se divisent également entre les époux ou leurs héritiers.

Pppp

Fig. 2 – Page from the annotated first edition of the Digest of 1808, signed by Moreau Lislet's, in the Hill Memorial Library of Louisiana State University, showing references to the *fueros* and the *recopilaciones*.

importance given to the number seven in the XIII and XIV centuries.[10]. Authorship is credited to Alfonso X in the prologue of the work, additionally; the letters of the Alfonso's name are used as the initial letter of each section to reinforce the notion of his authorship.[11] In reality the work was more than likely composed by a team of legal scholars including Fernando Martínez de Zamora, Maestre Roldán, and Jacobo de las Leyes.[12] The *Partidas* remained as effective law in Iberia until the end of the XIX century, in Latin America until the middle of the XX century, and it still influences present day law in those places as well as in the southern tier states of the United States.[13]

---

[10] The Seven Liberal Arts, the Seven Sacraments, the Seven Gifts of the Holy Spirit, the Seven Capital Sins, the Seven Joys and Sorrows of the Virgin Mary, the Seven Ages of Man, *etc.*

[11] Each section of the Partidas begins in this manner, forming the name Alfonso;

I.	A seruicio de Dios
II.	La ffe cathólica
III.	Fizo Nuestro Sennor Dios
IV.	Onras sennaladas
V.	Nascen entre los ommes
VI.	Sesudamente dixeron
VII.	Oliuidança et atreuimento

LAS SIETE PARTIDAS (Gregorio Lopez ed. Madrid 1789)

[12] O'CALLAGHAN, *supra* at xxxvii

[13] VAN KLEFFENS, *supra* at 164; See Summa Corp. v. California, 466 U.S. 198 (1984)

La Recopilación de Castilla and La Recopilación de Las Indias:

With the *Partidas*, Alfonso X began a codification effort with the intent of unifying and simplifying the legal picture in his kingdoms (the Kings of Castile were also Kings of León, two legally distinctive entities). His aim was to abrogate the old laws of his kingdoms and replace them with a set of comprehensive laws;[14] he failed in this attempt because his subjects, and his own son, were very jealous of their old rights and prerogatives and actively opposed him to maintain their traditional laws.[15] After Alfonso X's death, the traditional laws or *Fueros* returned to force in conjunction with the *Partidas* but the appeal of a consolidated Roman law to rule the kingdoms did not die with him. His great-grandson, Alfonso XI (reigned 1312-1250), recognized that the solution was not to abrogate the old laws but to compile and classify them, giving preferential treatment to some norms over others.[16] This system became characteristic of Spanish law and became the method of *recopilaciones*, not codification but collection of legal text in force and classification of those texts by priority or weight of authority.[17] In Castile these *recopilaciones* were the *Leyes de Toro* in 1505, the *Nueva Recopilación* in 1567, and the *Novísima Recopilación* in 1805;[18]

---

[14] VAN KLEFFENS, *supra* at 226
[15] *Supra* at 212-3
[16] *Supra* at 226
[17] *Supra* at 227
[18] *Supra* at 227, note 2

thus during Spanish domination of the territory of Orleans, the former two were in effect.

With the discovery of the New World, primarily a Castilian enterprise,[19] the Castilian *recopilaciones* came into effect in their overseas possessions,[20] just as the French had brought the *Coutume de Paris* to be the principal law in their possessions. In 1528, the Ordinances for the *Audiencia de La Hispaniola* decreed that Castilian law was to be followed in conformity with the *Leyes de Toro* of 1505.[21] This enactment, repeated in other *Audiencias* through out the New World, ensured that the system of *recopilaciones* would be in force and it led to the compilation in 1680 of the *Recopilación de leyes de los Reinos de las Indias*, a collection of pre-existing law to be followed in the Castilian overseas colonies and the primary source of Spanish colonial law.[22]

El Fuero Real de Castilla:

The *fueros* are a typical Iberian institution that are mainly a combination ancient customary law, traditional law, and special regional and local charters that governed the legal picture in localized

---

[19] The Papal Bull *Inter Caetera* issued by Alexander VI on 4 May 1493 granted the newly discovered lands as conjugal property of King Ferran of Aragon and Queen Isabel of Castile during their lifetimes but they were to pass to the Kingdoms of Castile and León on the death of either partner
[20] VAN KLEFFENS, *supra* at 235
[21] *Supra* at 263
[22] *Supra*

areas throughout the peninsula.[23] Over time, the term *fuero* acquired several meanings; charters given by the king for the governance of townships, special statutes granted to social groups or institutions, and sets of laws of general application to the kingdom.[24] The proliferation of the *fueros* after the fall of the Visigothic Kingdom in 711 created a situation ripe for conflicting sets of law.[25] Alfonso X had the *Fuero Real* created in 1255 as his initial attempt to unify the laws of his kingdoms.[26] The *Fuero Real* is a codification, by no means exhaustive, with subject matter and provisions deriving from the *Fuero Juzgo* (the law of the Visigothic Kingdom based on the Roman *ius commune*), Castilian local *fueros*, customary law, and some elements of Roman law.[27] After Alfonso X's not entirely successful attempt to replace the *Fuero Real* with the *Partidas*, it remained in effect along with the *Partidas* and was incorporated into the general law through the system of *recopilaciones*.

Curia Philipica:

The *Curia Philipica* (Fig. 3) is the work of Juan de Hevia Bolaños an Asturian legal scholar who worked in Latin America during the first half of the

---

[23] *Supra* at 18
[24] *Supra* at 125
[25] *Supra* at 135-44
[26] *Supra* at 167
[27] *Supra* at 167-8

XVII century. The Curia was first published in 1603, in Lima, and it quickly gained a reputation as a complete reference source. It was used as a basic legal text book in Latin American law

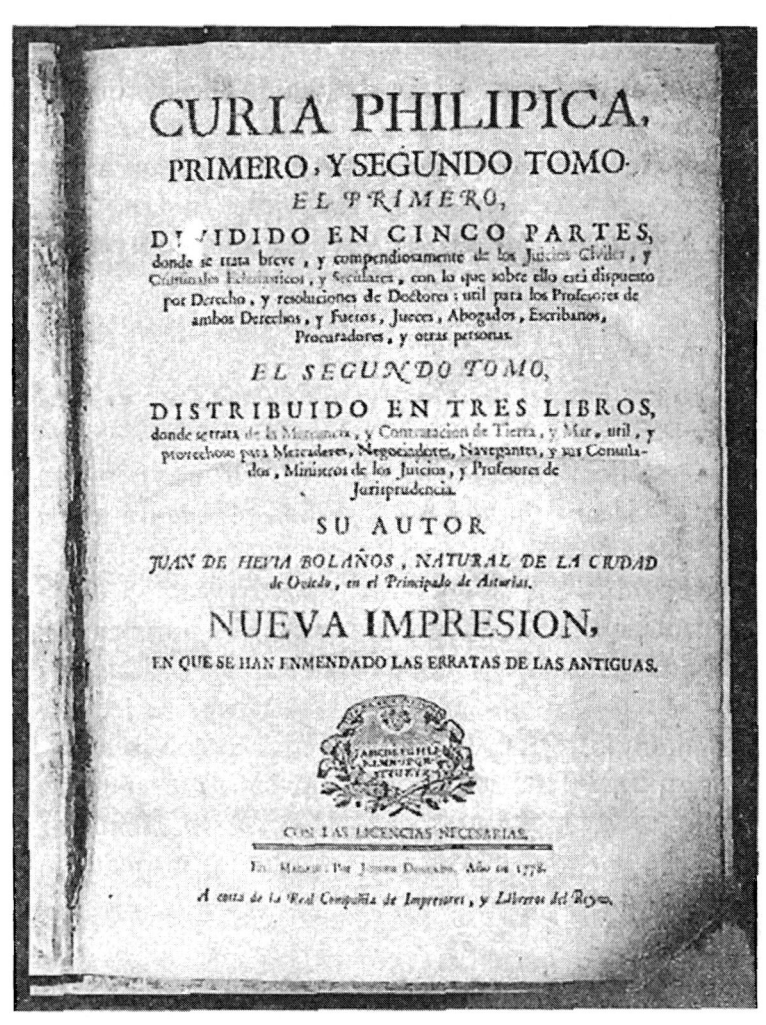

Fig. 3 – Title page of the 1778 Royal Edition of the *Curia Philipica*, held at the Rare Book Collection of the Paul M. Hebert Law Center Law Library.

schools until the beginning of the XX century. However, it's most important use in the context of the present inquiry, was as a guide for practitioners on the interpretation and practical application of the *fueros*, Partidas, and *recopilaciones*. In Louisiana the *Curia* continued to be used as an interpretative tool into the XIX century.[28]

Febrero Adicionado:

The *Febrero Adicionado* (Fig. 4) or simply *Febrero* is a practical guide written in 1769 by José Febrero, Royal Notary. It is a practice and procedure guide intended for use by practitioners in the application of Spanish civil law. It quickly gained wide acceptance and went through a number of reprintings with additional material being added as the interpretations of the law chance, hence the *adicionado* of the title. The *Febrero* continued in use in Spain and its former colonies as a reference source and practice guide while the *fueros*, Partidas, and *recopilaciones* held their position of primacy in Spanish law.

---

[28] *See e.g.* Reynaud's Heirs v. Peytavin's Ex'rs, 13 La. 121, 1839; Rowlett v. Shepherd, 7 Mart. (n.s.) 513, 1829; Keene v. Lizardi, 6 La. 315, 1834.

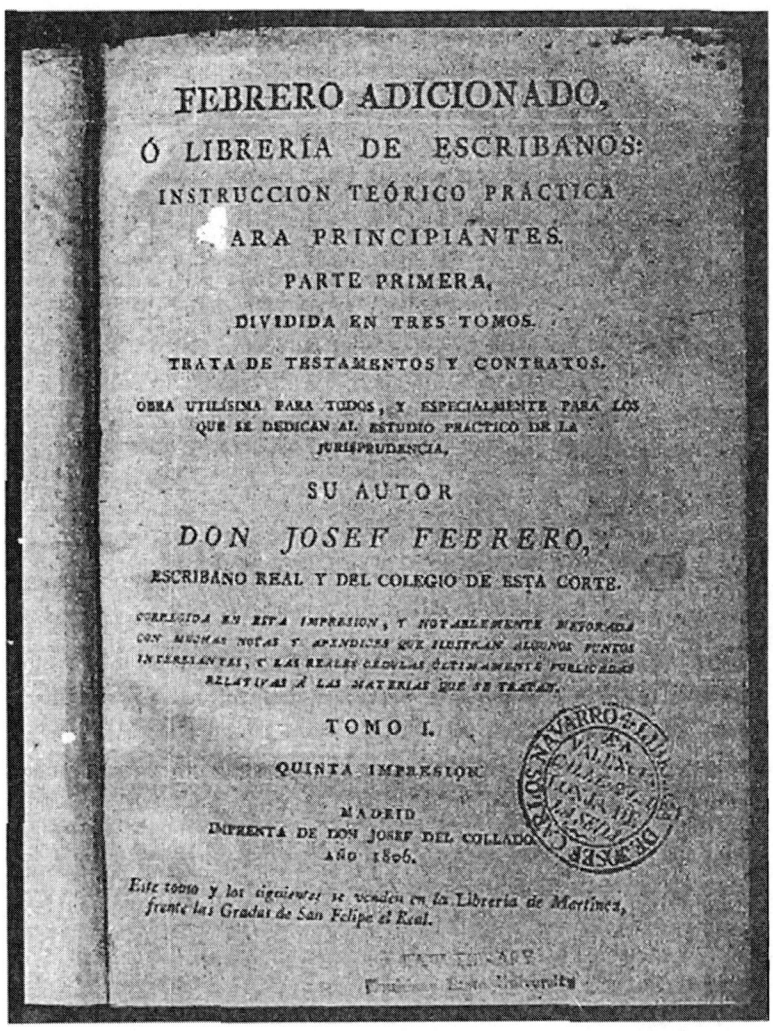

Fig. 4 – Title page of the 1806 edition of the *Febrero Adicionado*, held at the Rare Book Collection of the Paul M. Hebert Law Center Law Library.